The Thinking Game

Saint Peter's University Library
Withdrawn

W9-CEG-110

CHATHAM HOUSE STUDIES IN POLITICAL THINKING

SERIES EDITOR: George J. Graham, Jr.
Vanderbilt University

THE THINKING GAME
A Guide to Effective Study

EUGENE J. MEEHAN
*Curators' Professor in Political Science
and Public Policy Administration*
University of Missouri-St. Louis

CHATHAM HOUSE PUBLISHERS, INC.
Chatham, New Jersey

THE THINKING GAME
A Guide to Effective Study

CHATHAM HOUSE PUBLISHERS, INC.
Post Office Box One
Chatham, New Jersey 07928

Copyright © 1988 by Chatham House Publishers, Inc.

All rights reserved. No part of this publication may be reproduced, stored in a retrieval system, or transmitted in any form or by any means, electronic, mechanical, photocopying, recording, or otherwise, without prior permission of the publisher.

PUBLISHER: Edward Artinian
ILLUSTRATIONS: Adrienne Shubert
COVER DESIGN: Lawrence Ratzkin
COMPOSITION: Chatham Composer
PRINTING AND BINDING: Hamilton Printing Company

LIBRARY OF CONGRESS CATALOGING-IN-PUBLICATION DATA

Meehan, Eugene J.
    The thinking game.

    (Chatham House studies in political thinking)
    1. Critical thinking. 2. Decision-making.
3. Policy sciences. I. Title. II. Series.
LB1590.3.M44 1988 371.3   88-4335
ISBN 0-934540-64-0
ISBN 0-934540-63-2 (Instructor's ed.)

Manufactured in the United States of America
10 9 8 7 6 5 4 3 2 1

‹B
‹590.3
‹44
‹88

Contents

Acknowledgments

Various sorts of obligations have accumulated during the development of this volume that deserve recognition and thanks. To give publishers their due first, I am most grateful to the Greenwood Press (a division of Congressional Information Service, Inc.) for permission to plunder freely from an earlier book entitled *Reasoned Argument in Social Science: Linking Research to Policy*, which they published in 1981, and I must point out that the units dealing with policy were published by *Policy Sciences* as an integrated essay (18 [1985]: 291-311) under the title "Policy: Constructing a Definition."

A second major set of obligations is owed to the students who have struggled with earlier versions of the material, creating in the process the kind of information needed to improve the text, and to those friends and colleagues who have used the text in their own classes and made the results available freely and critically. In the latter group, special thanks are due to Larry Spence at Pennsylvania State University, who has been enormously helpful, and to Professor Maria de Wille and Abelardo Brenes of the University of Costa Rica for arranging translation into Spanish and promoting an experimental course at that institution.

Finally, a public "thank you" is due to Jan Frantzen and Lana Sink in the political science department of my own university for translating typescript into electronic impulses, thereby satisfying the perverse (in my view) requirements of contemporary publishing. None of those mentioned, obviously, bears any responsibility for the quality of the text.

The Thinking Game

1. Introduction

The physician treating a patient, the farmer cultivating crops, the student preparing a term paper, and the child going to the store for a loaf of bread all have one important thing in common: Each of them is "thinking to purpose," using knowledge to produce a desired result, and using knowledge to determine that the result is desired. In general everyday terms, most persons agree that knowledge plays a major role in human affairs. But precisely what that means—what role knowledge actually plays, and why it is able to do so—usually remains unexamined. Similarly, the need for systematic testing and criticism of the existing body of knowledge, for developing the capacity to separate valid knowledge from "beliefs" or "opinions," is generally accepted, but the criteria and procedures involved are rarely articulated or taught. Very little of human behavior is directed by instinct or natural inheritance, and human success in the world is almost entirely dependent on the creation, application, and improvement of knowledge. Nevertheless, the kind of knowledge needed to criticize and improve knowledge is not widely available, even among highly educated populations. Yet there seems no good reason to reserve such critical capacity to the privileged few and every reason to make it part of the general education of the citizenry, particularly in democratic society. This text is targeted at that gap in the educational system. It provides a generalized framework for developing, using, and criticizing knowledge in which the purposes that knowledge can serve are linked to the kind of knowledge required to fulfill them—those are the essential requirements for systematic criticism and improvement of knowledge and its uses or applications.

The key to criticism and improvement of knowledge claims is a clear and adequate conception of what *knowledge* means. That problem is not resolved by consulting a dictionary or some other authority. Perhaps the best point of departure is to clear away some of the mystique that has grown up around knowledge and thinking over the years, working out the basic elements involved in everyday terms. Far too many persons, young and old, tend to assume that they lack natural ability in "thinking," which they associate with formal schooling. By assuming the condition, they tend to make it come true, for thinking, like most human activities, improves with practice. Yet everyone can think, and most persons can think very well, but not everyone thinks equally well about every topic. Similarly, everyone has some knowledge; most persons have a lot of knowledge of very good quality; but not everyone has equal amounts of knowledge, of equal quality, on every subject. Neither knowledge nor thinking is reserved for the academic world, but both tend to remain unrecognized in everyday affairs.

In the most basic and useful sense, knowledge is nothing more than organized human experience, and thinking refers to the processes by which knowledge is developed, acquired, tested, and applied. In these terms, knowledge and thinking play a central role in everyone's behavior, at all times. The housewife selecting a cut of meat for the dish she will prepare for dinner uses the same *kind* of knowledge as the economist or meteorologist; the child who throws a temper tantrum to obtain money for ice cream is using the same kind of knowledge as the engineer who designs a rocket. The housewife and child are not likely to realize they are using knowledge of a particular kind, or to know how to go about testing and improving it. But most engineers are equally unaware of the type and quality of the knowledge they use in their work, or how to improve it. An individual can have knowledge and not be aware of it and may improve knowledge without knowing that an improvement has occurred. But such unsystematic activities are relatively inefficient and unreliable. The likelihood of improvements in the knowledge supply is greatly increased if knowledge can be examined self-consciously within a framework that allows qualitative criticism and suggests improvements. The purpose here is to produce such a framework and provide an opportunity to learn its uses and limitations. The framework is completely general and could be used by the child, the housewife, and the engineer as it stands. More important, it is intended to apply to everyday experience as well as academic affairs, and can therefore be tested by anyone in the day-to-day world.

Of course, there *are* significant differences between the kind of knowledge acquired and used in everyday life and the kind of knowledge that is available in such physical sciences as chemistry and physics. But those differences relate to the subject matter dealt with and the level of generality achieved and not to quality or type; they have nothing to do with one being "scientific" and therefore intrinsically superior, while the other is necessarily inferior in quality. Indeed, scientific knowledge, even in physics or chemistry, may in some cases be less accurate and reliable than everyday knowledge.

The key to criticism and evaluation is to focus on the purposes for which knowledge is employed. For any given purpose, the form of the knowledge required to fulfill it is the same regardless of the subject matter, and the criteria applied to the knowledge are identical. Criticism by reference to form and purpose can therefore make use of the same criteria in all fields. Most of the difference between personal knowledge and scientific knowledge is found in the scope or application and the subject matter. In most cases, personal knowledge refers to particular things or limited classes, to one particular mother (a class with one member) rather than all mothers. The knowledge produced in the physical sciences usually refers to different kinds of things, and to larger classes. The quality of knowledge does not depend on its scope or subject matter, however, but on uses or applications. The generalized knowledge of children that is available in society to sociologists, psychologists, and physicians would not be adequate for the mother engaged in raising a particular child. The mother must have the detailed knowledge that comes from close and sustained experience with a particular child. But if the child develops symptoms not included in the mother's experience, she then turns to the generalized knowledge available in society to find out whether the symptom has occurred before and what it portends. For raising children, then, both kinds of knowledge have their uses. Further, both are developed from the same foundations, find their validity in the same kind of evidence, and are criticized and improved using the same criteria and procedures.

The critical apparatus used for assessing knowledge must therefore be able to handle both the mother's knowledge of her specific child and the physician's knowledge of children as a class. That function is fulfilled by creating what is called a *metalanguage,* or second-order language. The meaning of this somewhat exotic term is best demonstrated in a familiar illustration, coaching athletics. It is commonplace that a casual spectator and a professional coach observing the same tennis match do not "see" the same things. The reason lies in the special language that the professional coaches have developed for criticizing and improving a player's performance in such activities. These "coaching languages" are a perfect example of the kind of metalanguage needed for criticizing and improving thinking and knowledge. In that context, the purpose of the text is to develop a coaching language for thinking—for developing, testing, criticizing, and applying knowledge to human affairs.

The reason why a coaching language is useful for improving performance, whether in sports or in thinking, is found in the function the language performs, in what it does. A coach is trying to assist the individual player to achieve the purposes of the game more efficiently and effectively. To do that, the coach focuses on the relation between the purposes of the game and the actions of the player. Comparison of the results achieved by the player with the purposes to be fulfilled in the game can suggest ways of modifying the player's actions and thus achieving results that better fulfill those purposes. Criticism of thinking requires a metalanguage developed from the same focus: The purposes sought through thinking are compared to the results achieved by thinking, seeking ways of improving performance, of achieving purposes more fully and efficiently.

Before entering into a detailed discussion of the purposes of the thinking "game" and their relations to the products of thinking, some other characteristics of systematic coaching in athletics, equally applicable to thinking, need to be pointed out. First, in most cases the individual who is being coached must learn the coaching language and its underlying rationale. Following orders to the letter is not usually enough because the player must adapt or interpret the coach's generalized instructions to fit the particular situation encountered in a real game. Players, in others words, should become self-coaching to the fullest extent possible. To do so, they must learn to stand aside and examine the results of their own performance, seeking to modify their actions in order to produce results that correspond more accurately to the game's purposes. Ultimately, that seems a worthwhile goal for every kind of instruction: Good coaching should produce self-coaching, for only in that way can coaching itself be improved. In other words, both the coach and the thinker must from time to time ask how well they are performing their own coaching functions. In the process, yet another metalanguage is created, a metalanguage that can be used to criticize and improve the metalanguage used in coaching. Stated abstractly, that may sound a little complex and confusing. But the difference between a program for training football players and a program for training football coaches can be sorted out very quickly with only modest amounts of information about the game.

How does an athletic coach go about producing an appropriate framework or metalanguage for criticizing and improving player performance? A brief summary of the major factors involved will suggest the basic requirements for a metalanguage that can be used to improve thinking. The heart of the process is a simple assumption, very widely accepted: *Human performance can be criticized or improved only by reference to the purpose(s) that performance is meant to achieve.* The proposition is readily tested, for it asserts that no individual, engaged in any kind of activity, whether physical or mental, can assess performance quality until the purpose of the performance is known. If the quality cannot be assessed, improvement is clearly impossible. Coaching, then, whether in sports or thinking, must begin with the purpose of the activity and work backward to the activity itself. Until a game has been specified, there is no possibility of creating a coaching program. Once the purposes of the game have been established, the problem for the prospective coach is to work out the necessary and sufficient conditions for fulfilling the purposes of the game as reliably and efficiently as possible. Such solutions must be worked out within three basic kinds of limits: (1) the rules of the game must be precise and unambiguous, and must remain fixed; (2) the capacities and limitations of the players cannot be exceeded, although they can be extended in various ways; and (3) other situational limits must be observed—the basketball coach cannot develop a coaching program that requires suspension of the law of gravity, for example.

Within that overall context, the coach must create a theory of play that will link the activities of the players to achievement of the purposes of the game. Golf, for example, has as its overriding purpose "winning" the match, which may refer to the number of strokes taken or the number of holes won. The overall purpose is fulfilled by first achieving a more limited purpose: striking a golf ball with a legal club in a way that will move it from its present resting place to a particular spot on the course, and eventually into a small hole surrounded by a relatively smooth grassy surface. Achieving that purpose, in a variety of circumstances, can in turn be linked to holding a particular club in a particular way, placing the feet in a particular position relative to the ball, swinging the club through a particular arc, and so on. If these activities are pursued regularly and systematically over time, with self-conscious attention to the relation between action and performance, a theory of play can develop that will suggest ways of achieving limited purposes in a wide range of situations. Training cannot guarantee success, and those who lack training may prove successful, but good coaching can produce measurable improvements in performance in various phases of the game, improvements that will be reflected in performance in real games—the only place where the quality of the coaching language can be assessed. Coaching develops out of experience in real games and is tested against experience in real, particular games. Player performance provides the information needed to adjust the theory of play. In significant real-world affairs, the process of developing and improving such coaching languages goes on endlessly.

Athletic coaching can also be used to illustrate some of the prime limits on what training in systematic criticism can accomplish, in sports or in thinking. First, coaching is not usually directed to motivating the player to practice or seek improvement; that must come from the player, perhaps with some prodding from the coach. Second, the coach can suggest ways of practicing that will improve performance, but practice itself is a function of individual effort. Third, good coaching should lead to self-coaching, and that implies a deliberate effort by the player to become self-critical, to learn to improve from experience without assistance. Fourth, coaching functions negatively, for the most part, correcting errors rather than demonstrating "correct" actions to be emulated precisely. Fifth, coaching is carried out in generalized terms; such instructions must always be adapted to specific individual capacity and particular real situations. Good coaching can and should lead to improved performance, but that assumes individual effort. Not everyone can become a professional golfer, but most individuals can be coached to a respectable level of performance. The expectations of both coach and player should incorporate enough reality control to avoid frustration while seeking to develop potential fully.

The text is designed to satisfy these conditions. The main body of the text develops the metalanguage for criticizing thinking, the theory of play, to be mastered by the prospective player. The purposes of the thinking "game" are derived from a conception of the human situation sketched briefly in unit 2. Since that conception of the human situation serves as a point of departure for both developing and improving the theory of play, the reader should test the construction against his or her own experience as systematically and carefully as possible. No critical apparatus should be accepted uncritically, particularly when it has far-reaching implications for both the individual and society. The overall theory, the critical apparatus, is summarized broadly in units 3 and 4; that overview should serve to locate each of the elements within the overall theory. In the text, the elements are examined in detail, including as much redundancy as was shown necessary in past experience teaching the course. Finally, each unit of material includes a set of exercises, each divided into two parts: (1) A set of review questions is used to call attention to the primary elements in the theory and serve as a check on reading accuracy and comprehension; and (2) a set of discussion questions suggests some of the applications of the critical apparatus in everyday affairs and provides an opportunity to relate the abstract mechanism to concrete experience.

Exercises

Review Questions

1. Identify the precise meaning of each of the following terms as they are used in the text:
   a. knowledge
   b. criticism
   c. metalanguage

2. In your own words, describe the function performed by a competent coach in athletics.

3. Given two training programs, one for training dogs and the other for training people to train dogs, list some of the topics that would be covered in both courses and others that would appear in one course but not in the other. Discuss the way in which the actual behavior of dogs is linked to the content of the course at various points.

4. What is meant by a "self-coaching" player?

5. How is rote learning or memorizing used in athletic coaching?

Discussion

1. If you were coaching a golf team, would you seek to avoid mistakes or concentrate on correcting them? Why?

2. Describe a single play in any sport known to you from the perspective of
   a. a spectator who knows nothing of the game
   b. a player
   c. a good coach

3. What advantages and disadvantages would you associate with learning how to play a game from books and lectures? Would these same advantages and disadvantages appear in efforts to learn how to improve thinking performance? Give reasons for your answer.

4. How can an athletic coach assess the quality of his or her own coaching? To what extent is winning the game an adequate basis for assessing the performance of either player or coach?

2. The Human Situation and Human Purposes

In athletics, coaching and criticism require a theory of play that is able to link the actions of players to the achievement of the purpose set by those who control the rules of the game. In the apparatus, the overall purpose of the game is broken down analytically to show contingent purposes whose fulfillment contributes to the overall purpose, other purposes that contribute to achieving these, and so on. For coaching critical thinking, the purposes of the game must be created, and justified, by the prospective coach. They are not established by authority or found in nature.

The task turns out to be much easier than might be expected because of the overriding significance of human life in human affairs generally. *The fundamental human purpose to be achieved through systematic thinking is always and everywhere to maintain and improve the conditions of life of some human population.* Without a human reference point, there can be no acceptable basis for criticizing human actions, physical or intellectual. The practical problem is to identify the set of secondary purposes whose achievement is necessary and/or sufficient for achieving the primary goal. Once a set of purposes has been established, development of an analytic or critical framework, a theory of play, can proceed as in athletics. As it turns out, only three major first-order purposes seem to be required for fulfilling the overall purpose.

The Three Prime Purposes

Given humans as they appear, and the world as it is currently understood, maintaining and improving the human situation depends on the fulfillment of only three first-order purposes. Although it may prove necessary, or useful, to extend or augment those three purposes in due course, they seem for the moment to be both necessary and sufficient for fulfilling the overall purpose accepted for human thinking. That they are *necessary* means the purpose cannot be achieved unless they have been satisfied; that they are *sufficient* means that once they have been satisfied, the purpose will be achieved. For example, if burning cannot occur without oxygen, then oxygen is a necessary condition for burning. If burning will occur given oxygen, flammable material, and a high enough temperature, other things equal, these are the sufficient conditions for burning.

1. In order to survive, humans must be able to *anticipate* events that have not yet been observed, to *predict* observations that have not yet been made or are not yet known. The predicted event may lie in either the future or the past, as long as it has not yet been observed. That is, expecting that today's rain will produce flooding tomorrow is precisely equivalent to expecting that yesterday's snow has blocked the road over the mountain. Both kinds of expectations or predictions are produced and justified in the same way using the same criteria.

2. Survival and prosperity also require the capacity to *control* future events by present human actions in predictable ways—to cause events to occur or prevent them from occurring by deliberate actions. Without some capacity to control the future (if only to escape drowning by moving to higher ground), human life could hardly continue. Predictions of future events, coupled with some capacity for control, allow the individual to adapt the self to expected future situations. The ability to control events makes it possible to adapt natural conditions to human needs and preferences. The development of human capacity to control the flow of events, mainly through the natural sciences, accounts for human dominance over the other living things on earth.

3. The capacity to control events, to produce foreseeable outcomes by deliberate action, forces humans to *choose* or *act*; the third major intellectual requirement is for the apparatus required to make and justify such choices. To be able to control future events is to have the capacity to produce one situation in the world rather than another. It follows that any person with the capacity to alter the flow of events is actually forced to make a choice. No positive action is required; if the capacity to act is real, not to act still serves to produce a world that is in some way different from what it would be had the capacity been exercised. The meaning of *choice* is defined by reference to the capacity to produce change by voluntary action. Otherwise, failure to act would not be considered an "action," or choice. Yet the physician who ignores the injured person whose life he could readily have saved "causes" the death of that person as surely as if he had severed the jugular. An analytic or critical framework must take

that situation into account. Choices are therefore unavoidable any time that a human actor can alter the flow of events by voluntary action. The outcomes that could be achieved by acting, plus the outcome expected to follow from the drift course of events, constitute the content of the choice. That usage may seem a little complex, but it avoids a great deal of confusion in the analysis of action.

For criticizing and improving human thinking, a theory is needed that can show how these three primary human purposes can be achieved by real-world people in real situations. Put another way, the theory comprises the set of assumptions required for achieving those purposes. The meaning of *knowledge* can then be identified with the instruments required for satisfying the same three purposes. Such a theory can be tested and improved in the same way as the theory of play in athletics: by training individuals in ways implied by the theory and then evaluating their real-world performance.

Of course, human interactions with an environment that includes both the subjective self and many other persons involve purposes other than anticipating and controlling events and making choices. Individuals go to the environment in all manner of contexts, whether seeking amusement or merely passing the time away. There are various involuntary interactions with the outside world, such as breathing, which are controlled autonomically. The three primary purposes that bound the applications of the analytic framework to be developed here are necessary and sufficient only for meeting the overall objective of maintaining and improving the human condition.

Limits and Possibilities

In thinking, as in athletics, the theory of play used to improve performance must function under real-world game conditions and not merely in imagination or even in a laboratory. A theory of knowledge that demanded capacity no human possessed would be useless, and a theory that ignored the constraints imposed by real-world conditions would not work. Human capacity and limitations must be respected. The relevant factors will range from the attributes of the human nervous system to the various ways in which the "natural" world is known to function. It is unlikely that all the underlying assumptions in a complex theory can be identified, but the major limits and possibilities can be noted briefly.

The central problem that an adequate theory of knowledge must somehow resolve or circumvent before the three primary human purposes can be achieved is readily stated. Each individual lives in an unending flow of time at the border between past and future, *facing backward* toward the past. Since it is usually assumed that each person is wholly dependent on the sensory system for information about the environment, and the sensory system is focused on the immediate present, all the information available to the individual refers strictly to the past. But the focus of human life lies in the future and not in the past. The results of present actions appear in the future; the hopes and fears experienced in the present, as well as the aspirations, are frustrated or realized in the future. Humans direct their lives by reference to the future to a surprising degree, and that creates a basic dilemma. Human needs, and the thinking that seeks to satisfy them, are oriented almost entirely to the future; the sensory apparatus is tuned to the past and cannot be changed. Moreover, the future cannot be inferred from the past using formal logic because that operation is forbidden by the rules. In effect, some means must be found for dealing with the human future, of fulfilling human purposes, using information about the past alone. How that can be done, and at what cost, occupy the remainder of the text. For the moment, some other aspects of the human situation that either complicate the problem and make it harder to solve or contribute to a possible solution need to be identified briefly.

Most of the perplexities facing the prospective coach in systematic thinking are created by the operating characteristics of the human sensory and nervous systems. The sensory system, the eyes and ears and other sensors, lies between the external environment and the knowledge-creating central nervous system, or brain. Three points are particularly important for dealing with the problem of knowledge. First, the information that enters the brain combines the effects of the external world/transmission medium with the operation of the sensory mechanism into an inseparable, integrated whole. Direct observation therefore says nothing about the character of the external world alone. Knowledge of the world therefore cannot be tested by comparing it directly to what is "out there." The "real world" lies beyond reach. Some other means of testing and justifying knowledge must be found. As we see later in the text, a solution can be found in the relation between action and purpose, in the use of pragmatic criteria of adequacy, but only at a price.

The second important characteristic of data provided by the senses, already noted in passing, is that they refer only to the past. And statements that refer to the future, which are essential for dealing with the primary purposes set for the intellectual enterprise, cannot be inferred or deduced from statements about the past—which could be justified by sensory evidence. The separation of past and future is only logical; observations or experience must somehow provide support and justification for knowledge claims that refer to the future, for there is no alternative source of evidence. The relation between the two cannot, however, be completely formal and logical.

The third point to be noted about sensory information is that it is always static, like a single frame in a motion picture film. Change, which is an essential concept for dealing with human affairs, is actually inferred from differences among observations of what is assumed to be "the same" situation at different points in time—it cannot be observed directly. Taken together, these three factors make up the principal obstacles to success in the effort to fulfill human purposes accurately and reliably. They are formidable, but they can be overcome or circumvented.

On the positive side, the human species is not without advantages. Four well-established human attributes, taken in combination with two of the basic features of the natural environment, make possible the fulfillment of the primary purposes in reliable ways at reasonable cost.

1. Humans are able to *discriminate* perceptions into things perceived, to separate out elements in the environment and group them according to their similarities and differences. The world does not appear as an undifferentiated blur in space and time but as a collection of discrete things that can be related in both time and space. That kind of organization of perceptions is the first step toward a solution of the problem of dealing with the future using information about the past.

2. Humans are able to *generalize* their perceptions, or experiences, into patterns divorced from particular times and places. No one knows exactly how such generalizations are produced, and the capacity is not always exercised very carefully, but generalization does occur frequently, and it provides a way of bridging the logical gap between past and future. Two kinds of patterns are created by generalization. First, perceptions are organized or grouped to create *classifications,* sets of "things" that share common properties—dogs and mothers and typewriters and so on. Second, patterns are created that link or relate things in various ways: Fertilizer applications are linked to the production of cereal crops, falling from considerable heights is linked to serious injuries, specific choices are linked to a more acceptable way of life, and so on. Generalization produces patterns that may be either empirical or normative; those patterns can be used to order past experience and to deal with the future. They make possible an evasion of the limits imposed by the sensory apparatus.

3. Humans are able to *calculate.* They can create abstract patterns (logics or calculi) consisting of symbols and strict rules that control the meaning of the symbols and their interactions. Algebra, geometry, arithmetic, formal logic, and a host of mathematical systems are included in this group. Within a calculus, the implications of specific changes in the relations among symbols can be calculated precisely and completely. Suitably linked to observation, those calculations can be transferred to real-world affairs. The dynamic force that drives systematic thinking is created by harnessing the calculating power of a formal calculus to the generalized patterns that appear in observation. If the connections are properly established, calculations made within the logic can be used to anticipate or control events, and make choices. A simple example occurs when the logic labeled arithmetic is combined with observation. If two apples are placed in a basket, then two more apples are added to the first pair, a simple calculation tells us there are now four apples in the basket—there is no need to look. Looking, however, provides confirmation for the application of that logic (arithmetic) to that situation, and for the accuracy of the calculation. Similarly, calculation tells us that the general statement "All dogs have two ears" contains or implies the particular statement "If X is a dog, then X has two ears." Such particular statements can be tested against observation or experience, thus providing confirming evidence for the general statement. In effect, calculation makes it possible to test general statements against past experience and thus provide the reasons needed for accepting general statements. It enables us to explore the content of general statements and test that content against experience.

4. Finally, humans *react* affectively; they like or dislike, prefer or reject different things. It *matters* to individual humans whether the world has one set of characteristics or another. Without such preferences, there could be no basis for making choices, and no reason to want to choose. The effort to produce and improve knowledge, in other words, makes sense only in a situation where humans strive deliberately to remain alive or improve their life situations, in a world that can be molded to some degree by human preferences.

Taken together, the human capacities to discriminate, generalize, calculate, and react affectively provide the foundation on which an adequate theory of knowledge can be constructed. They are not, however, sufficient for fulfilling the primary human purposes. Two more characteristics of humanity and the human situation must be added. Both are commonplace, and therefore easily overlooked, but each is essential for developing the kind of knowledge that maintaining and improving the human situation demands.

First, each human individual is born into an ongoing system; there is no need to begin from a blank slate. This is very fortunate, for if humanity had to begin anew with each generation, survival would be extremely uncertain. Humans survive readily at one point in time because other humans survived at an earlier time; they cannot survive alone. Being born is testimonial advertising for human success. And since success is clearly contingent on the creation of the knowledge required for survival, that gives us good reasons to believe that such knowledge lies within human capacity. That is encouraging, if only in the long run. Further, much of the requisite knowledge must be available, captured in language, culture, history, and practice. Past experience provides humanity's principal treasure trove, an enormous storehouse that can be searched for knowledge useful for dealing with current problems. Of course, the storehouse cannot be used efficiently without critical capacity, the ability to separate what is valuable and valid from what is not. Argument and criticism, based on an adequate coaching language, are the keys that unlock the storehouse and help build an even better storehouse for future generations.

Second, the knowledge required, particularly for predicting and controlling events, need deal only with recurring events, with repetitions. There is no way to deal with events that have not occurred before and cannot be anticipated; there is no need to deal with events that will never again recur once they have happened. The point is a trifle complex but very important. In some respects, every observed event is unique. Each event has its own time and place, at the least. Yet, every event is in some respects like other events. The critical question is whether the events that have the greatest impact on the human situation are enough alike to be dealt with by a common procedure or practice—whether a coaching language can be developed for the activity. Childbirth, for example, is treated as a recurring event by physicians and a unique event by mothers. Both perspectives are valid; each can contribute usefully to the human enterprise, and there need be no conflict between them. Indeed, the physician should be sensitive to the unique aspects of each birth, and the mother should realize that what has been learned about childbirth generally can be of great value to herself and the child. If both perspectives are honored, the mother and child should be better off—healthier and safer—and the physician's knowledge of childbirth should be improved and reinforced.

Experience suggests that in an ongoing system of human interactions, the ability to deal with recurring events is sufficient to maintain and improve the human situation. That is good news, since human capacity cannot extend beyond the abilty to handle recurrences, but not surprising—if such knowledge were insufficient, there would be no humans to be surprised. That does not mean that humans have no capacity whatever to deal with events that do not recur; so long as an event is not completely unique, so long as there is some past human experience that can be transferred to the particular case, a better-than-random performance in dealing with unusual or nonrecurring events remains possible.

Against this background of requirements, possibilities, and constraints, discussion can turn to the theory of knowledge needed to show how the primary purposes can be achieved. An overview of the structure, and the processes involved, is sketched in units 3 and 4. The treatment is summary, and meant to provide a brief account of the major elements involved and show how they relate. Details of structure and process are covered in the main body of the text. Examples and illustrations are taken mainly from the natural sciences: in general, they are simpler, clearer, and less likely to arouse controversy than examples taken from political, social, or economic affairs.

Exercises

Review Questions

1. What overriding human purpose is used here to control development of the critical apparatus or theory of knowledge? Can you think of any significant problems that lie outside its boundaries?

2. What are the primary first-order purposes that must be satisfied before the overall purpose in human affairs can be achieved? Again, can you think of any important concerns that would not be included in that arena?

3. Differentiate the necessary and the sufficient conditions for an event to occur. Illustrate each from your own experience.

4. What does "generalize" mean? Illustrate from experience.

5. What is the central logical problem that a theory of knowledge must resolve or evade?

6. What are the three primary implications of having to base human knowledge on sensory data?

7. The induction problem can be avoided, and knowledge produced that will allow fulfillment of the basic human purposes, because of certain basic characteristics of the human species and their life situation. What are they?

Discussion

1. Is it possible to deal effectively with an event that is completely unique? With an event that will not recur? Illustrate.

2. Is it appropriate to think of language as a communication device like a telephone or is language something more than a tool?

3. Explain why human survival would be unlikely if humans did not react affectively to differences in the environment.

3. The Theory of Knowledge I

Given the set of capacities and limitations that characterize the human situation, a relatively simple procedure is sufficient for fulfilling the three primary purposes of anticipating, controlling, and choosing. A generalized pattern of relations is created out of past experience—"All robins migrate," for example. That pattern is combined with a particular observation by making an assumption ("that bird" is a robin) and the implication of the combination is calculated, producing an expectation—"that bird" will migrate. Human knowledge is made up of an enormous number of such patterns, of varying scope, complexity, and power. The patterns must be created; they cannot be produced logically or discovered in nature. They must also be testable, subject to quality control, else they could not be relied on nor improved. Bearing in mind that there can be a great many different kinds of patterns, this fairly simple procedure is able to account for the achievements of the physical sciences as well as success in the conduct of personal affairs. It serves as the foundation on which the theory used in argument and criticism is built.

Creating and using a generalized pattern of experience to achieve a purpose in the environment require a four-step procedure that can be followed regardless of the purpose sought or the kind of pattern employed. It is illustrated here using a classification to predict future events, but the same steps are used for controlling events or choosing. It must be assumed that the purpose sought has already been determined by the inquirer.

In the first step, the purpose sought in the environment is identified within the theory of knowledge. That purpose must lie within the boundaries of anticipating, controlling, or choosing, for the theory does not function if other purposes are being pursued. The purpose, however, may be to contribute to achieving a primary purpose—by producing a description, for example—and not to predict or control events directly. If a very striking bird is observed in the neighborhood, for example, and an observer wishes to know whether or not it will remain in the area through the coming winter, the purpose in hand is to make a prediction (the bird will or will not migrate), and a pattern of generalized experience is needed that can fulfill that purpose.

The second step in fulfilling a purpose is to locate or create a suitable pattern. For the moment, let us assume that the necessary pattern is already available; otherwise, it would have to be created, and that involves complexities and uncertainties best avoided in this introductory material. If a classification is already available that applies to the bird observed, and if that classification is known to the observer (he or she knows about "that kind of bird"), the problem can be solved and the purpose achieved. A major function of education, whether in school or on the streets, is to familiarize the individual with the patterns in use in the various areas of human activity. In complex academic fields such as chemistry or medicine, where the number of patterns and variations is extremely large, specialization—concentration on one part of the field—is unavoidable.

The third step is to assume that the pattern in hand fits the observed situation. In the illustration, it must be assumed that the bird belongs to the species for which a classification is available; in effect, the observer assumes that a bird of species X has been seen. The effect of the assumption is to allow a transfer of calculations from the formal pattern to the world of observation. In the case of a classification, the pattern consists of all characteristics shared by members of the class: size, shape, color, eating and mating habits, and so on. By assuming that the thing observed belongs to the class, the observer is entitled to transfer all the known characteristics of the class to the thing observed. If the bird is a robin, it can be expected to look like and behave like a robin. If the observer is uncertain about the diagnosis, a tentative assumption can be made and tested: "*If* this is a robin, it should look and act as follows." If those expectations are fulfilled, that confirms the diagnosis and the other characteristics of that class of birds can then be transferred to the case in hand.

The logic by which predictions are produced from classifications and observations is quite simple. The classification consists of generalized statements about the shared attributes of class members, produced inductively from observations and tested against further observations. For example, one of the shared attributes of a given class of birds may be annual migration, in which case the classification contains the statement "All birds of class C migrate annually." A combination of observation and diagnosis (assumption) produces a particular statement, "This bird is a member of class C." They combine to form an elementary syllogism:

PROPOSITION 1. *All birds of class C migrate annually.*

PROPOSITION 2. *This bird is a member of class C.*
∴ *This bird will migrate annually.*

The conclusion is logically inescapable once the two initial propositions are accepted. Past experience provides the evidence that justifies the first proposition. The adequacy of the diagnosis is a more complex problem, for the diagnosis may be correct yet the conclusion may not appear in the observed world—there are always exceptions, and the bird observed may not in fact migrate that year. Although judgments are involved, and mistakes are possible, the procedure can in practice produce very reliable and accurate results; it can fulfill the original purpose of the observer. Note particularly that the prediction is not generated *within* a pattern but by combining pattern and observation. A device that creates predictions without reference to specific observations is a prophecy generator rather than a predictor.

One step remains: to justify acceptance of the expectation. In that step, which is the heart of systematic criticism, attention is focused on two fundamental points: (1) the selection of a pattern, the assumption that the particular case observed belongs to the class of cases generalized by the pattern; and (2) the validity of the pattern, the extent to which past experience supports it. Valid prediction depends on selecting a pattern that is both appropriate to the situation and adequately established; mistakes can occur at either point. In the example, if the observer assumed that the bird was a robin, and robins migrate annually, it would be justifiable to expect the particular bird to migrate as well. The critic, however, can raise two questions about the argument: First, was the diagnosis correct? Was the bird really a robin? Obviously, if the bird was not a robin, there would be no justification for expecting it to migrate. Second, was the classification accurate? Do robins really migrate each year? Such questions are easily answered with respect to well-known species of birds such as robins. But if the classification refers to the voting habits of members of particular economic or religious groups, the reliability of the classification may be much more doubtful.

Assessment of justifications for predictions is complicated by the fact that applying a pattern actually tests *two* factors, the assumption of class membership and the validity of the class. Interpretation can be a tricky business. The bird observed may not be a robin, for example, but still belong to a migrating species, in which case the prediction will be correct but for the wrong reasons. Further, if robins actually did *not* migrate, and the observer mistakenly assumed that they did, that would further compound the problem. Asking yourself how such errors could be detected, or even where they are likely to occur, will tell you a great deal about the kinds of problems involved in developing and using knowledge in rigorous ways.

The justification for accepting and using a pattern of generalized experience does not refer to the procedures used to create the pattern. Outside of logic and mathematics, procedures cannot guarantee the quality of the product generated by the procedure. Nor does the justification depend on the qualities of the person who produced or endorsed the generalization. Justification is always a function of evidence and experience. Because knowledge patterns are formed of generalized experience, it is safe to assume that persons with no experience in an area are very unlikely to create valid generalizations about it, but the amount of experience that a person has had does not, in itself, justify accepting the generalization. In the last analysis, justifications depend on testing in use, either directly or indirectly. It can be shown by direct test that a particular chemical kills a particular type of weed, for example, but the effect of changing the tilt of the earth with reference to the sun on the earth's climate can be justified only indirectly—by reference to patterns that have been tested through application.

How human knowledge is created, how experience is generalized to form patterns, simply is not known. There are strategies that can be expected to stimulate such creativity, and factors that inhibit it, but there is no method, scientific or nonscientific, that can guarantee results. That condition does not pose any special problems for systematic criticism. In the past, human creativity has appeared frequently and regularly in every area of human activity, and there is no reason to suppose it will stop— and some reason to expect it might increase because of increased opportunities. Creativity must be assumed, but it seems a safe assumption, and in any event there is no choice in the matter. It may be wise to try to remove obstacles to creativity, or to stimulate it by any available means, but that is another point. Criticism must focus on the products of creativity, on the generalized patterns suggested for organizing human experience, not on the methods used to produce them. In many ways, the most important test facing any new pattern or generalization is its compatibility with the body of knowledge that has already been accepted—suitably augmented by evidence obtained from testing and experimenting. Existing knowledge serves as both the primary testing ground for new proposals and as a launching pad for efforts to generate them. That is the underlying reason why careful study of present knowledge, and its historical development, is such an important part of systematic training, in academic life or in everyday affairs.

Organizing and Generalizing Experience

The reason why simple patterns can be used to fulfill vital human purposes is found in the results of the process labeled *generalizing*. There is no magic involved in the process, though it cannot be formalized. Patterns are used to organize experience; experience, when organized, is available in patterns. The process is necessarily cumulative. If there were no knowledge available at the start, very little would be accomplished. That is the reason why the ongoing character of the human enterprise is so important. The more experience available in generalized form, other things equal, the easier the task of fulfilling specified human purposes. Less time is spent charting blind passageways as more passageways are known to be blind. There is a potential danger here, of course, for if the past controls the future too strongly, it may discourage innovation. But in general, the old adage often applied to wealth, perhaps wrongly, is clearly applicable with respect to knowledge: the more that is available, the more that is likely to be produced, and the more quickly it is likely to appear.

The effects of generalization are best illustrated by comparing a description, which is particular and static, with a generalization, which is unrestricted with respect to time and place. All of human experience begins as a flow of raw perceptions into the central nervous system—the system is, of course, self-stimulating in some degree. An initial organization of those perceptions produces a description, which is analogous to a still photograph or a snapshot taken with a particular camera lens and film at a particular time and place. Aside from language, which is too complex to be examined here and must be taken as given, only two kinds of instruments are needed for describing events. First, a set of concepts that identify the "things" observed—the birds, typewriters, atoms, and so on. Such concepts are already generalized forms or classifications, and a good supply is available in every language. Second, an instrument is needed that expresses the various kinds of relations that hold among the "things" observed—such "relational terms" include anything from "larger" or "to the left of" to "earlier" or "quicker."

Concepts and relational terms make up the spectacles through which humans "see" the world. They are the lenses and film used to make still photographs of the world around (and within) individuals. A description summarizes what is observed at a particular time and place using a particular set of spectacles; concepts and relational terms serve to "organize" the incoming flow of raw perceptions. The content of a description is a function of the concepts employed and the environment observed—plus the competence of the observer. If a concept such as *sand* is applied in

21

SAINT PETER'S COLLEGE LIBRARY
JERSEY CITY, NEW JERSEY 07306

a jungle environment, the resulting description would be simply "There is no sand here." If such concepts as *trees, vines,* and *leaves* were used to describe the same environment, the resulting description would be lengthy and detailed. Both descriptions would be equally valid; they are fully compatible. Both can be justified, and if observations are made carefully by trained observers using precise concepts and perhaps mechanical measuring tools, such justifications are perhaps the strongest available to humans. The validity or accuracy of a description does not, however, establish its value; that is a function of the use that can be made of its content.

Generalization is the most important step in the development of useful knowledge. It can take a number of different forms: All birds have wings; as temperature increases, the density of the atmosphere decreases; some deer have antlers; my mother is a very happy person; and so on. One can generalize the attributes of a single person or thing or generalize the attributes of a class of things; the relations among things that can be generalized range from physical and temporal links to normative preferences. The process depends on experience, but the amount of experience seems not to be crucial. There is a good illustration of the point in astronomy: Tycho Brahe, a sixteenth-century Danish astronomer, observed and recorded the movements of the stars for years but it was Johannes Kepler, using Brahe's observations, who generalized them into the laws of planetary motion that are still in use today. We have no grounds for predicting that Kepler would create those general propositions and Brahe would not.

The result of generalization is a proposition that relates two or more things in a particular way. The relation is expected to hold any time the things are observed. If a classification of dogs asserts that "All dogs have two ears," that expectation applies to every dog, past or future, that is encountered. The proposition is not time bound. If the relations do not hold when the things are observed, the generalization is mistaken. In practice, there will almost always be discrepancies. Dogs occasionally lose an ear, or perhaps fail to develop one. If the discrepancies are numerous, a limitation will be imposed on the general statement: "All dogs have two ears *except. . . .*"

The value of such timeless propositions can hardly be exaggerated. They provide the bridge between readily justifiable and testable statements about the past and the kinds of statements about the future that are needed for predicting, controlling, and choosing. Of course, generalized statements are always in some degree problematic or uncertain. Even predictions based on the law of gravity would fail, for example, if all of the molecules in a solid object were for an instant moving in the same direction—a possibility, however remote. But generalization marks one limit of human capacity, and the success already achieved in using generalizations, and the absence of any reliable alternative, suggests continued efforts to develop more — and to acquire the capacity to use them critically.

In addition to providing a bridge between past and future, generalization adds enormously to the *content* of the knowledge system, the amount of knowledge available. For generalizations contain *more* information than the sum of all the descriptive accounts from which they were developed. The extra content must be assumed, and the assumption may be mistaken. But the extra content added by generalization plays a vital role in human efforts to deal systematically and effectively with the environment.

Two basic kinds of generalizations are found in every supply of knowledge: The first generalizes the attributes of individuals or classes; the second generalizes relationships among things or classes. The first type, consisting of classifications or concepts, has already been examined. Relational generalizations can be broken into a number of subdivisions. In some cases, the relation generalized is static; other propositions generalize the effects of change. Some relations refer to empirical matters, such as the relation between temperature and level of discomfort; others will refer to normative matters, such as the relative desirability of wealth and happiness. The content of the generalization, obviously, determines the kinds of purposes for which it can be used. Conversely, the purpose sought determines the kinds of generalizations required to fulfill it.

There are two prime limits on the generalization process. First, no more can be included in a generalization than experience warrants. That is obvious when positive observations are generalized, for traits or relations that do not appear cannot be included in general statements. Judgment is more difficult, however, when the absence of a trait or relation is generalized; the question how many members of a class must be observed before it is safe to assume that *no* members of that class have a particular trait or characteristic is very difficult to answer satisfactorily.

The second major limitation on generalization, which seems to function in every classification scheme thus far devised, is sometimes referred to as the *index number problem.* As the scope of a class increases, as the class is defined with increasing looseness and wider boundaries, the amount of information that is contained in the generalized attributes of the class diminishes. Eventually, that leads to saying nothing about everything. Conversely, as the class is narrowed, defined more precisely and rigorously, class membership decreases until everything can be said about nothing. Neither extreme, obviously, is very useful.

What kind of evidence or justification can be offered, and should be accepted, for a generalization? Because the justification must be produced *before* the generalization is accepted and acted on, and since the general statement must hold in the future and not just in the past, justification is always incomplete and imperfect. But since generalizations occur in an ongoing system, and are produced by persons familiar with the events generalized, it is unlikely that no evidence, direct or indirect, is available to support them.

The kind of justification that generalization requires depends, of course, on the content of the generalization, the nature of the claim, and that point is examined in detail in the main body of the text. More broadly, three aspects of generalizations need to be examined by the critic or user; an illustration will show their importance. Assume a field of corn is being damaged by insects. A particular insecticide is suggested for ridding the field of the insects. Should the insecticide be applied? What factors need to be examined before that question can be answered? Obviously, the farmer cannot be indifferent to the outcome, else the question is meaningless. The use of the insecticide presumes a prior decision preferring a field without insects to a field in which they are present. Once that decision is made, the farmer faces a diagnostic problem: Will the use of the insecticide solve the farmer's problem? Application of the insecticide must be expected to produce an acceptable outcome for the farmer.

If the insecticide is in fact expected to produce the desired result, are there any side effects that would inhibit use? Spoiling the crop, or rendering it inedible, would be too high a price to pay for eliminating the insects. If there are no worrisome side effects, the farmer must then ask what actions must be taken to bring about the desired result. In a simple case of this kind, the user merely follows instructions. In more complex situations, such as brain surgery or repairing an automobile that has been badly damaged, a complex chain of actions may be required to implement the decision.

If the actions are feasible, the farmer may wonder whether the assumption that they will in fact produce his preferred outcome is well grounded. For evidence, he could turn to the manufacturer, to other farmers, or to his own past experience, seeking historical data about the relation between the use of the insecticide and the effect on the insects, or even more sophisticated data relating the chemical characteristics of the insecticide to the life-sustaining processes within the insect. If all these questions can be answered satisfactorily, that provides a justification for applying the material, and the application in turn becomes a test of the sequence of assumptions that influenced the decision.

Exercises

Review Questions

1. Sketch briefly the basic procedure used in fulfilling the primary human purposes.

2. Outline the four-step procedure required in efforts to fulfill human purposes through reasoned and defensible actions.

3. Identify the two fundamental points to be examined when seeking to justify a generalized pattern.

4. What are the more important limitations on generalization?

5. Identify the basic tools used in description and illustrate each one from personal experience.

6. Summarize the similarities and differences between descriptions and generalizations.

7. Identify the two main kinds of generalizations available for fulfilling human purposes and illustrate each one from personal experience.

Discussion

1. What is meant by the "diagnosis problem," and why is it important? Illustrate from experience.

2. How does a description resemble a snapshot or still photo, and in what ways are they different?

3. In what sense is it true to say that the ultimate test of any knowledge claim is application or use for achieving human purposes?

4. State one general proposition and one descriptive proposition about someone you know well. Then provide a justification for accepting each statement. In what ways are the two justifications similar and different?

4. The Theory of Knowledge II

Summarizing briefly, the theory being developed here is intended to show how to create, apply, and test the knowledge required to maintain and improve the conditions of life of some human population. Assuming that criticism and improvement depend on the purposes for which knowledge is to be used, three primary purposes are identified as necessary and sufficient for achieving the overall goal: predicting and controlling future events and making choices. The theory asserts that those purposes can be achieved within the constraints that govern the human enterprise by organizing and generalizing human experience into patterns, combining those patterns with observations, and calculating the implications of the combination. Assuming an adequate language, an ongoing human population, and a capacity for logic or calculation, only five kinds of patterns are needed to fulfill those purposes, and each pattern is common in every aspect of human affairs. They are summarized in this unit and examined in detail in the main body of the text.

Notation

Each of the patterns that constitutes the body of human knowledge consists of a set of two or more elements or things and a set of relations linking them together. The structure and function of the various kinds of patterns is clarified in a very useful way by using a simple notation system. Each element in a pattern will be called a *variable* and will be written as *(V)*. Such concepts as size, shape, color, eating habits, and so on would be considered variables in a descriptive account of a bird, for example; a pattern used to predict weather would include such variables as wind direction, temperature, humidity, or cloud coverage. Each variable will have a *value,* determined by measuring the thing observed on an appropriate scale or measuring unit. The height of a bird, for example, can be measured in inches, centimeters, or even by comparison with another object. The value of the "height" variable will be the result of that measurement—that is, so many inches, centimeters, or "larger than that stick." The special problems associated with such measurements are considered later.

The relations among the elements in a pattern are stated in the form of rules that are symbolized as *(R)*. Two kinds of rules are needed in the knowledge system. The first type identifies the range of values that can be taken by the different variables included in a set; the second links the values of a set of variables into a calculable relation. The first type of rule is used in classifications to state the shared attributes of class members. One rule in a classification system for birds, for example, will state the range of heights for a particular species of birds; others will state the range of colors, migrating habits, and so on. In a forecast, on the other hand, the rules will link the values of the variables in a calculable relation. The rule may state that the measured value of one variable will always be twice the measured value of another, for example, and stipulate the unit of measurement to be used—that the number of units of a given product sold by a store will always be twice the number of units of another product sold.

Patterns that incorporate calculable rules relating the values of the variables will be enclosed in parentheses ( ). Ohm's law, for example, is written as $(E = IR)$, meaning that the voltage in electrical circuits, measured in volts *(E)*, is the sum of the current *(I)*, measured in amperes, and the resistance of the circuit *(R)*, measured in ohms. If any two of these values are known, the value of the third variable can be calculated, and that is indicated by the use of parentheses with the pattern. Patterns that cannot be calculated in this way are enclosed in square brackets [ ], indicating that the rules show the selection of variables included in the set or the range of values they can be expected to take. Each pattern, regardless of the type of rules it includes, carries a set of limiting conditions governing application, conditions that must be satisfied before the pattern can be expected to hold. Ohm's law, for example, will not operate if the electrical circuit is connected to the ground or submerged in water, among other things.

We proceed now to the five basic patterns used for fulfilling the primary purposes required of a knowledge supply. They are grouped according to the purposes for which they can be used, since it is the purpose that matters rather than the characteristics of the instrument.

Generating Expectations/Predicting

Three of the five basic forms of organized experience can be used to make predictions or generate expectations. The first, already used to illustrate the general process, is a *classification* or concept. The others, which relate members of two or more classes by calculable rule under specified limiting conditions, may be either a *forecast* or a *theory* depending on the additional assumptions they contain.

A classification generalizes information obtained by observing members of a class of things in the environment; its rules state the shared attributes or characteristics of members of the class, such as physical characteristics, relations with other things, and so on. Development of the instrument begins always with observations of a particular thing, separating it from the rest of what is observed and recording its characteristics. Additional members of the same class must then be sought and observed. The classification emerges as a generalized statement of the attributes observed in every class member. Those shared attributes become the defining characteristics of the class. If the classification has significance in some human life (separates edible and nonedible birds, for example) and is sufficiently accurate, then a valuable tool has been created. It is essential that both the accuracy and the significance of classifications be examined; it is relatively easy to produce accurate but utterly useless classifications.

Structurally, a classification consists of a set of variables, each referring to one of the shared attributes of class members, and a set of rules that state the range of values each variable can take. In the notation system used here, a classification appears as

$$[V_1 \ V_2 \ V_3 \ldots V_n \ R_1 \ R_2 \ldots R_n].$$

The reason for using square brackets is that each rule is established separately and the value of each variable is a function of the appropriate rule. The rules do not link the values of the variables, they establish a range of possible values for one variable. A common example of classification is found in the market where meats are graded to show quality, nutritional value, and so on. A classification summarizes what is known about particular kinds of things, taken collectively; if accurate, anything identified as a member of the class will have all the attributes included in the classification; if significant, that information will be useful to someone for purposes of action. It is important to note that classifications need not include everything that is known about any particular class member, or even everything that is true of every class member, and that there will almost always be aberrations and discrepancies—class members that do not always demonstrate all the established characteristics of the classification.

The procedure by which classifications are used to generate expectations or predictions that can be justified in advance has already been touched on and is sketched here only briefly. Summarily, a "thing" is observed and its characteristics noted, it is assumed to be a member of a specific class on the basis of those observations, and that assumption allows the transfer of generalizations from the classification to the particular case. Three conditions must be fulfilled before the classification can be used to make successful predictions: (1) class membership must be identified correctly; (2) the classification must be valid; and (3) the logical calculations must be correct. If the prediction fails, one or more of the three conditions has not been satisfied, or the observer may be dealing with an exceptional case or aberration. Classifications are widely used for predicting in everyday affairs, particularly in purchasing, and an important part of marketing is devoted to developing in the prospective purchaser's mind a "classification" that will lead to the purchase of a particular product — automobile advertising provides some of the better examples of that practice currently available.

The second kind of instrument used to produce justified expectations or predictions consists of two or more variables whose values are linked by rule subject to specified limiting conditions. One of the variables will refer to the event being predicted; the other will provide the cue, the observation that triggers the prediction or expectation. An instrument used for predicting rain, for example, will include as one of its variables the concept rain or precipitation, linking its value (rain or no rain) to the value of some other variable(s) such as temperature or humidity or both.

Two different instruments are available for such predicting. They have precisely the same structure (two or more variables whose values are linked by rule), but they embody different assumptions about the nature of the relationship between the variables and can therefore be used for different purposes. In the simple form, it is assumed that the values of the two variables covary or change in a particular way if they are not interfered with. It follows that if the value of one variable is known, the value of the second can be predicted using the rule included in the pattern. Such structures are labeled *forecasts*. If it is assumed that the variables in the pattern are linked causally, related in such manner that deliberately changing the value of one variable will cause the value of the second variable to change according to rule, the structure will be labeled a *theory*. Theories provide a basis for action and play a major part in human efforts to improve their conditions of life. They can also be used for making predictions in precisely the same manner as a forecast.

A forecast is created by locating two or more things in the observed world, two or more variables, whose values have covaried systematically in the past. That relation is generalized to create the forecast. To take a very simple example, suppose that in the past flowers of type B have bloomed about two weeks after flowers of type A. Generalized, that relation becomes a simple forecast: Flower B will bloom about two weeks after flower A. The forecast can be tested against past experience prior to use, and since it was generated out of that experience, it can be expected to fit. That provides some justification for accepting and using it, even if no additional information is available. Other possible procedures for increasing confidence in the forecast are discussed below.

Under suitable conditions, the pattern can be combined with observation to generate a valid and useful prediction. Thus, if flower A is observed to bloom, accepting the forecast leads to the prediction that flower B will bloom in about two weeks if nothing interferes. The calculation is quite simple:

$B = A$ *plus two weeks* (the forecast).
$A =$ *today* (observed).
PREDICTION. *B will bloom in about two weeks' time.*

Since the forecast contains no causal assumption, it cannot be acted on and therefore cannot be tested experimentally; it is the assumption contained in the generalized proposition that is actually tested by an experiment and not the action flowing from that assumption. The justification for forecasts consists entirely in references to past experience. Single forecasts can be strengthened by making several forecasts of the same event using different relations. Nevertheless, as those who predict elections have learned to their sorrow, past experience is not always an adequate guide for the future. And in no case can a forecast be used as a basis for action, as a device for controlling events. Forecasts are adequate only for predicting.

Controlling Events

To control an event means to act in a way that will either produce or inhibit some event in the future; past events are beyond human control. A valid theory is required to fulfill that purpose. Theories have exactly the same structure as forecasts, consisting of a set of two or more variables linked by rule in a closed and calculable set and a set of limiting conditions governing application. In addition, a theory assumes a causal relation, which may be unidirectional or reciprocal, between the variables. That causal assumption provides a basis for action since it implies that the rule of change will hold regardless of the way in which the initial change is induced. That is not true for a forecast: If flower A in the example used earlier were force-fed or provided with artificial light in order to speed the flowering of B, the action would be unjustified, and unlikely to be successful.

Including a causal assumption in theories increases their power and usefulness but makes them more difficult to justify; the evidentiary requirements are much more severe for theories than for forecasts. Yet, because the causal connection provides a link between deliberate action and expected outcome, it opens the way for experimental testing—and provides the base for action needed to adapt the world to human needs and preferences. In most cases, theories are justified ultimately by reference to the results obtained from deliberate action or test, either experimentally in laboratories or in the real-world environment. There is no need for a large laboratory and complex equipment to demonstrate the principle involved, however. If a causal link is assumed between placing a dead fish in each hill of corn at planting time and the yield obtained from the hill, a simple but perfectly adequate theory has been created. It can be tested by actually placing fish in some hills of corn and comparing the yield to yields obtained from hills that have not been so treated. The theory may be crude and the test informal, but all the requirements have been fully satisfied, and the structure could be used to increase corn production in real cases.

Theories play such a major role in the fulfillment of human purposes that they are worth examining from a range of different perspectives, each of which illuminates a different aspect of this invaluable intellectual tool. In the usual mode of analysis, a theory is a set of variables whose values are linked by rule. That set of variables has been "isolated" from the rest of the environment and incorporated into a pattern; within the pattern, changes in the value of any variable can be accounted for *completely*, in principle at least, by changes in the values of the other variables, given the rules included in the pattern. In the real world, outside interferences on a selection of variables cannot be eliminated completely, even in highly sophisticated laboratories. The influence of these external factors on the operation of the theory is readily managed by inserting a "Fudge Factor," or *ceteris paribus* (other things equal) clause between the environment and the theory. The strength of the influences lumped together in the Fudge Factor is a measure of the theory's reliability. Since those influences are lumped and need not be identified, this greatly simplifies the theorist's task without undercutting the validity of the theory. If the theory is not reliable enough, some of the influences incorporated into the Fudge Factor will have to be isolated and brought into the theory, or more likely, included in the set of limiting conditions that control application of the theory.

Theories are also usefully construed as statements of the necessary and/or sufficient conditions for an event to occur. Knowing what is necessary for an event to occur provides a way of preventing it, assuming the requisite technology is available. Knowing the sufficient conditions for an event to occur allows the event to be brought about deliberately, again assuming the technical capacity. From another perspective, a theory is a logical pattern or overlay that can be fitted to observations in much the same way that a map is fitted to the observed world and used to direct movement. Finally, a theory can be construed as an unbroken chain of causal links connecting an action with some future event. A good illustration is found in the chain that connects oiling the water in stagnant pools to the life cycle of the malaria-carrying mosquito and through them to the prevention of the disease. The usefulness of these various perspectives on theory is explored more fully in later discussions.

Choices

The structures and processes involved in making choices that can be justified are more complex than those used for predicting and controlling events, although the overall principles are the same. Choices begin with persons who have the capacity to produce change in the environment. If that capacity is available, choice is forced, for failure to exercise the capacity produces an environment that is different than it could have been had the capacity been exercised, hence can be attributed to the actor. In that context, the content of a choice is defined by the outcomes an actor can produce. Obviously, the content of those outcomes must be known before a defensible choice can be made, and that requires valid theories. And making the choice necessarily involved a rank ordering of the possible outcomes, an indication of preference. Such preferences or priorities must be justified from experience, as with any other intellectual instrument. The justification will include two basic elements: (1) the individual's direct or affective reaction to the various outcomes or situations available for choice; and (2) an intellectual projection of the wider implications of choosing one of the outcomes rather than the others—a marshalling of evidence not open to direct experience and affective reactions. In most cases, intellectual considerations serve to modify and direct affective reactions: The patient accepts the pain associated with medical treatment to obtain the long-run benefits because of an intellectual and not an affective decision. Even very simple choices may involve complex sets of factors and difficult weighting of outcomes, and these questions must be left for detailed discussion later.

The basic principle remains the same: Within the context provided by the overall purpose of maintaining and improving the human situation for some population, relevant experience is organized to create a priority that can serve to direct action and therefore be tested in action—by further experience—and thereby improved or reinforced. As in theorizing, there is always a body of past experience and current practice available as a testing point and launching pad for further efforts.

Structurally, three different instruments are involved in choices or actions. First, theories must be available for projecting the set of future outcomes lying within the actor's capacity and therefore available for choice. Since theories are always in some degree uncertain, the risk involved in the projection must be taken into account when options are weighed. Until the content of the options has been agreed, and that is an empirical rather than a normative question, there can be neither agreement or disagreement about choices. Disagreements about preference require prior agreement on the precise content of what can be chosen.

The second instrument required for choice is a priority, a generalized statement of preferences created from and justified by past experience—both affective and intellectual. Each element in the priority will be a complete outcome, the full chain of events expected to follow if capacity to act is exercised in a particular way.

Finally, a program of action or *policy* is needed to apply the priority to the particular case and thus produce the preferred outcome. An example may clarify the function of policies in action or choice. Good reasons can be offered for preferring good health to poor health, other things equal. A person in poor health who accepts that priority must have available ways of producing good health, otherwise the choice is not real. That implies in turn a program of action that can lead from the present situation, however characterized, to a situation in which the individual's health is good. That treatment program corresponds exactly to a *policy* as the term will be used here.

That ends the overview of the structures and processes involved in developing the tools required for fulfilling the stipulated overall human purpose in the environment—by way of fulfilling the three primary first-order purposes. The discussion can now shift to a detailed examination of the basic structures in the system, beginning with descriptions.

Exercises

Review Questions

1. What is the difference between a variable and its value? Illustrate.

2. What is the difference between a set of variables enclosed by parentheses ( ) and a set enclosed in square brackets [ ]? Which would you use for a theory? A classification?

3. What are the three kinds of instruments that can be used for predicting?

4. What is the difference between generalizing and averaging?

5. What is the difference between the rules incorporated into a forecast and those found in a classification?

6. What is the difference between the way classifications are produced and the way forecasts are created?

7. What differentiates a forecast from a theory?

8. Explain the role played by a "Fudge Factor" in a theory.

9. What are the minimum requirements for making a reasoned choice?

10. Explain why a pattern that includes a causal assumption is more useful in human affairs than a pattern that does not.

Discussion

1. What are the major differences between organizing experience to produce a forecast, a theory, and a priority?

2. What human capacities are required for making defensible choices?

3. What grounds would be adequate to justify a causal assumption? Give an example.

4. Why is neither a forecast nor a classification an adequate basis for action?

5. Description: Introductory

In a theory of knowledge intended to show how human experience can be organized for maintaining and improving the human situation, two points are crucial. First, a set of purposes must be identified whose fulfillment is necessary and sufficient for satisfying the overall purposes of inquiry; second, the various forms in which experience must be organized to achieve those purposes have to be established, and the problems involved in creating, testing, justifying, and applying them examined systematically. In the critical apparatus being developed here, three primary purposes provide the basic focus of concern (predicting, controlling, choosing) and five patterns are needed to fulfill them (classifications, forecasts, theories, priorities, and policies). Criticism and improvement of performance (intellectual coaching) require that the performer's purpose be identified within the analytic framework; knowing the instrument required, and the problems, limitations, and pitfalls associated with the development and use of each instrument, provides a base for improvement.

All the intellectual instruments are formed by organizing human experience; experience in turn is based on the flow of raw perceptions entering the nervous system. The organization proceeds through several stages, and in most cases, instruments created at one stage are used in the development of the next. The final product, the theory or priority actually applied, is the result of a complex set of interactions. The quality of each product is no better than the quality of the elements used to construct it. For that reason, we begin with the initial organization of perceptions into descriptive accounts, then follow the development of more complex instruments from that base.

Description

A description is a statement of what has been observed, of what is or was the case at a given time and place. "It is raining," "There is an elephant in the back yard," and "It was cold yesterday" are all descriptive statements.

They are created from, and justified by, what was "perceived," by reference to the incoming flow of perceptions into the central nervous system. It is extremely important to keep a description separate from the perceptions from which it was created because the relation between the two must be understood before the uses and limitations of descriptions can be appreciated. The flow of raw perceptions into the central nervous system is both enormous and continuous; much of the information entering the system is ignored or discarded. Humans perceive very selectively. A description, then, is based on a *selection* of incoming perceptions; it is not a detailed record of everything observed or of everything in the environment. The selectivity that characterizes descriptions can have a profound effect on the quality of the instruments that depend on them. Moreover, descriptive accounts of what has been observed are sometimes colored or modified by the internal apparatus to reflect attitudes and preferences or prior training, and that source of potential distortion may require examination in systematic criticism.

Descriptions are particular and they are static, limited to a single time and place; those restrictions reflect the operating characteristics of the nervous system. Descriptions alone are not adequate for fulfilling human purposes but they do play a central role in developing, testing, and applying the basic patterns. Purposes are fulfilled by combining an established pattern with a descriptive statement—with the results of observation. The projected results of applying or using knowledge will normally appear in descriptive form. That is, to say "It will rain tomorrow" is to claim that on the following day a competent observer at a particular place will be able to describe what is observed as "rain." Similarly, the future outcome of action projected by a theory is a descriptive account of a future state. Nevertheless, such projected "descriptions" only share a common form with real descriptions. The latter are justified by past observations; the former are justified by a different body of evidence.

Observation or description goes on almost uninterrupted while human individuals are awake and conscious. Much of the information exchanged among individuals is descriptive, answering such questions as "What is the weather like?" "Where is my coat?" or "How do you feel?" Descriptive accounts can be very accurate and reliable, particularly if they employ instruments able to make precise measurements. They are widely, and correctly, regarded as the most reliable source of knowledge and evidence available to the human species. They are not, however, infallible, and psychologists have shown very decisively that observers often produce widely varied and incompatible accounts of quite simple events, particularly under stress. Nevertheless, if seeing does not lead to believing on every occasion, and the sensory apparatus can be deceptive, observation remains the best available basis for belief, and descriptions find their justification mainly in observation.

The Descriptive Process

In everyday discussion, description appears as a simple and even "natural" process, very much like taking pictures with a still camera. The human observer makes a record of what has been seen in much the same way that a camera records what is observed through a particular lens. In some respects, a description *is* like a still photograph, but in other respects the two are quite different, and those differences make a great deal of difference in the way descriptions are criticized or evaluated.

The key point for criticism is that a description is not a record of what is really "out there" to be seen or heard or felt, nor is it a simple and complete record of what has been observed. The observer does not see an elephant because there is "really" an elephant there, although it can be assumed that if there were nothing there, an elephant would not be seen except, perhaps, by alcoholics. Technically, the observer *interprets*, selectively, the flow of perceptions to mean "That is an elephant." The proposition "There is an elephant in the yard" is an assumption; the assumption can be justified by referring to observations. That may sound needlessly complicated, but there are good reasons for treating descriptions in that way. Between the "thing" perceived and a descriptive statement lies a set of structures and processes; understanding what they are and how they function is essential for valid criticism.

The two primary structures used for the preliminary organization of perceptions contained in descriptions are the *concept* and the *relational term*. Concepts identify or bound the things observed; relational terms, as might be expected, show how things relate—in time, space, and along other continua. They are human creations, built out of experience. The concept *tiger,* for example, includes the tiger's tail because observers have found it necessary to identify tigers in ways that include that appendage; the tiger can provide very good reasons indeed for doing so. Concepts and relational terms, which are plentiful and diverse, serve as the spectacles through which the world is observed; they are the selective mechanism that determines what is recorded in observation. Without an appropriate concept, "what is seen" cannot be identified, and may not even be seen as a "something."

The nature of the observation process, much simplified in the account given here, has great significance for a knowledge system built on the organization of experience. It means that what is seen and described is a function of two factors: (1) what is actually "out there" to be seen; and (2) the particular set of lenses or spectacles used for observation. The person who knows an elephant when he or she sees one cannot record an elephant in experience unless it is actually there—and a target of the perceptory apparatus. The person without a concept of *elephant* cannot see an elephant even if the elephant is present, although "something" will be seen and perhaps described, using the concepts and relational terms that are available to the person.

One final corollary bears mentioning: There are many ways of "seeing" the same thing and many different things to be seen in the same place. To take a common example, a trained biologist and a city dweller "see" quite different things in an open field in the countryside. They wear different sets of spectacles—make use of different concepts and relational terms in their observations. Asked to describe the content of the field, they will produce descriptions that differ, often quite radically. Both descriptions may be accurate, but their content will vary; therefore their value or usefulness will vary. For systematic criticism, that kind of difference is very important. The use that can be made of a description, and the adequacy of actions based on it, will depend on what is included and excluded, and that is a function of the conceptual apparatus employed in observation. The world is like a stage on which many different plays are going on simultaneously; the play that is seen depends on the spectacles taken to the theater. When a choice is made self-consciously, the spectacles selected will depend on the purpose for which the theater trip is made.

Accuracy and Adequacy

For critical purposes, a description consists of sets of propositions in the form "X is the case," or "X was the case." The propositions are assumed; the assumption is justified by referring to specific observations. The parallel to still photography is useful, for it suggests two major areas of potential weakness that need to be explored—the two kinds of faults that appear in photography. First, the camera may be inadequate; the lens may be distorted, the machinery may not function properly. In such cases, the result is a picture that is *inaccurate*. A parallel situation appears in description if the concepts and relational terms are of poor quality, or if the observations are carelessly made. In the second case, the camera is of good quality and functioning properly but the photographer uses it badly, pointing it in the wrong direction or taking pictures at the wrong time. The use will be "wrong" if the result does not further the purpose of the photographer who is taking the pictures. The content of the photograph may be clear, but the information will not be relevant. Such pictures are accurate but *inadequate*. In description, if the wrong set of spectacles is used to observe, the content of the resulting description may be clear and accurate, but it will not serve the purposes for which it is needed.

The distinction between accuracy and adequacy is very important. To illustrate, if an ambulance attendant is describing an accident victim to a physician at the hospital by radio, and the pulse rate is stated to be 75 when it is actually 55 per minute, the description is inaccurate and potentially dangerous. If the attendant fails to notice a symptom that would inform the physician of a serious injury for which the hospital should make some special preparations, then the description is inadequate and perhaps even more dangerous. Evaluation of descriptive quality must take both kinds of potential error into account.

Structural Characteristics

Structurally, a description consists of a set of concepts that identify the things observed and sets of relational terms that show the connections observed among them, plus any other terms required by the rules of the language. Each of the concepts can be identified as a variable *(V)*; the value of each variable is set by observation, which also determines which of the relational terms is appropriate. Both the concepts and relational terms are generalized; they refer to classes of things. Description, therefore, requires the observer to make judgments, to determine whether or not what is observed is a member of a particular class—that a "tree" has been seen or the color "green" observed.

To illustrate, the descriptive statement "There is a green tree in that field" uses three major concepts (*tree, green,* and *field*), one relational term (*in*) and a time-determining concept (the verb *is*, which implies the present). By asserting the proposition, an observer claims that three points can be supported by observations made at a specific time and place: first, that a member of the class "trees" can be observed; second, that the tree belongs to the color class "green"; and third, that the tree lies "in" the boundaries of a field. Four judgments have been made; three relate to class membership and one to relation or location. Can those judgments be justified? In such a simple case, common sense suggests that they can, barring exceptional circumstances such as color blindness. But if the concepts are more complex, and identification of class members (diagnosis) is more difficult, judgments may be much more difficult to justify. A typical illustration is found in the difficulties encountered in efforts to identify the "aggressor" nation in a case of armed conflict, or to determine "who started it" in a school brawl.

The strongest justification for a description comes from multiple observations made by competent observers using measuring instruments. If a description is supported by several competent observers, each with normal sensory equipment and trained to know the meaning of the concepts and relational terms employed, such testimony would be difficult to refuse. Yet there is always the possibility of error, even if adequacy is ignored. A description is an assumption, based on a set of judgments, and not a simple "hard fact." Just as a camera can err (by showing that a stick "bends" when placed in water), the human observer can be mistaken—and even instrumental observations may distort or mislead. And, ultimately, every description breaks down at some level of precision; measurement capacity always fails at some point, and it becomes impossible to say what is the case beyond that level. Nevertheless, good reasons can be produced for accepting and using all sorts of descriptions, and they remain the strongest element in the chain of relations on which knowledge depends. The purpose of the analysis is to produce awareness of potential weak spots, not to create skeptics. Descriptions can be tested or checked, and knowing that testing is needed and possible, and knowing where to look for errors, is a basic requirement for developing and improving knowledge.

Some Problem Areas

Some of the common errors that occur in the discussion and use of descriptions will be touched on briefly in the remainder of this unit. For one thing, there can be no definitive description of any situation; a new description can always be created by changing concepts. For another, accuracy is not enough, and the significance of a description depends on the purposes of the user. Again, what is omitted from a description may be as important as what is included, yet it is very difficult to know the selection principles employed. One of the more exasperating aspects of historical studies, for example, is not being able to determine whether a particular datum does not appear because the event did not occur or because the historian chose to ignore it or was not aware of it. Since descriptions always refer to the past, they are always stated using verbs in the past tense—a description made in the here and now actually refers to the past at the time it is articulated, strictly speaking.

Descriptions are static and particular, like single frames in motion picture films. Change must be inferred, assumed on the basis of differences in two descriptive accounts. Those accounts must refer to *the same* object, and that can be very difficult to establish. If John had red hair at age twenty and white hair at seventy, it seems reasonable to say that the color of John's hair has changed. Similarly, a middle-class residential neighborhood in a large city may in due course take on the appearance of an awful slum, in which case it is said "The neighborhood has really changed in recent years." Every change implies an *it*, a thing that changes. In the case of neighborhoods and individuals, the thing that changes is easy to identify. But if John is mistaken for his twin brother, who is bald, then the assumption of change will be mistaken. In fact, if there is reason to doubt that the same *it* has been captured in all descriptions, the evidence for change is uncertain.

Collective bodies, such as legislatures or the Supreme Court of the United States, can be particularly troublesome in this context. If the Supreme Court upholds a particular exercise of the police power in 1970 and reverses the decision in 1980, is it true to say that "the Court" has reversed itself? Suppose that more than half of the justices had been appointed to the Court in the ten-year period? Is that the same as confusing identities? The question is important because change is one of the things to be controlled by the development and application of knowledge, or at least anticipated and provided against.

Descriptive errors are in some cases a function of the processes used to make them. Descriptions cannot include aesthetic or evaluative terms, although they may include statements about affective reactions on the part of the individual. "That is a beautiful picture" is an aesthetic judgment. "That picture makes me want to destroy it" is a descriptive account of an internal state. Such distinctions are not always easily made. The physician can say with some confidence, "That is a very sick man," but can a layman do so? Are such statements descriptive accounts or judgments? And what of such statements as "That smells very bad," applied to a very old egg, broken accidentally? In some cases, they contain judgments or opinions; in other cases, they are only descriptive accounts of internal states and can be treated as facts, subject to the usual reservations about subjective reporting.

Subjectivity, which is unavoidable, is responsible for a number of the major problems in description, and justification. In one sense, every observation is carried out within the person; what is perceived may lie within the person or externally, may be wholly private or in some degree exposed to other observers. Descriptions of internal states take the same form, and make use of the same kind of evidence, as descriptions of the external world. The problem is finding some means of validating the description, of protecting against errors in judgment or measurement. If I claim to have a stomachache, who can say I do not have one? Should I be believed? I could be lying or hallucinating or experiencing a psychic illness. There may be grounds for suspicion, but wholly convincing evidence one way or the other is not always accessible.

Observations of public events can usually be tested by using a second observer, or more if needed, and that strengthens the justification for propositions based on such observations. Even in such cases, the strength of the justification depends on the competence of the observers, their ability to use the conceptual apparatus. For example, suppose that several observers agree on the proposition "There is a dog in the yard." To test validity further, a number of supplementary questions would have to be explored. Do they all mean exactly the same thing by the terms *dog, yard,* and *in,* for example? If not, they have not observed the same thing. The likelihood of differences can be reduced by testing eyes, narrowing the meaning of concepts, employing measuring instruments, and so on. It might even be possible to devise tests that would require each observer to translate the meaning of key terms into suitable actions—place a number of animals in an enclosed area and ask the observer to select the dog, or ask for strict definitions of other terms. When all has been done that can be done, and in these cases it would not be necessary, there will remain some element of uncertainty. There is no way to be positive that two observers "saw" exactly the same thing, or mean exactly the same thing by a descriptive statement.

Consistency with other currently accepted knowledge also provides a test of descriptive propositions. To say "There was an oggleygy in the library this morning" is to speak nonsense, although in descriptive form. (I just now invented the term.) Claiming that an alligator was observed to speak fluent Spanish is to invite psychiatric observation rather than agreement. Asserting that a dog five miles down the road is carrying a red flea may be descriptive in form, but the sensory apparatus needed to make such observations is not available to humans.

Finally, no matter how accurate a description may be, its adequacy can still be questioned, and that is a function of purpose. Description is rarely if ever without any purpose at all. People do not return to their homes and give descriptive accounts of passing automobiles or routine events. Normally, they refer to something that is unusual, puzzling, amusing, or in some fashion interesting. The describer's purpose, which may be no more than amusing the audience, will determine what is included in the description. Relating description to purpose serves to establish the adequacy of what is included, and to suggest what could have been omitted or should have been added. It also serves to expose bias in the observer, deliberate or not. For example, a description of criminal activity in the city meant to be used as evidence for expanding the police force would be inadequate if it omitted to say that the electricity had failed during the time period in question.

Exercises

Review Questions

1. Sketch briefly the role of description in the theory of knowledge.

2. Why is it possible for two descriptions of the same situation to be accurate but different?

3. What are the main structural characteristics of descriptions?

4. Differentiate between an inaccurate and an inadequate description. Illustrate each error from your own experience.

5. Why is it impossible to produce a complete description of any event?

6. Why are descriptions always in some measure uncertain?

7. If changes cannot be described, what is the character of such phenomena?

8. State the problems created by subjectivity in description and suggest means of avoiding major errors.

9. What grounds other than direct observation are available for justifying or opposing descriptions?

Discussion

1. How does an observer decide *what* to describe?

2. What determines what is included and excluded from a description?

3. When should an observer note that something is missing from the scene? Provide an illustration.

4. Why is accuracy an insufficient criterion for criticizing descriptions?

5. Discuss the special problems involved in describing the actions of collectivities or aggregates.

6. Description: Concepts and Indicators

Humans observe the world around them through sets of spectacles or lenses called *concepts* and *relational terms*. Concepts identify the things observed; relational terms specify the physical or other relations between and among them. Both concepts and relational terms are generalized and must be applied to specific cases. The application requires judgments that can be mistaken. Concepts range from "simples," like the color yellow, which have no other attributes, to very complex structures, such as electrons or psychic states, which involve the use of a great many other concepts. Relational terms may specify physical relations such as distance or direction, temporal relations, or complex interactions such as destroying. Concepts are usually defined by the use of other concepts and relational terms. The class *robins,* for example, will be defined with concepts that specify size, colors, or weight, as well as the relations of class members to other birds or to the environment generally—mating or nesting habits, for example. The rules that define the meaning of a concept, that specify the shared attributes of class members, will state the range of values that can be taken by the set of variables used to measure class attributes. Applying those rules to observations provides the grounds for deciding whether or not the thing observed is a class member—sometimes a very difficult question. The classification itself is a discriminating device, ruling out as class members some of the things perceived as well as ruling others in.

A distinction is needed between the *meaning* of a concept, which is its full definition, and the set of *indicators* for the concept, the observable variables that cue its use in organizing perceptions. The meaning of such concepts as *heat*, for example, is probably best stated within molecular theory and the language of thermodynamics. The indicators that lead us to say things such as "My, it is very hot today" include such observables as thermometer readings, perspiration, and subjective feelings of discomfort. Obviously, the meaning of a concept must be related to the indicators used with it; in most cases, that relation is established theoretically, through a chain of relations linking indicators to the set of attributes that make up the full meaning. A good illustration is found in the concept *viscosity*. It means the amount of friction between the molecules in a liquid. Friction of that nature cannot be measured directly. Therefore, the indicator for the concept is the rate of flow of different liquids through a tube of given size, which can be measured accurately and compared. The reasoning on which the indicator depends is straightforward: The greater the viscosity of a liquid, the greater the amount of friction among the molecules, the more slowly the liquid will flow. No absolute measure of viscosity can be obtained by measuring flow rates, but a standard can be adopted, and the rate of flow of each liquid can be indexed by reference to that standard. Indicators provide a way of measuring the value of a concept or variable; they also tell us when it is appropriate to use the concept. The meaning of a concept will assert what can be expected in the environment if the concept is present; the indicators for the concept are used in diagnosing presence. Indicators are adequate only for diagnosis; meaning must be used in treatments.

Languages are not equally well supplied with concepts, and the quantity and quality of the concepts available in various aspects of everyday life as well as in the different academic fields vary widely. Over time, the supply of concepts fluctuates as old terms are dropped, new terms are added, and meanings are changed. Flexibility in meaning is valuable, since it allows refinement to increase precision, although it opens the way to serious abuse. In just a few decades, for example, the meaning of *cancer* within medicine has been almost completely redefined—and vastly enriched. The absence of change can also create problems, particularly in fields such as political science where the concepts in use have a long history and have accumulated a range of meanings. A closer look at the function that concepts perform in description, and at the way they are developed and improved, may pinpoint some of the more common weaknesses in the existing conceptual apparatus, particularly in social science.

An Illustration of Conceptual Development

Tracing the course of development of a particular concept, hypothetically in this case, can be a very illuminating exercise. Since a concept is a set of rules for organizing perceptions, and the content of the rules depends on the kinds of perceptions to be organized, it is clear that perceptions must *precede* development of the concept. That is, observation of a dog

or a horse must come before the concept is created—excluding the generation of classes by analogy, and the complex concepts used to deal with
other existing concepts, such as theoretical terms. Conceptual development
therefore begins with the first appearance of some new thing in the environment. For simplicity, assume that what is now called a dog makes
an appearance in an isolated village where no dog has ever been seen. Are
the villagers completely helpless in the face of the new creature? Probably
not, unless the village had no experience whatever with animals of any
kind, and that seems unlikely. Familiarity with other living creatures, particularly those that walk on four feet, would provide a crude and perhaps
uncertain base for dealing with the dog. Such prior experience might suggest that living creatures could be dangerous, that the dog might attack
or bite if approached or annoyed. It would also imply that living creatures
usually eat, and food might be offered on the basis of the kinds of food
consumed by other living creatures known in the village. If the dog remained
in the village, new information about the particular thing would be gathered
from observations and could be generalized. Two kinds of information are
most likely to appear first, the personal attributes of the creature (color,
size, smell, and so on) and its relations with other things (eating habits,
behavior toward humans, or behavior toward other animals). In some cases,
the animal might be stimulated deliberately to provide essential information (be threatened, for example, to determine reactions, in a crude form
of experimenting).

To this point, the dog could be described, differentiated from other
allied things, and some of its attributes could be generalized; it would constitute the sole member of a class that could be labeled *the creature*, for
example. The classification or concept, however, would coincide precisely
with the label. The information available might grow quite rich and plentiful over time. Indeed, the dog might be made useful, employed as an early-
warning device if it was learned that the dog barked when strangers approached the village and was aware of the approach long before the human
population. In some ways, conceptual development in very young children
resembles the process by which information about a new species of animals
is developed. The child's information about the world is rich but specific,
directed to a very limited population. As the child matures, information
is generalized about an increasingly wider range of things, often with surprising facility and accuracy—the pointed comments that children make
about relatives provide a good illustration.

The essentials of conceptual development begin to emerge when a second dog appears in the village. If it closely resembled the first dog, say

with respect to size, color, and shape, would it be recognized as "just like the creature" or classified as "another one of them"? Much depends on the range and kind of similarities and differences between the two animals, and the question requires a psychological rather than a methodological answer in any case. But there are good reasons to believe that, under some conditions at least, information about the first animal would be transferred to the second; the two would be treated collectively. The class that had previously had only one member would now have two, and it would no longer be the case that any observation made of one member would transfer automatically to the class. Where the first dog's ears were straight, the second dog's ears could hang downward, and so on. Not all the characteristics of the first dog could be shared by the second; some features of the second would also be unique. Learning what was unique to each, and what was common to both, would require a slightly different focus than before. Indeed, one danger to be avoided would be the unwarranted transfer of attributes from one dog to the class. Assuming that because the first dog was friendly to humans, the second dog would share the same attribute could have tragic consequences. Such premature transfer of attributes of a particular specimen to the class as a whole is so common that it has been given a special label in logic — *hasty generalization* — indicating a transfer made without sufficient warrant or justification.

The shared properties of the two dogs would make up the meaning of the concept *dog*, at that stage in development. The word "dog" would be a convenience, a label that facilitated discussion. Precisely the same effect is achieved if the class was identified as "them" so long as everyone knew the referent. If still more dogs appeared, some of the attributes shared by the first two dogs might have to be discarded, but no new attributes could be added; the meaning of the class is limited to the attributes shared by every member. Tracing out the steps by which a very broad concept such as "dogs" is developed, and noting the conditions under which a subclassification can and should be introduced (say, between hounds and sheepdogs) and then further subdivided, can provide valuable insight into the problems of conceptualization. When a concept remains in use for a very long time, meaning is likely to be full and rich but at some cost in precision.

Vagueness and Ambiguity

The two major problems encountered in conceptual development and use are vagueness and ambiguity. A concept is *vague* if its meaning cannot be determined accurately; a concept is *ambiguous* if it has more than one meaning, both meanings are clear, but the meaning intended in use cannot be determined. For example, the meaning of *boskis* is vague if the implications of saying "John has boskis" cannot be determined or the question "Does John have boskis?" cannot be answered on adequate grounds. The meaning of *green* in such statements as "That apple is green" is ambiguous because it may mean either "That apple is green in color" or "That apple isn't ripe," and there is no way to determine which meaning is intended from the proposition as stated. Further information is needed before meaning can be determined.

Both vagueness and ambiguity are undesirable characteristics of concepts, but of the two, ambiguity is far and away the more serious problem. In fact, some vagueness of meaning is probably unavoidable and may even be useful, particularly when a new field of inquiry is being developed. For example, suppose that students of management found that a certain kind of worker-job relation seriously reduced productivity, but they were unable to agree on precisely what kind of relation was involved. They might create a vague concept to identify that relation, give it a label such as *comportance,* but provide an incomplete statement of meaning. That would allow time to explore the relation further and develop a more precise definition or meaning for it, and appropriate indicators. A vague concept is useful for marking out new territory without defining the boundaries and limits too closely. If vagueness remains unresolved over time, however, the concept is unusable. Vague concepts are points of departure for conceptual development. It is not helpful to know that workers whose relation to work is not comportant will not produce effectively if such workers cannot be identified. Similarly, it would be pointless to identify the relation between a worker and the work done in terms of comportance if the effects remain unknown. A concept must be provided with a meaning that has human significance and a basis for accurate diagnosis in due course, or it should be abandoned.

Ambiguity is a more serious problem in conceptualization because propositions that include such concepts are literally without meaning until the ambiguity is resolved; they cannot be justified or criticized. Further, the ambiguity may be unrecognized, or may be exploited deliberately by one party to a discussion. Ambiguities appear in various forms and guises, but three are so important in the conduct of human affairs that they deserve special treatment. In the first case, a concept has more than one meaning, and the meaning intended cannot be determined from context. In such instances, it is very easy to slip from one meaning to the other and thus avoid criticism. To take the earlier example, if a person passing a fruit stand says to his companion, "Those apples are really green" and is then threatened with bodily harm by the vendor, he need only reply, "I meant that they were a lovely green color." That leaves the vendor without a basis for criticism, or fisticuffs.

One way of avoiding such problems, widely practiced in physical science, is *conceptual standardization*—the use of technical terms. In extreme cases, central concepts have been defined operationally, by reference to the set of operations needed to produce the phenomenon being defined. In some areas of human activity, that practice would probably be very helpful; the physical sciences have clearly benefited from their technical languages. But in everyday affairs, technical jargon is less obviously an improvement over everyday usage. The richness of meaning, subtleties, and nuances that can be conveyed in everyday language makes for a kind of communication between humans that rigorous scientific language does not allow. Further, conceptual standardization serves to fix the meaning of concepts at present positions; in the social sciences, that seems unwise and premature, since there are good reasons to suppose that the apparatus in place is not really adequate. Moreover, most of the great advances in human knowledge have involved a restructuring of the conceptual apparatus used for dealing with some part of the environment—creating new spectacles for seeing the world. It would be a great loss if the freedom to speculate and innovate that has produced past theoretical developments was sacrificed through the imposition of standard conceptualization on everyone. In such matters, diversity seems a virtue, well worth the price paid in uncertainty in use.

The two other major forms of conceptual ambiguity occur in the use of aggregates or collective terms—in discussions of football teams, watches, automobile accidents, or legislatures, for example. In the first case, ambiguity is produced because the distinction between the features of an aggregate and the characteristics of its parts is not maintained. Every aggregate, taken as a whole, will have features that are not shared by all of the parts: A crowd may be noisy, for example, even if some of its members make no noise. The problem is again so common that it has earned a special label from logicians. When the properties of an aggregate, such as the noisiness of crowds, is transferred illegitimately to one of its parts, that is called a *division fallacy*. A second major source of ambiguity involves much the same error, with directions reversed. When the properties of some part of an aggregate are transferred to the whole structure wrongly, that is called a *composition fallacy*. Both are extremely common, not least in public discussion of public issues.

To illustrate the ease with which the two fallacies are committed, and the consequences for the unwary, suppose that a young reporter is asked to write a brief account of the arrival of a shipment of hogs at the local market. If the shipment contains ten large white hogs, each weighing about 500 pounds, and fifty small black hogs, each weighing about 200 pounds, and the reporter writes that "the white hogs weigh more than the black hogs," the report is hopelessly ambiguous. If it means that each white hog weighs more than any one of the black hogs, then it is correct. But if it means that the white hogs, taken collectively, weigh more than the black hogs, also taken collectively, then the report is mistaken. Imagine the effect on a farmer seeking a large white hog for his farm.

A parallel form of ambiguity occurs in such statements as "Men are found everywhere on earth," which is accurate with respect to men as a whole but mistaken if the class is subdivided. A slightly different form of the same mistake occurs when the parts of a collectivity are confused with its overall features. A common example is attacking a legislator because Congress failed to pass a particular measure, even though the legislator voted for it. A more subtle form of the mistake is made if a single legislator is given credit for legislation passed through the whole legislature *because* he or she voted for it. The meaning of the legislator's action, the individual vote for a measure, may be completely divorced from the meaning of the vote to the individual who favors the measure. The congressman who votes for a bill because he or she wishes to be reelected should not necessarily be given credit for supporting the content of the bill; the legislator might oppose the bill but believe that open opposition would lead to defeat at the next election and be more opposed to being defeated than to voting for the bill. Such considerations are not reflected in the bare arithmetic of voting.

The third major conceptual problem associated with the use of aggregate concepts is somewhat more difficult to explain, therefore discussion begins with an example. Suppose that the number of automobile accidents in the country was rising rapidly each year. To know that the number of members of the class of events "automobile accidents occurring annually" is increasing rapidly is to know something important, of course, and for some persons at least, to have reason to want to do something about it. The concept employed to demonstrate the problem (automobile accidents) is useless for trying to do something about it. A different kind of concept is needed as a base for action. Similarly, no physician can cure a case of "sickness," nor can a legislature do anything with "the poor" or "the homeless." Until such concepts can be linked to specific causes and cures, there is no way to attack them as a class. Pneumonia, on the other hand, can be dealt with systematically because a cause can be identified for all members of the class; diabetes can also be dealt with, not because a cause is known but because all persons with the disease respond more or less identically to treatment with insulin. For purposes of action, then, concepts must be of the same type as pneumonia or diabetes, rather than sickness or poverty. In effect, the concept must group populations affected in the same way by a common action. We shall return to the problem in the discussion of policy making.

Although the use of aggregate concepts and collective terms causes a great many conceptual problems, they cannot be purged from the vocabulary; they are far too useful for that. Consider how very difficult it would be to make the following statement without the use of collective terms: "Congress today passed a law forbidding the use of more than one pair of headlights on any automobile." Moreover, it is essential to be able to say such things as "Congress is at present reluctant to deal with the issue of abortion," "The U.S. Supreme Court is today a more conservative body than it was twenty years ago," and so on. Aggregate concepts must be used carefully, and misuse is unlikely to stop in the future, but they are far too valuable in the development and use of knowledge to be abandoned completely.

Exercises

Review Questions

1. Identify and differentiate "concept" and "relational term."

2. Describe briefly the role played by concepts in description.

3. Illustrate the difference between the meaning of a concept and the indicators for a concept.

4. Explain and illustrate the way in which concepts organize perceptions.

5. What is the difference between a concept that is vague and a concept that is ambiguous? Illustrate.

6. Assess the value of conceptual standardization in the social sciences.

7. Discuss the major problems involved in the use of aggregate terms, illustrating each one with an example of your own.

8. What is meant by the "fallacy of composition" and the "fallacy of division"? Illustrate.

Discussion

1. How might conceptual needs vary from culture to culture? Illustrate.

2. Illustrate the reasons that might lead to a subdivision of an existing classification.

3. Differentiate a concept that can be used to call attention to a problem from a concept that can be used to solve the problem. Illustrate.

4. Trace the development of a concept from the initial perception of the thing to which it refers.

7. Description: Conceptual Frameworks

An analysis of the descriptive process that is adequate for systematic criticism must separate the observer from the things observed. Human observations are always made through a complex set of lenses, of concepts and relational terms. Descriptions based on those observations consist of propositions that are assumed, then justified by referring to the content of the observations. Such propositions are criticized with respect to both their accuracy and their adequacy. Accuracy is a function of the quality of the concepts, indicators, and measurements used in making the description; adequacy depends on the relation between the content of the description and the purpose for which it is used. A crucial factor in descriptive accuracy is the quality of the concepts employed in observation; adequacy depends on the selection of concepts. The selection depends mainly on the *conceptual framework* employed by the observer. This unit focuses on those frameworks and their role in systematic inquiries.

Conceptual Frameworks

No observer can notice and record everything in the environment, or even everything that is included in the incoming flow of perceptions; not everything in the environment is important, given the purposes of the observer. Observation is necessarily selective, and that is both efficient and potentially dangerous. No observer goes to the environment with a handful of randomly chosen concepts and applies them to what is observed there. Observation is a highly structured process when it is linked to a purpose in the world, and even casual observation tends to be structured by past experience. Releasing the central nervous system from its own internal structure is extremely difficult, even with the use of drugs or alcohol.

The concepts actually used for observation tend to be grouped or clustered together into what will be called *conceptual frameworks*, sets of concepts or variables that experience has shown to be required for dealing with certain kinds of events or activities or that have been inculcated by past training. They are most clearly visible in work or occupation, but they control activity in family affairs, recreation, and virtually all other forms of behavior. What identifies an individual as a dentist or an electrician, even more accurately than clothing or income, is the set of concepts used in daily work. An electrician at work thinks and acts in terms of wires, fuses, circuits, switches, connections, and so on because the nature of the work requires attention to these dimensions of the world. An electrician who gets into an automobile to go for a drive refocuses attention to those matters that are important for safe and efficient movement on the highways.

Functions

A conceptual framework focuses attention on some aspects of the world and screens out others. Which elements are included or blocked depends on the concepts employed; they in turn depend on the nature of the activity around which the conceptual framework develops. Their influence is well known, and they are widely used, although not always explicitly recognized. For example, even a casual reader scanning a newspaper tends to look for "eye-catching" materials or "stand-out" headlines. That is, certain configurations on the page tend to capture attention and call into play a set of concepts that is then used while reading the material. Those who organize the materials printed in newspapers, whether commercial advertisers or editors, are aware of this human characteristic and design their materials accordingly.

Conceptual frameworks can be regarded as very complex spectacles for viewing the environment, spectacles that are "multifocal" because they incorporate a number of different lenses or concepts. Each individual develops a large collection of these frameworks over a lifetime and learns to switch from one to the other with remarkable skill and speed. A chemistry instructor moving from one experiment to another in a laboratory may change conceptual frameworks a dozen times in as many minutes. And the effect of a very pretty girl on a construction crew in a city suggests the way in which external factors can cause a shift in conceptual apparatus —much humor is built on such switching. Daydreaming, which usually means free-floating contemplation not linked to any particular purpose, may produce strange modifications in the conceptual apparatus, combining and recombining them in peculiar—and sometimes very useful—ways.

A major function of the conceptual framework is to call attention to significant events in the perceived environment, internal or external. A peculiar pain felt internally calls to the fore very quickly such medical capacity as the individual possesses, and may lead to a visit to another person with a better-developed conceptual apparatus. The physician responds immediately to symptoms of serious illness; the layman may attach no significance whatever to the same symptoms. The ornithologist reacts strongly to the sight of a rare bird; the bird is passed casually by those who do not know that it is rare. Such unusual or eye-catching sights, which usually serve as a point of departure for systematic activity, acquire their status by virtue of the conceptual framework of the individual who makes the observation. That implies a close relation between a set of purposes or activities and a particular set of concepts. It follows that the content of the framework will change over time as a field of inquiry develops. In dentistry, for example, new concepts have been added as technical capacity has grown; in the process, the meaning and significance attached to specific observations has also had to change. An observation that formerly meant that a tooth should be pulled may now mean that a particular technique or treatment should be employed that will save the tooth.

In general, the quality of the conceptual frameworks attached to a field of study depends on the state of theory in the field. In areas where theory is relatively weak, the kinds of inquiries undertaken will tend to be governed by fad and fashion, or by strict tradition, rather than by the evolving purposes that theoretical considerations suggest. The contrast with theoretically powerful physical sciences such as physics is striking. Further, the different elements in the overall conceptual apparatus employed by those working in the same general area will not be integrated and mutually supportive. Good illustrations are found in the lack of coherence among the theories used to deal with crime, housing, and welfare. Some of the effects of such theoretical inadequacies are extremely unfortunate: poor families placed in housing they cannot afford to maintain or lack the knowledge needed to manage; transportation systems that contribute to the congestion and pollution they were intended to reduce; programs for improving low-income housing that actually force the poor out of cheaper housing and require them to pay more for shelter; and so on.

Uses and Limitations
Focusing on the development and use of conceptual frameworks in contemporary society turns out to be a very useful and illuminating exercise. A major function of the educational system, for example, is to provide the young with the conceptual apparatus needed for dealing with the variety of occupational, familial, and social situations they can expect to encounter

in society. The extent to which those concepts are being supplied is a good indicator of the adequacy of the overall educational system, and locating the areas where adequate concepts are not available will suggest points where improvements are needed. For society as a whole, the range of conceptual frameworks required for competent citizenship is usually a good index to the level of development achieved; the extent to which those frameworks are distributed within society will suggest the adequacy of political education. Finally, the mixture of conceptual frameworks found within society provides a great deal of information about the conditions of life there. Highly advanced industrial societies usually require the development and transmission of large and sophisticated conceptual/theoretical structures that may take years to master. The less developed societies have a much larger supply of conceptual frameworks that are readily mastered and widely shared. Detailed specialization characterizes the developed society; generalization is more common among societies that are less developed. A corollary of specialization is, of course, increased interdependence. Highly specialized technicians, such as astronomers, dentists, or neural surgeons, cannot use many of their concepts and technical skills outside their own fields of work. And when frameworks are so complex that only one or two can be mastered in a lifetime, the pressure on youth to choose correctly at the outset is much increased.

Not enough is known about the way in which conceptual frameworks develop, about the influence of culture and tradition on that development, or even about similarities and differences among the more important shared conceptual frameworks within a single society. Yet the scope of their influence on daily life is incalcuable. Without conceptual frameworks to sort and identify the incoming flood of perceptions, the central nervous system would literally be swamped. Some apparatus must be available for locating the significant factors in the environment, allowing the intellectual apparatus to concentrate on them. The individual who spends five minutes adjusting a necktie in the face of rising floodwaters or an oncoming hurricane is unlikely to survive unscathed, and unlikely to elicit much sympathy for damage done. The initial stages of intellectual development in children are usually taken up with acquisition of conceptual frameworks for identifying the life-supporting and the dangerous, aided, of course, by the prior knowledge of the family. By maturity, most individuals, particularly in industrialized societies, have acquired an astonishing range of conceptual structures, and learned how to use them quite efficiently.

What makes the study of conceptual frameworks and their influence particularly difficult is that not all of them are public, explicit, or even self-consciously held. Most of the time, most people rely on an apparatus developed more or less subconsciously over time. Its elements will be derived from traditions and legends, hearsay and rumor, fact and fiction, hunches and intuitions, folklore, common sense, and science. The great size and capacity of the human brain allows this smorgasbord to live in peace, even though its elements may not be consistent. It is usually impossible to say what part of the conceptual apparatus is functioning in any particular case excepting highly technical activities. That makes criticism and improvement of performance exceptionally difficult. This is both an indication of the importance of socialization, particularly in the early years, of the habits of thinking employed in everyday affairs and a warning that systematic criticism will have to be satisfied with limited improvements rather than revolutionary transformations.

Hazards

Conceptual frameworks perform an invaluable service for the individual, and they exert a powerful influence on daily performance. Instruments with such power can be dangerous as well as beneficial. When an intellectual construct takes substantial periods of time to master, the result is likely to be firmly fixed, and if the individual is barely aware of the existence of the structure, self-conscious modification is increasingly unlikely. Such conceptual stability is in some respects desirable, but in a rapidly changing society, it can be disastrous, leading to needless friction among generations and between societies. The tendency to walk the well-worn trails in thinking is well known. That may indeed be the reason why young persons, those who have not yet carved grooves into their thinking patterns, tend to do most of the really creative work in science or mathematics.

Finally, conceptual frameworks are the instrument through which unacceptable bias and invidious distinctions most readily are intruded into human behavior. An illustration may help to clarify the point. Assume that the children in an elementary school located in a badly blighted slum area inhabited by people of very low incomes are found to suffer from serious malnutrition. If it is agreed that such conditions are unacceptable and that society should accept responsibility for the situation and provide a remedy, means must be found for changing the children's nutritional state, and it is likely that the source of the problem will be sought in order to eliminate it and thus prevent a recurrence. Consider what is likely to happen if the problem is attacked using a number of different conceptual frameworks.

First, using the conceptual framework of a nutritionist, the children's condition will be described using concepts that relate to dietary intake in the past; the problem will be defined by reference to food intake; and a remedy will be sought in the various channels available for altering the children's diet. Using the nutritionist's conceptual apparatus, nothing can be said about the source of the problem beyond the characteristics of dietary intake; no person or institution in society can be held responsible or required to provide a remedy. The remedy itself cannot alter whatever the personal and institutional arrangements might have been that produced the problem in the first place. Although the report produced using these concepts could be used to improve the children's condition, for a change in diet would certainly eliminate malnutrition, it could go no further. The approach, although necessary for identifying the kinds of changes in diet that the elimination of malnutrition requires, would be insufficient for introducing changes into society that would prevent the condition from recurring.

If the problem is approached from the perspective of the social worker specializing in the effects of parental neglect, a quite different conceptual framework will be employed, and both remedy and cause will take on a different appearance. In that conceptual apparatus, the condition of the children will be linked to parental actions. Dietary deficiency serves as the indicator of activity in another arena, and physical abuse might serve equally well for the social worker's purposes. Responsibility is focused automatically on the parents, and the perspective is likely to foster some hostility toward the parents for failing to care properly for their children. Proposals for remedying the situation will focus, not on the children's diet, but on ways and means of enforcing parental responsibility. The effects of such social institutions as the employment market, and the responsibilities of government generally for the welfare of the weak and helpless, are likely to be ignored or overlooked because they are not part of the conceptual apparatus.

Approaching the same problem using the conceptual framework of a specialist in governmental welfare programs and the responsibilities of social authority for those living in abject poverty will produce yet another account of the situation, a different assignment of responsibility, and a different solution. The poverty of the children's parents is now linked causally to the children's malnutrition, in contrast to prior links between food intake or parental responsibility and failure to develop normally. The primary cause for the children's condition is assigned to the failure of relevant social institutions. The primary responsibility for the state of affairs is then reasonably assigned to government. The conceptualization will tend to generate sympathy for the parents and children, hostility to public authority, and a demand for collective action.

Built-in bias of this kind is virtually impossible to eliminate from thinking. A description of the children's situation produced with each of these conceptual frameworks, however accurate it may be, will unavoidably reflect the bias built into the selection of concepts. The search for cause and remedy will be biased along precisely the same lines. In general, social problems cannot be resolved until responsibility for action is assigned to some specific point in society. In one sense, that assignment is a function of public authority. But it cannot be assumed that public authority will in every case assign responsibility to itself, any more than it can be assumed that in no case will remedial action be left for a public agency. The selection of a conceptual framework for researching the problem will alter the locus of responsibility and in all likelihood influence the extent to which the problem can be resolved in the present and prevented from recurring in the future.

Put another way, the conceptual framework used to deal with real-world situations will tend to determine the amount and kind of learning that takes place. Experience does not always produce learning, of course, but what is learned depends heavily on the conceptual apparatus used for examining experience. A student who took part in a twenty-four-hour simulation of the United Nations organization's efforts to deal with an international crisis, for example, responded to the question "What was the most important thing you learned from the simulation?" by saying, "I learned how to roller skate." As it happened, the student was assigned a job as a courier, a carrier of information; to speed operations, the couriers were provided with rubber-wheeled roller skates. The young man, who had never used this means of transportation before, mastered the use of the skates during his period on duty. The response was legitimate, and meaningful, although not precisely what those responsible for the simulation had expected.

The reason why the conceptual apparatus has a great influence on learning is found in the theoretical connections that determine the concepts included in the structure. Again, an imaginary illustration can clarify the relationship. Consider a cave dweller living long ago who had never before seen a snake. Confronted with a large and poisonous reptile, what will be learned from the interaction? If the cave dweller simply runs away, and the action is successful in the sense that no harm is done, learning is very limited; the new "thing" can be described but only in general terms. If the individual remains in sight of the animal, or moves closer to it, that allows for a more detailed physical description and perhaps some account of behavior as well. If an effort is made to capture the creature, and the individual is bitten solidly, that may be the end of the matter; the cave dweller may have learned something new and important, but if death intervenes, nothing will be passed along to the next generation. If another person observes the sequence of events, using a similar conceptual apparatus, many of the same limitations hold. It may seem reasonable, with the advantages of hindsight, to assume that the death of the person will be linked to the bite of the reptile, but there is no way to be certain of it. Folklore says that a child once burned is twice shy of hot stoves; my own parent insisted that, in fact, the connection between pain and the hot stove was not made and the burning incident was repeated. The reader is left to draw his or her own inferences from that bit of information.

Exercises

Review Questions

1. What is meant by a "conceptual framework"? Identify a particular framework and some of the concepts that it includes.

2. How does the conceptual framework influence the accuracy and adequacy of a description?

3. What are some of the similarities and differences you would expect to find between the conceptual framework of a policeman and that of a burglar?

4. How is the conceptual framework affected if the theoretical base from which it derives is very weak?

5. Identify some of the major problems arising out of the need to use conceptual frameworks. Illustrate from experience.

6. What can be learned about society or culture from a study of the conceptual frameworks found there?

Discussion

1. Which would you expect to develop first, concepts or conceptual frameworks?

2. How can errors or bias in a conceptual framework be detected and corrected?

3. Enumerate the major errors in conceptualization encountered thus far in the text.

4. Discuss the problems expected when a new conceptual framework is being introduced into a society. In what ways would this be similar to changing the rules of play in a well-established game such as football?

8. Description: Definitions and Measurements

Two major aspects of description remain to be examined: (1) the way in which the concepts (variables) used in descriptions are defined; and (2) the kinds of measurements used to determine the values taken by those variables. Both factors influence the quality of the description produced. If terms are not adequately defined, both the descriptions and the other knowledge patterns that depend on them will be faulty. And the quality of the measurements determines both the accuracy of the description and the amount of information that it contains.

Definitions

The meaning of a concept is contained in its definition. There are many different ways to define concepts, however, and not all of them are acceptable if the purpose of inquiry is to provide a basis for action. It is often said, for example, that terms can be defined in any way the user wishes, as long as they are consistently used. That is only partly true, and the limits on such definitions must be clearly understood. No physician, for example, is allowed to define a disease without regard to both past experience and current usage in medicine. The reasons for restricting the freedom to define, and the criteria of adequacy to be applied to definitions of such concepts, are matters of great importance for systematic criticism.

Kinds of Definitions

The most efficient way to deal with the problem of definition is to summarize the basic kinds of definitions, indicating their uses and limitations. The most common source of definitions or meanings is the dictionary. The *lexical* definitions found there summarize current usage only; the quality of the definition is not considered. If a word is used in a particular way in society, that usage is included in the dictionary. Such definitions are often inadequate for rigorous inquiry or criticism.

When greater accuracy is required, everyday usage can be limited or sharpened in a particular way, producing what is called a *precising* definition. For example, a student of government may limit the meaning of the concept *party member* to those persons who contribute in time or money to the activities of a political party. Such precising definitions are quite useful as long as they are used consistently and understood by the reader or listener. The principal danger involved in their use is that either author or listener will forget the special meaning, particularly if the term is common in everyday use, and will revert to everyday meaning. If an author writes of "party members" while thinking of persons who contribute money or time to party activity, and the reader has in mind anyone who *claims* to belong to a political party, confusion and disagreement over propositions are unavoidable.

When a new concept is being introduced, it is first given a *stipulative*, or *nominal*, definition: The meaning is asserted by the creator, and the concept is given an appropriate label. Suppose, for example, that a student of politics believes that the ratio between the number of legal voters in a district and the number of votes actually cast in elections is a very important indicator of a successful democratic process. A new concept, say *Citizenship Index,* can be invented and defined as the ratio between the two numbers. The danger here, obviously, is that the label attached to the new concept has everyday connotations that differ from the meaning attached to the concept by the author. The meaning of the proposed concept is clear enough, and its value can be measured quite precisely, but it is not clear that the ratio of voters to eligible citizens is a good measure of citizenship levels, and that is a source of potential disagreement.

This raises what is probably the most important distinction in definitions needed for concepts used to deal with real-world affairs, the difference between *real* and *nominal* (or stipulative) definitions. The point is a little complex, but its importance is so great that the extra effort needed to learn how to use it is amply repaid in both academic study and everyday affairs. Concepts that refer to events in the observable world are defined, ultimately, by reference to experience or observation—are given a real definition. The meaning of the concept is developed inductively, by making observations and generalizing the results. The best examples of such definitions appear in the meanings attached to such concepts as *measles* in medical dictionaries. Since real definitions are created from experience, they can be challenged by reference to experience. That is, if one physician claims

- Description: Definitions and Measurements

that measles has a particular characteristic, another physician may dispute that claim, and the disagreement (and definition) will be decided on the basis of past experience with real cases of measles.

There is another way of giving meaning to concepts, a way already encountered in the discussion of stipulative definitions and typified in the meaning given to terms in mathematics. These nominal definitions simply state the intention of the user to substitute one word or phrase or symbol for another. When we say, "Let X be the total amount of money in the economy," or, "Let us define a 'great power' conflict as an opposing vote on a nonprocedural resolution in the United Nations Security Council," we are providing nominal definitions for "X" and "great power conflict" respectively. Terms defined in this way do not refer to experience and cannot be challenged on experiential grounds. A nominally defined term means what its definer says it means; no other reason or justification is required. If a zoologist stated that the word *robin* would be used henceforth (by him) to designate a four-footed reptile with specified characteristics, it would be pointless to challenge the definition by referring to experience, as long as the zoologist insisted that it was intended as a nominal definition. But, and it is a very important *but*, other zoologists would necessarily ignore that individual's discussion of "robins" for the very good reason that it would make no sense in terms of past experience and current usage. The price of using nominal definitions, in other words, is that what is said then does not apply to the world of experience except accidentally.

If nominally defined concepts are so limited and dangerous, why not abandon them entirely? Unfortunately, they perform a number of very useful functions in systematic inquiry and cannot be discarded altogether. It is necessary to guard against abuse rather than cease employment, like an irreplaceable employee who has an unfortunate propensity to steal. For one thing, nominal definitions provide a way of introducing new terms into systematic inquiry in the form of stipulative definitions. Second, they are invaluable for simplifying complex formulas, as in mathematics or chemistry, much facilitating discussion and clarification of the topic. Third, terms that are nominally defined can be used to avoid the bias and affective coloring built into ordinary language; discussing the relations between state A and state B avoids some of the problems associated with the use of real labels, particularly in discussions with persons directly involved with the topic.

The principal danger associated with the use of nominal definitions arises when the label attached to the term has a real-world meaning of its own, and the two meanings are different. If the user forgets that the concept has no real-world meaning and begins making statements about real-world affairs using the nominal definition, the result is unacceptable. Unfortunately, that situation occurs often. Consider the following illustration, adapted from a real case published in the press. A young fascist is arguing with a young advocate of democracy about the merits of the democratic process. The crux of the argument is as follows: "You can keep your form of democracy. Democracies elect their rulers. What of it? In many of the world's countries, rulers are popularly elected, yet people live in great poverty and suffer serious repression. Who wants to live in such a political system?" There are various ways of identifying the error involved, but one of the most useful is to realize that "democracy" has been given a nominal definition in the second sentence (democracies elect their rulers). As a real definition of democracy, it is as inadequate as a definition of measles limited to "a disease that causes spots to appear on the body." In the remainder of the argument, that nominal definition is treated as though it were real. For that reason, even if it were less simplistic and more persuasive, as it would probably be in a real case, it would remain illegitimate and unconvincing.

Measurements

Description depends on the use of observations to measure the value of a specified set of variables at particular times and places. There are various ways of making the measurements; they produce different results, in terms of the amount of information contained in the description, the quality of that information, and the kind of mathematical treatment that it can sustain.

Kinds of Measures

Measurement, or *scaling*, as it is often called, is usually divided into four basic kinds; graded from weakest to strongest, they are labeled nominal, ordinal, interval, and ratio measurements. How they function, and how they relate to the amount and quality of the information produced, should be clearly understood by the prospective user or critic. Those who are already familiar with scaling procedures can skim this discussion quickly, for it is quite elementary.

An observer who sees two birds and notes that "one bird is different from the other" has made a *nominal* measurement. The two objects have been compared and found different. *How* they differ, *how much* they differ, and *to what extent* they are similar cannot be determined from the description produced from the measurement. The process depends on direct comparison of two or more things; there is no external scale that is applied to each in turn. The amount of information supplied is minimal. Although such measures may be useful, particularly in a preconstrained context (an eye examination, for example), the principal use for the results is likely to be suggesting that further measurements are needed.

In the next kind of measurement, the two birds are compared, but this time along a specific dimension or continuum, leading to the statement "One bird is larger than the other." The amount of information has been increased, for one dimension of the difference between the birds is now known (size). The amount of difference, the absolute size of the two birds, and other similarities or differences remain unknown. Again, the measurement depends on comparison, but along a specified continuum; if that continuum is important, the information may be valuable. Choosing a chicken for Sunday's dinner from the family chicken coop may involve no more than such measures if a choice must be made between two birds and the larger specimen is desired. These are *ordinal* measurements.

To improve on ordinal measurements, a continuum or dimension of the thing to be measured is selected (presumably because it is important in context), and a standard unit is created for measuring along that continuum—for measuring that characteristic or attribute. There are many different units of measurement already available, of course, for dealing with such physical dimensions of things as weight, size, or duration, and other units for measuring less tangible things, such as temperature or intelligence. Two basic kinds of units, or two basic kinds of scales, can be created; since they differ greatly in terms of usefulness, they need to be separated carefully.

In the simpler case, a standard unit is created on what is called an *interval* scale; a more powerful scale, but more difficult to produce, creates units on a *ratio* scale. The primary difference between them is that there is no "zero point" on an interval scale, meaning that a zero measurement of the thing being measured is not conceivable. Measurements of intelligence, and of temperature, are made on such interval scales. A ratio scale, in contrast, does contain a zero point; size and weight are measured using such ratio scales. The importance of the zero point, as the name suggests, is that things measured on a ratio scale can be compared by ratios, while measurements made on an interval scale cannot. For example, if one pot of water measured 25°C and a second measured 50°C, it would be incorrect to say that one pot was *twice as hot* as the other because both were measured on an interval scale (temperature). Similarly, intelligence scores, and most grades in school, cannot be compared as ratio expressions. But, if one chicken weighs 2 pounds and the other weighs 4 pounds, it is quite correct, and very useful, to say that one weighs twice as much as the other.

Since the difference between an interval and a ratio measurement sometimes causes serious problems for students, an illustration may help to clarify the difference between them. Suppose that two piles of identical blocks are observed standing on a table. If each block is the same size, it can be considered a standard unit of measurement. But is it a unit on an interval scale or a ratio scale? It depends on the presence or absence of a zero point, and that depends on what is actually seen by the observer. If the table top is visible, and there are two blocks in one pile and four blocks in the other, the surface of the table provides a "zero point" and the units can be used to measure and compare the height of the two columns. In that case, each block is a unit in a ratio scale, and it is legitimate to say that one pile of blocks is twice as high as the other. Availability of a zero point has made it possible to measure the *length of the two columns*. Moreover, if the number of blocks in each pile is halved, the ratio between the two lengths will not be disturbed, which suggests one of the main advantages of being able to develop ratio scales: They allow for more complex mathematical manipulations, other things equal, than do the results of interval scaling. In effect, a ratio scale provides more information than an interval scale.

The effect of eliminating the zero point from measurement can be illustrated by observing the two piles of blocks through a window that obscures the view of the table top. Each block remains a standard unit, but the length of the pile can no longer be measured—it cannot be seen! The observer can still see two blocks in one pile and four blocks in the other, and the length of *what can be seen* remains measurable. But what can be seen may differ from what is actually there. The amount of information provided by the observation has been reduced. Since what can be seen does not include the height of the total column, the two columns cannot be compared. Having a zero point, or starting point, means that total length is comparable, and comparisons of total length can be expressed as ratios.

There are various ways of expressing the importance of the kind of scale used for measuring. The two most important implications of scaling are the amount of information that observation provides and the kinds of calculations that can be carried out on the resulting data. They are closely related, of course, since the result of logical manipulation is to bring out additional information contained in observation or measurement. Nominal and ordinal scalings produce very little information; or, to put the matter another way, mathematical manipulation of nominal and ordinal data is very restricted—little if any additional information can be extracted by formal calculation. Such data are not trivial, for it is often useful to know, say, that one person is more impetuous, or more aggressive, than another. But the very powerful tools in a knowledge system require information that has been measured with an interval, or better, a ratio scale. In fact, some experts restrict the use of the term *measurement* to interval and ratio scaling.

The kinds of measurements that can be made, the kinds of scales or units of measurement that can be developed, depend on the character of the concept being measured, the type of continuum involved. It is obviously difficult to create a standard unit for measuring such things as strength of feeling, or even intelligence; most such measures function indirectly, in the same way as measures of viscosity. And with human subjects it is very difficult to get a measurement of a single trait; human actions usually reflect the influence of a complex of factors rather than a single element. For most dimensions of human action, ratio scaling has proved impossible to achieve. Systems have been devised for attaching numbers to a variety of concepts, but attaching numbers is not the same as making measurements using a standard unit.

The philosopher Abraham Kaplan has provided four useful rules for determining whether or not the requirements for additive measurements, or ratio scaling, have been satisfied in any particular case. First, the outcome of any combination of measurements will be the same regardless of the point at which the combination begins. Second, the results of combining elements should not be affected by the order or arrangement of the things measured. Third, when equivalents are combined with equivalents, the result should remain equivalent. And finally, when one of two equivalents is combined with a third element, the result is no longer equivalent. Measurements that can meet these requirements are genuinely additive, have been made on a scale with a zero point, and can be treated using a wide range of mathematical techniques.

Additive measures are highly desirable, whether in social or physical science or in everyday life. Unfortunately, the question whether or not they can be developed is not a matter controlled by the wishes of the inquirer. It depends on the meaning of the concept being measured. Psychological testing illustrates the fundamental difficulties involved in devising measures of human attributes very nicely. There is much quantified information available about individual responses to the kinds of questions asked on intelligence tests. What has proved difficult is to create a theoretical link between those responses (indicators) and a meaningful conception of intelligence. The data have proved useful for predicting success in school, but the meaning of intelligence remains uncertain, and there is no agreement on how it can be measured precisely. Doubtless, techniques will improve, but for now, an adequate concept has proved elusive.

Exercises

Review Questions

1. What is meant by a "definition"? How does it relate to meaning?

2. Better definitions can be produced by limiting everyday meaning in a specified way. Why is the practice dangerous?

3. Distinguish between a real and a nominal definition and explain why the difference is important.

4. Why do concepts require a real definition?

5. Enumerate the legitimate uses that can be made of nominal definitions.

6. What is a "measurement"? How is it related to observations? To indicators and concepts?

7. Identify each of the four measurement scales and provide an everyday illustration.

8. How can interval and ratio measurements be distinguished? What is the significance of the difference?

9. Enumerate Kaplan's criteria for genuine additive measures and explain why they are desirable.

Discussion

1. If knowledge is organized human experience, and description is a way of storing experience, then knowledge is dependent on the quality of the definitions and measurements employed in description. Can you justify that statement?

2. Any term can be defined in any way that a person wishes as long as it is used consistently. Do you agree? Why?

3. Illustrate the difference between interval and ratio scaling by counting railroad ties set the same distance apart. In each case, count fifty ties.

4. Prepare a checklist of the major points in a description where quality can be lost.

9. Generating Expectations I

In everyday usage, to *expect* means to look forward to or predict some event that has not yet been observed. The claim contained in an expectation is that an observation made at some specified time and place will support a particular description. Usually, expectations and predictions refer to the future, but they can also refer to the unobserved past or to the present. That is, to expect that a member of the family has already returned home on seeing an automobile or bicycle in the yard or noticing activity in one of the rooms of the house is quite reasonable. Of course, it would be wrong to say, "I expect Larkspur will win the big horse race today," if the result is already known to the person making the statement. An expectation must refer to something not yet observed by the person entertaining the expectation.

Propositions that state expectations need not make use of the verb *expect*. Saying "It should rain tomorrow," "I believe that it will rain tomorrow," or simply "It will rain tomorrow" means the same thing in each case. Usually, what is anticipated or expected in the future is a change in the environment: The pond will be frozen over by morning; the snow will melt by nightfall, and so on. But expectations can also refer to the absence of change, to continued stability—expecting that the house will still be in place in the morning, for example. The change that is expected may result from the natural course of events or from human activity. The kind of instrument needed to generate justified expectation depends in some degree on the source of change. Predictions about the natural course of events can be made with classifications, forecasts, or theories; predictions of the effects of human actions, in contrast, require a bona fide theory.

Generating Justified Expectations

An expectation can be defined very loosely as a prediction about the content of an observation that has not been made, or whose results are not known. As long as expectations do not have to be argued or justified, they can be generated quickly and easily. But a prediction that can be defended with adequate reasons in advance of the predicted event must be generated using a particular kind of instrument under specified conditions. To predict that it will rain the next day but have no reason for saying so is to make a prophecy. Such predictions cannot be criticized, except by comparing them to a justified prediction; hence there is no good reason to accept them or take them seriously. Of course, when a long-time resident of an area predicts rain for the next day, and all the local residents carry their umbrellas, it may be the course of wisdom to follow suit. An individual with a very good record of past performance is often worth listening to, but the knowledge on which such predictions depends dies with the person. It cannot be transferred to others, improved and tested systematically, or subjected to criticism; criticism focuses on the reasons for, rather than the substance of, the prediction. For developing and improving the human capacity to predict accurately and reliably, such personal knowledge is not an adequate base.

The generalized procedure used to fulfill any of the primary human purposes is followed in arguing and justifying expectations or predictions as well. That is, a pattern must be created by organizing past experience with particular events. Combining that pattern with an observation, and assuming that it applies to the situation observed, generates an expectation by formal logical inference or calculation. The expectation is justified by referring to the pattern, the observation made, and the calculation. If the pattern is queried, the experience from which it was created must be examined. How that can be done in an adequate manner is the question to be answered in this unit.

Put another way, reasoned or justified expectations are produced by linking one description (the observation that cues the prediction) to a second descriptive account (the expectation or prediction) through a formal pattern assumed to apply to the case in hand. Each description consists of a set of variables whose values are fixed, by observation in the first case and by calculation in the second. The variables included in the cue and those found in the expectation need not be the same, for it is reasonable to expect a change in the condition of a dirt road if heavy rain is predicted for the following day. But the pattern that links cue to expectation must contain *both* sets of variables. The values of the variables in cue and expectation will be linked by the rules incorporated into the pattern. The rules must include all the variables.

A simple example will help to clarify the process. If the temperature is expected to drop well below freezing during the night, the water standing in the road can be expected to freeze—to turn to ice. The reason is found in the well-known scientific rule that water freezes, changes from liquid to solid, if the temperature drops below 32°F or 0°C, other things equal. Structurally, the process by which that expectation is generated is as follows:

Cue	Pattern	Expectation
Water observed in liquid form. Vwater is liquid. Temperature expected to fall below 32°F.	As Vtemp falls below 32°F, Vwater changes from liquid to solid.	Vwater will change from liquid to solid.

The example is very simple, even obvious. But it illustrates the core of the process. All that the pattern must do is connect the values of the variables in the cue to the values of the variables in the expectation by rule.

Two basic kinds of patterns can be used to perform that function: (1) a classification, which states the range of values that a given selection of variables can take (that define a class); and (2) a forecast or theory that links the values of two or more variables by rule under specified limiting conditions. With respect to each form, two points are critical. First, given the observed cue and established pattern, has the expectation or prediction been calculated correctly? Second, is the pattern employed valid? Has it been justified adequately by reference to prior experience? Prediction using each of these kinds of patterns can now be examined in more detail.

Predicting with Classifications

The use of classifications to generate expectations or predictions has already been touched on briefly. A classification, to review, is a generalized statement of the properties shared by all members of some class of things. Because classifications are generalized, they apply to future events as well as to the past, and that gives them predictive capacity. Because they are created by generalizing past experience with members of the class of things designated, they are a form of stored past experience that can be tested against present and future experience, and that gives them legitimacy or justification.

Structurally, a classification consists of a set of variables and rules for specifying the limits of the values that each variable can take. For example, one of the variables used to identify the class *robins* will certainly be the size of the bird; therefore, one of the rules that define the class will state the measurements that a bird can be expected to have. How precisely the rules can state these limits depends on the characteristics of the things classified, on experience gained from observation of individual members of the class. For a class such as robins, there may be substantial differences among specific birds with respect to any particular variable that defines the class.

If the exceptions are numerous, the class may have to be subdivided. Young robins, for example, differ from mature birds in plumage, in coloration, in chest markings, and so on. They are far more likely to be confused with other members of the thrush family than are mature birds. And when a phrase such as "young robins" is employed, it is in fact used to identify such a subclass. At the boundaries of almost every classification, there will always be difficult decisions to make about membership: A few minor discrepancies can usually be ignored; a large number of deviations may call for reclassification.

The key to using classifications to produce reliable expectations is found in their structure. Each classification consists of a set of variables and a set of rules that set the limits of their values. The total structure can be shown within a set of square brackets in the following way:

Class: $[V_1 \ V_2 \ V_3 \ \ldots \ V_n \ \ R_1 \ R_2 \ \ldots \ R_n]$
V = the concepts that identify shared attributes.
R = rules that specify the range of values for each variable.

It is worth emphasizing again at this point that the content of the classification, the selection of variables and the rules, has its own independent base in experience. The concepts employed must have real definitions; the rules generalize past experience with class members. The classification is tested by applying it to present and future members of the class and checking the fit, or by comparing it to recorded experience with earlier class members. Anything that has all the attributes of a class is a member of that class; anything that does not is excluded. Barring minor discrepancies, all class members share all the class attributes.

Assuming that a classification has been established and tested, an expectation or prediction can be generated by a simple three-step process. First, the use of the classification must be cued by an observation made in the present or past but prior in all cases to the expectation. Some "thing" must be observed to have at least some of the defining attributes of a class member. With respect to birds, for example, the cue might be observation of a bird with particular coloration. In the second step, it is assumed that what has been observed is a member of the particular class. The reason for the assumption is simple. If *all* the attributes of a class member have been observed, then class membership is certain and no assumption is needed.

But the classification would then predict nothing whatever; its strength would be exhausted. Prediction using classifications depends on the capacity of the observer to identify a class member *before* all of the class attributes have been observed. The machinery can then be used to predict the remaining class attributes. Once the assumption of class membership is made, formal inference will justify assuming that the remaining attributes will be observed in due course. The logic is as follows:

1. *All members of class C have property P* (classification).
2. *A is a member of class C* (assumed on observing properties other than property *P*).
3. *Therefore, A will have property P.*

Note that (1) comes directly from the classification, (2) is the assumption made on the basis of a partial enumeration of class properties, and (3) is a formal deduction from the two initial premises. In everyday language, if all members of a class share certain properties, and the thing I see is a member of that class, then it must also share those properties. The prediction or expectation consists in the other properties established for the class.

Uses and Limitations

Most of the problems and possibilities involved in the use of classifications to generate expectations can be demonstrated within the context of that simple example. First, the process depends on the availability of a valid classification, and the instrument must have certain characteristics before it can perform the predictive function. In particular, it must be generalized from experience, must serve as a storehouse for past experience with class members. It functions in some respects like a storage battery. There is no magic in the procedure. The classification predicts because it is assumed that the past performance of class members will be repeated. If experience suggests the assumption is valid, it will continue to be made. Obviously, the structure may fail; hence predictions should always be regarded as uncertain or problematic. Nevertheless, such instruments have proved their worth many times over, and if care is exercised, they provide one reliable and improvable base for generating expectations.

Second, prediction depends on the ability of the observer to identify a member of a class before all its properties have been observed. If a class is defined by only four properties, no more than three properties can be used in identification, else there is nothing left to predict. The limit on what can be predicted with a classification is the list of established properties minus one. How effectively diagnosis can be made depends on the class and its relations with other classes. In some cases, a particular kind of bird can be identified positively if one characteristic is observed—a coloring or configuration shared by no other bird, for example. It should be possible to identify an elephant on observation of the trunk alone, although a tapir has a somewhat similar shape. Other cases are more difficult, as medical diagnosis so often shows. And even experts can be confused by the similarities among the various spring and fall warblers.

As might be expected, two major errors can occur in the use of classifications for generating expectations. In the first case, the diagnosis of class membership, the assumption that a member of a particular class has been observed, is mistaken. Usually, if the classification is misread, some at least of the expectations projected on the future will be mistaken. Indeed, if the expectations did not go beyond the characteristics displayed, the mistake would not be discovered. Ordinarily, diagnostic errors, and the classification errors often associated with them, are discovered if an expectation remains unfulfilled or something not expected occurs. Physicians are trained to be particularly alert to such variations from the norms. When a prescribed mode of treatment fails to produce the expected effect, or a patient undergoing treatment exhibits unexpected symptoms, a careful rediagnosis is generally called for, unless the case in question is minor and trivial.

A second kind of error appears if the quality of the classification is poor. That is, if an attribute assumed to be part of the classification actually is not shared by all members of the class, expectations relating to that attribute may not be fulfilled. If, for example, it is believed that birds of a particular species migrate, but in fact some do not, then an expectation generated with respect to a particular bird may be mistaken, even though the bird was identified correctly. For a long time, for example, it was taken for granted that all swans were white. In due course, black swans, birds that were truly swans but black in color, were discovered in Australia. Expectations about the color of swans had to be modified accordingly.

When such situations arise, the taxonomist (classifier), as well as the person who makes use of the classification, faces a serious dilemma. Has the error occurred in diagnosis? Or is the classification itself at fault? How should predictive failure be interpreted? There are several possibilities to be explored. First, the diagnosis may be correct and the classification may be of good quality, but the particular class member observed may be aberrant in one or more respects from class norms. In such cases, the failure is written off, and procedures and instruments remain unchanged. Second, the diagnosis may be mistaken; the thing observed may not be a member of the class. That raises two further possibilities. Either the observer may need to check criteria or obtain further training, or the classification may need tightening. If a class is too loosely defined, it may be properly applied yet lead to mistaken diagnoses, identification of things as class members that share all the class attributes yet do not really belong to the class. Further observations would be needed to determine the source of error and suggest a remedy. Finally, the diagnosis could be correct, but the classification could be wrong. If an attribute is not genuinely shared by all class members, expectations with respect to that attribute are bound to be disappointed in some cases. Again, modification of the classification is required, and that depends on the results of future observation.

In effect, the use of a classification as a predictive device serves as a test of a combination of factors. Predictive failure may be due to one factor or several. The application tests the validity of the classification, the descriptive powers and diagnostic capacity of the observer, and the calculating capacity of the person who actually generates the prediction. Working out the source of error and specifying a corrective action can in some cases be a very complex and time-consuming problem.

The primary factor in most decisions about the acceptability of a classification is probably the significance of the purpose for which the classification is used. A physician will accept and use a program of treatment that is successful only 5 percent of the time if the only other alternative is death for the patient. Improvements can occur in three ways: (1) the range of variation allowed for each variable can be narrowed; (2) the number of variables used to define the class can be increased; (3) the limiting conditions governing application of the pattern can be augmented. Whether or not improvements can be made may depend in part on the ingenuity and creativeness of the classifier, but in the end the matter is decided by the kind of experience acquired over time with the "things" being classified.

Exercises

Review Questions

1. State a precise meaning for "expecting" and relate it to description.

2. Differentiate prediction from prophecy. Illustrate.

3. Outline the procedure used to generate an expectation with a classification using an example from everyday experience.

4. Illustrate the way in which the purpose for which a classification is made influences its content.

5. Sketch the role played by formal logic in the development of a prediction using a classification.

6. What are the major problems encountered in the use of classifications for making predictions?

7. If a prediction derived from a classification fails to materialize, outline the points where the cause of the failure could be found.

8. Is accurate prediction an adequate test for classifications? Explain.

9. Enumerate the assumptions required before a classification can be used to make a prediction.

10. At what point in classification does generalization occur?

Discussion

1. What are the implications of the "index number problem" for the future development of classifications? Illustrate.

2. How can successful prophecy be accounted for, particularly if it recurs?

3. Is there any reason why classification of humans, or of human actions, should be less accurate and reliable than classifications of animals or of inanimates?

10. Generating Expectations II

Two basic procedures can be followed when organizing human experience into patterns that can be used to generate justifiable expectations. The first, which has already been discussed, is to identify a class of things in the environment and collect information about individual members of the class systematically; that information can be generalized to create a pattern called a classification. Combined with observations, such patterns can be used to make predictions. The procedure is widely applicable, whether to natural artifacts, living things, or human individuals and groups. But the predictions generated using classifications apply only to members of the class, and there remain a great many kinds of purposes that cannot be fulfilled by such instruments.

A more powerful and flexible procedure is to collect information about the relations between two or more classes of things or events over time. Such information can also be generalized to form patterns in which two or more classes of things are related by rule. That is, a rule is generalized that links the values of two or more variables or observables. Once that pattern has been established, observation of members of one of the classes can be used to make predictions about members of the second class. To repeat an example, if the relation between air temperature and the physical state of water is observed over time, it will be found that if the temperature of the air remains below 32°F for some time, water will change from a liquid to a solid state. That information can be generalized into a pattern in which air temperature is linked to the physical state of water. The limiting conditions within which the pattern holds can be established from the same kinds of observations. Thus, the relationship will not hold if the water is saturated with salt, and some time may be required if the body of water is large and the temperature is barely below 32°F. When the pattern has been limited and refined, it can be combined with observations in the same manner as a classification and used to generate predictions. That is, if water is exposed to temperatures below 32°F for an appropriate period of time, the observer is entitled to expect that it will convert from a liquid to a solid state.

Two different kinds of patterns can be created by this procedure. They are identical in structure but differ with respect to the assumptions made about the relation they express. If a causal relation is assumed to hold between the variables, then a change in the value of one variable can be expected to produce a change in the value of the other(s) according to the rules in the pattern. Such patterns are here called *theories*. If no causal assumption is included in the pattern, it is labeled a *forecast*. Both instruments can be used to make forecasts or predictions; only theories can be used to control future events in the environment.

Forecasts and theories consist of a selection of two or more variables related by rule; the rule links the values of the variables. Each instrument is accompanied by a set of limiting conditions that must be satisfied before it will function as expected. In the example relating air temperature to the physical state of water, there are two variables; if air temperature *(AT)* is measured and found to be less than 32°F, then measurement of physical state *(PS)* will show it to be solid. The rule also covers changes in the values of the variables. That is, if the value of *(AT)* changes from more than 32°F to less than 32°F, the value of *(PS)* will change from liquid to solid. The essentials of theories and forecasts are contained in the rules: Each rule must link two or more variables; in combination, the rules must connect *all* the variables included in the structure. Since they generate expectations in precisely the same way, forecasts and theories can be examined together.

Note: Confusion sometimes arises over the difference between asking of a given instrument, "Is it a forecast or a theory?" and asking the different question, "For that purpose, what is needed, a forecast or a theory?" What makes an instrument a theory or a forecast is the set of assumptions it includes and the evidence that supports those assumptions; what sets the instrumental requirements is the purpose of the user. Those requirements control the evidence needed to justify a particular use of the instrument. An individual who wishes to make a prediction, for example, may use a genuine theory for that purpose. In evidentiary terms, however, all that need be shown to justify the use of the instrument is that it fulfills the requirements for a forecast.

Predicting with Forecasts or Theories

The simplest way to deal with predictions based on forecasts and theories yet maintain the essential distinctions between the two instruments is through an example. This unit therefore pursues a commonplace example of the kind of forecasting regularly used in business, first to illustrate and underscore the differences between forecasts and theories and second to illustrate the processes and considerations involved in prediction or forecasting.

Assume a contemporary businessman who manufactures trousers. Typically, he needs a way to predict future sales of the product so that storage costs can be minimized, turnover rates optimized, and so on. He discovers that sales for any given month in the past could have been predicted very accurately by relating the number of sales per month to the price of a particular stock on the Stock Exchange sixty days prior to the beginning of that month. That relation is easily generalized into a formula, tested against history, and used to produce the required predictions. If, however, the manufacturer wishes to increase sales rather than predict them, and uses the same apparatus as a basis for action, the apparatus will be inadequate. That is, if friends and relatives are organized into a financial group and large blocks of the stock are purchased in order to increase the price and thus increase trouser sales, the manufacturer is likely to be condemned by friends and perhaps attacked by the investors, although that same kind of error is surprisingly common in human affairs. The stock purchase would make sense only if there was some reason to believe that the stock price and monthly sales were somehow causally connected — an unlikely event, other things equal.

In general, relations among variables that can be used for predicting are very much easier to find than causal links. In fact, forecasts are based on a simple principle and are usually easy to construct and apply. They range in size and complexity from simple two-variable structures linked by a single rule with minimal limitations to the enormous models used to forecast national economic activity, models that may incorporate hundreds of variables and use millions of computations. Basically, all forecasts function by projecting trends located in the past upon the future. The past trend is generalized into a relation, expressed by rule, linking the values of two or more variables. Applying the rule, by combining it with a present observation, serves to project the past relation onto the future.

To illustrate, assume that the trouser manufacturer wishes an estimate of future sales, by month, for a period of one year — a purpose readily fulfilled by either a theory or a forecast but impossible for a classification. In the simplest case, the manufacturer takes past sales information for a period of time, say five years, and charts it month by month. If the volume of sales has increased about 10 percent each year for the past five years, and the increase has been distributed in a particular pattern over the twelve months of the year, the raw material needed to contruct a forecast is available. Two rules can be used to generalize prior sales experience: (1) "Sales in any given year are equal to sales in the preceding year plus 10 percent"; and (2) "One-half percent of the increase appears in each of the first four months of the year; the increase in each other month amounts to 1 percent of the previous year's total." That relatively simple apparatus suffices to predict future sales into the indefinite future.

The businessman now has the needed predictions but is faced with the difficult problem of evaluating them. How reliable is the forecast likely to be? What are the limiting conditions that must be satisfied before it will hold? What kinds of events or changes would be likely to destroy its predictive value? Such questions are likely to be very difficult to answer and justify. It is fairly obvious that the business must continue to function, that the overall economy must not break down completely, that foreign competition must not capture the international trouser market, and so on. Less obvious influences may not be noticed. The structure can be tested against past experience, of course, but since it was generated out of past experience, there are not likely to be serious discrepancies if the forecast was created by a competent person.

How can confidence in the forecast be increased? The quality of the predictions, their accuracy and reliability, need to be known *before* they are acted on. Unfortunately, forecasts cannot be tested experimentally; they lack the causal assumption that makes experimentation possible. They can be tested only against past history. All that can be varied is the amount of history probed and the way in which that history can be organized alternatively. The evidence for a forecast is always "more of the same," although "the same" can be packaged differently.

Other things equal, then, the strength of the justification offered for a forecast will depend on such things as the period of historical time to which the forecast applies, the number of cases included, and the character of the historical period from which the data were derived. Obviously, that procedure has limits. The businessman who explores his own experience into the remote past may find that external business conditions have changed so drastically that only recent history is relevant to current possibilities. A pattern valid a half century earlier may not hold very well in the present and may be superseded by a pattern established during the past year or two.

Other techniques are available, of course. Thus far, the manufacturer has produced a forecast based on direct projection of past sales history. The easiest way to strengthen confidence in its predictions is to increase the number of factors taken into account by the forecast—in effect, to create multiple forecasts focused on the same factor (trouser sales) but linked to different time series, different bodies of information, or different kinds of events. Again, past history must be searched for readily accessible numerical records that can be linked to trouser sales over time (generating new data can be very expensive). In practice, forecasters will try to use data that are somehow linked to clothing sales, whether by folklore and tradition or by systematic inquiries—seasons, number of persons leaving school, sales of other items, and so on. The forecast does not depend on the plausibility of the real-world relation between the elements it includes, however, and if the number of tins of sardines imported from Norway into the United States each month turned out to be the best available predictor of trouser sales, the forecaster would use it gladly and without asking questions.

The relation would, however, be tested historically. Suppose, for simplicity's sake, that the value of sardine imports into the United States from Norway was exactly 100 times the number of pairs of trousers sold by the manufacturer in the succeeding month. That relation can be generalized to produce a simple two-variable forecast containing a single rule: $(V_1 \ V_2 \ R_1)$ Where

V_1 = value of sardines imported, month A.

V_2 = number of pairs of trousers sold, month A + 1.

$R_1 = V_1 = 100 \ V_2$

The forecast is applied by inserting the real number for the value of sardine imports for any given month and calculating expected trouser sales in the following month. Again, the forecast would be applied to the historical records to determine the precision of fit with past experience. But now that a second forecast is available, a different comparison can be made: between the two projected figures for future sales. If they agree on the number of trouser sales to be expected in a given time period, that increases confidence in the prediction. In real cases, a number of different forecasts will be generated routinely, and perhaps averaged, before a final figure is set, particularly in matters of some significance.

Beyond an extension of the historical period from which the evidence used to create a forecast is drawn, and an increase in the number of variables linked to the variable whose value is to be forecast, there are some additional sources of evidence relating to the accuracy and reliability of forecasts. If there have been no counterexamples, no cases in history where the relations expressed in the forecast failed to hold, that is considered evidence in support of the instrument. Where counterexamples do occur, they can be studied to determine the factors responsible, and those factors can be incorporated into the limiting conditions governing use of the instrument. In some cases, counterexamples may actually strengthen confidence in a forecast by serving as a "natural state experiment" of sorts. To take an obvious example, if a forecasting pattern is broken by a major disaster, and the pattern is reestablished once the course of events returns to normal, that is evidence for the stability of the forecasting relation that cannot be obtained in any other way. The factors that caused the breakdown can be added to the limiting conditions.

Confidence in forecasts can be justified to some extent by careful consideration of the influence of known or suspected causal relations between external events and the predictions being made. A trouser manufacturer will know from past experience the kinds of events that influence trouser sales; other events, national and international, will be known to affect business firms of all sorts. Such events can be monitored, often by companies that specialize in one particular area, and the results used to develop an assessment of future business conditions that might influence the operations of particular businesses. For example, businesses whose operations are affected seriously by changes in the price of petroleum will keep a watchful eye on events in the oil-producing regions of the world, particularly on projected future trends that may influence oil prices. Wheat producers and traders attend carefully to long-range weather predictions and reports of crop failures or natural disasters known to influence levels of production. Although such considerations do not usually permit very accurate estimates of the amount of impact, it may be possible to predict the direction of change, which can serve as a rough basis for action if nothing more detailed and precise is available.

Finally, it may be possible to transfer or transpose events from one area to another, sometimes in geographic terms and in other cases by reference to the influence of common factors on disparate activities. Those who live in the lower Mississippi River valley in the United States, for example, can use flooding in the river's northern regions as an indicator of impending flooding, and even estimate the amount of flooding that can be expected. Such predictions are produced regularly by governmental agencies and used as a basis for flood-preparation activities. In a similar way, manufacturers of steel include sales of automobiles and other items that involve the use of steel products in predictions relating to their own sales. In that sense, both products are influenced by common factors, but the effect of, say, a change in buying trends, may be felt first in one area — automobile sales earlier than steel sales, for example.

Good forecasting, whether of business patterns or the weather, the outcome of elections or the outcome of football games, goes beyond simple calculations from the historical records. There is plenty of room for imagination and creativity, and plenty of margin for error. What can actually be accomplished depends on the subject matter, the use to be made of the forecast, the amount of information available about past performance, awareness of the various factors that influence the occurrence of the events as predicted, and the ability of the forecaster to organize selected parts of that information into patterns that hold up against the test of history.

Exercises

Review Questions

1. Outline the procedures by which forecasting devices are created and tested.

2. Sketch the steps by which a forecast is used to produce an expectation or prediction. Illustrate.

3. Discuss the means by which confidence in a forecast can be increased before the forecast is actually applied.

4. Under what circumstances would a forecast that has predicted well in the past fail to predict in the present? Illustrate.

5. Does an established causal relation increase confidence in the accuracy and reliablity of a prediction? Explain.

Discussion

1. Why do forecasts, like theories, include a statement of limiting conditions? Give an example.

2. Design an experiment that will provide a test for a proposed forecast in advance of use.

3. Explain why extending the historical time period on which a forecast is based may actually decrease the accuracy and reliability of the instrument. Illustrate.

4. Classifications are often produced with no particular purpose in mind. Can a forecast be produced without reference to a particular purpose? Explain and justify your answer.

5. Is contingency forecasting, predicting weather in one region on the basis of weather in another, for example, based on causal relations or on correlation patterns? Explain.

11. Controlling Events I

The importance of being able to control events in the environment, to produce or inhibit changes by deliberate actions, is literally beyond exaggeration. Without some capacity to control events in the future, human survival would be highly problematic. That capacity is expressed in human actions that range from simple food gathering or avoidance to the more complex feats of modern engineering such as placing a man on the moon or controlling diseases like pneumonia or diabetes. Control over the course of events depends on the availability of knowledge, obviously, which in turn requires an organization of experience that will both formulate and fulfill specific human purposes. The knowledge on which control over events depends may not be self-conscious, but if the human capacity to exercise such control is to be expanded, refined, and improved, the structures and processes involved, and the dangers to be avoided, need to be widely known and understood.

Causality

The key to exercising human control over events is to develop or identify causal linkages. If experience can be organized in patterns that capture a causal relation between two events, the structure can be used to control events in foreseeable ways. Here, any instrument that incorporates such a causal link, whose rules of interaction express causal relations, will be labeled a *theory*. Such usage corresponds reasonably well with the meaning of theory in the experimental sciences, but not every construct that is labeled a theory actually incorporates a causal link, even in the physical sciences.

A causal relation is only an assumption; that assumption must in due course be justified. Happily, the nature of the assumption allows the structure to be tested in action, either experimentally under laboratory conditions or in real-world use. The results of such testing make up the strongest element in the evidence used to support theories.

The meaning of *causal relation* is extremely limited. Two or more variables or factors are said to relate causally if their values are linked by rule in such a manner that deliberately changing the value of one variable will change the value of the other variables in predictable ways. In principle, that provides an instrument sufficient for controlling events in the environment, a basis for reasoned intervention to produce or prevent a particular outcome in the future. The technology needed to make use of the causal link may not be available, but the basic requirement for theory has been satisfied. Such structures can provide, and justify, answers to three important types of questions. First, what caused a particular change to occur? Second, how can a particular situation be changed? Third, what result can be expected to follow if a particular change is introduced into a stipulated situation? If these questions can be answered, then humans can exercise some measure of control over future events. The central concern is with the effects of deliberate human actions in a given situation. For if a causal link is assumed, then changing one of the elements in the pattern will produce a change in the second, however that first change may be induced. Such instruments are necessary, though not sufficient as an intellectual base for reasoned and defensible actions.

Note that the causal assumption asserts no more than that a change in the value of one variable will *produce* a change in the second. Nothing more is required or provided. A theory does not identify the "original" cause of any event; it provides a base for producing or inhibiting the event, and in principle only. Of course, it is often useful to know the "origins" of a particular condition, such as illness, but in future-oriented action, the focus of concern is necessarily on cures rather than causes. Given the uncontrollable nature of the time sequences in which human life is embedded, the question raised in action is always "Where do we go from here?" Asking "How did we get here in the first place?" is necessary in some cases, perhaps, but not in every case. The cause of diabetes or cancer, for example, is at present unknown, yet the first of these diseases can be controlled effectively and the second can in some cases be cured. In a systematic effort to articulate the intellectual foundations of action, the emphasis is placed on the development of cures and action programs directed at the future instead of tracing present conditions to their roots. Even if origins are pursued, the likelihood is that the inquirer will be caught in an infinite regress, unable to identify the original, or ultimate, cause even if it is uncovered.

Because a theory links two or more variables causally, it always suggests an intervention strategy for producing certain outcomes, a way of acting to produce or inhibit some event. Whether that strategy can be implemented or not depends on the state of technology, but in principle, every theory provides an adequate guide to action. Thus, if bread mold is linked causally to the elimination of infection, the intervention strategy used to eliminate infection is clear: Apply bread mold in some form. If the technology needed to apply a theory is not available, that does not affect the validity of the theory. It is easy to show that if the Gulf Stream could be diverted away from the eastern coast of the United States, the climate there would change dramatically. At present, there is no technology adequate to test the theory, and very little impulse to do so. But the theory can be justified by reference to other theories that *have* been tested in action, and that is sufficient for most purposes.

Preventing/Producing Change

The instruments needed to provide reasoned control over events in the world are created by exactly the same processes, using much the same criteria, as those employed to develop forecasts. Experience must be organized into patterns that link two or more variables; that experience must suffice to justify the causal relation assumed to connect them. Assuming that the pattern fits a particular situation allows the user to combine it with human *actions*, based on calculation of the implications of combining pattern and observation, to produce a foreseeable outcome. As with forecasts, the limiting conditions attached to use of the instrument must be satisfied.

There are two major kinds of causal relations, and each provides a basis for action, but the results that can be achieved using theories of the two types are different. In the first case, a theory incorporates the conditions that are *necessary* for an event to occur (the general form is: No X unless Y, under limiting conditions C); such theories can be used to inhibit but not to produce a particular event. If the *sufficient* conditions for an event to occur can be established (form: If A, then B, under conditions C), the theory has greater power and flexibility and can be used to produce particular events. In short, theories that identify the necessary conditions for change are useful for preventing change, usually in conjunction with another theory. Eliminating oxygen from an area will stop a fire burning because the presence of oxygen is a necessary condition for burning, to take a common example. In contrast, if a patient is to be cured of a disease caused by a particular germ, development of an appropriate medicine requires knowledge of the sufficient conditions for killing it— one hopes within specified limits on acceptable side effects. Usually, to say that someone "knows how to do" something carries the implication of knowing the sufficient conditions for effecting a change or bringing about a specified condition, but usage varies and precise meaning may be different.

Although theories are generalized in form, not limited in time and place of application, the search for theory begins with the particular case and is tested against the particular case. The clearest illustrations of the reason for starting at that point are found in medicine. Until a person appears with a particular disease, efforts to obtain a cure would be pointless or misplaced. And given the future orientation of the human species, once the disease does appear, the primary focus of concern is a mode of treatment, a solution to the particular case, rather than the origins or causes. The search for causes begins when it is learned that treatment requires knowledge of causes; more often, the search for causes and cures proceeds concurrently. Cures or treatments, if arrived at first, can be tested independently of knowledge of causes and can pursue an independent existence. Of course, knowledge of causes, or of the chain of causal links leading to a particular situation, can be invaluable for developing efficient treatments. A good example is found in the treatment of malaria, where knowledge of the chain of events leading to the infection of the person allows for different ways of preventing the infection—killing the larvae of the mosquito, killing the live mosquito, or simply avoiding mosquitos.

Structures and Process

Structurally, a theory consists of a set of two or more variables whose values are linked by a set of rules, together with a statement of the limiting conditions governing application or use. The change that a theory can be used to produce is usually called a *phenomenon;* in fact, any one of the changes that can take place *within* a theory can serve as phenomenon. A theory, in other words, can be used to deal with any situation that appears within its boundaries—in effect, with changes in the values of the variables that make up its elements. In principle, once a theory is established, the rules can account for any change that takes place in the value of any of the variables. Ohm's law, which links voltage, current, and resistance in a direct-current electrical circuit, can be used to deal with changes in any of those three elements.

Taken together, the rules incorporated into a theory make up a logic or calculus. That logic supplies the dynamic power for the structure. In that perspective, theorizing is only a special form of applied logic or applied mathematics, although it should be noted that the application of logic or mathematics is not in itself a logical or mathematical problem. In most cases, theories are based on rules derived from an existing form of logic or mathematics—algebra or calculus, for example. In some instances, however, a new branch of mathematics must be created to deal with a particular problem—as Leibniz invented calculus to deal with certain questions that concerned him. To harness the power of the logic to the fulfillment of human purposes, the logical structure must be linked to observation in a particular way. A logic consists in sets of rules for manipulating formally defined symbols. Those symbols are defined nominally: Their sole meaning is found within the logic. To apply the logic to real-world affairs, the symbols, and the rules of manipulation, must be given meaning in the world of observation. Arithmetic is used in everyday affairs, for example, by giving the symbol "one" an observable meaning (to designate a member of the class *apples*, say) and linking the meaning of "add" to real-world processes. Once that is done, the arithmetic can be used to add or subtract apples rather than just numbers (symbols).

The key to applying logic to real-world affairs is to find a situation in the observable world that is isomorphic to, that fits, the mathematical structure. If the earth is considered flat, as it can be over short distances, then the geometry of plane surfaces can be applied there. If that same geometry is applied to very large parts of the earth's surface—used to plot a flight from New York City to Los Angeles, for example—the result will be badly mistaken; the destination will be missed by a considerable distance. Similarly, arithmetical addition can be applied to apples, or to pears, but apples and pears cannot be added. Why? Because the meaning of addition is "counting the elements or units in a class of common units," and since apples and pears are two different kinds of units, they cannot be counted. Of course, both can be converted to another class of things, such as *fruit*, in which case counting can proceed. But what is counted in this case is "units of fruit" and not apples or pears. The logical structure must fit observation completely; it is not enough to identify the symbols within the logic with particular observables. Otherwise, the results of calculation cannot be transferred to the world of experience

Imperfections of Fit and the Fudge Factor

A theory isolates or separates a set of variables or factors from the rest of the world and links them by a set of rules in such a way that the effects of introducing a change into the set can be calculated perfectly using the rules. In principle, theories function in that manner. In the world of experience, however, it is probably impossible to isolate any set of variables from the rest of the world completely, even under the most stringent laboratory conditions possible. There are always some influences from outside the set to mar the results expected from calculation; the disparities can be reduced but not wholly eliminated. As measurements increase in precision, the influence of these external factors will emerge and increase. Eventually, every theory breaks down and becomes indeterminate—cannot be made more precise without losing isomorphism with observation. In effect, no theory achieves a perfect fit with experience, and there remains an unbridgeable gap between experience and logic. The results of observation will never fit theoretical calculations perfectly. If they did, measurement error would suggest that a mistake had been made somewhere. To that extent, a theory is an idealized pattern, an imperfect but calculable model of the world that appears in experience. That does not lead physical scientists to reject the law of gravity or the other scientific theories that have been created. It leads instead to the realization that the fit need not be perfect for the theory to be functionally useful.

The imperfect fit between theory and observation creates two primary problems for systematic inquiry. First, it leads to a logic problem a little like the one created by efforts to add apples and pears. When generalized experience is stated in propositional form, it can be put in absolute terms *(All A is B)* or in relative terms *(Some A is B; n% of A is B)*. Absolute propositions are readily calculated. But when general statements in relative terms are handed to logicians for calculation, it turns out that very little can be done with them. Excepting a few special cases involving very large numbers or relations among known majorities, nothing can be deduced about particulars from probabilistic statements. Second, the prospective user of a theory is then faced with the problem of dealing with the influence of factors not included in the theory on the outcome being controlled.

Both problems can be solved by a very simple device. A Fudge Factor is inserted into the application of the theory, placed between the calculations made within the theoretical structure and the observed situation where it is applied. All the external influences on the theory, which need not be identified, are lumped together into the Fudge Factor. Acting on the theory will produce data for measuring its reliability, and that can serve as a measure of the strength of all external influences. If the theory works 90 percent of the time, the factors included in the Fudge Factor account for the rest.

Because the Fudge Factor remains *outside* the theory, lies between theory and environment and refers to applications, the generalizations inside the theory (rules of interaction) can be stated in universal terms *(All A is B)*.

Calculation can proceed as usual. The influence of the Fudge Factor, the measure of reliability, then provides the user with a way of discounting the theory, adjusting expectations in terms of the likelihood that the theory will function as expected. Since every theory has a probability of less than one, no theoretical statement, no generalization, can have a probability of 100 percent. It follows that no statement in the form *All A is B* can reflect observation perfectly. The Fudge Factor simply extends the usual scientific practice of discounting or adjusting theory for measurement and other errors in a more general way.

In disciplines such as the social sciences, where it is very difficult if not impossible at present to produce generalizations that are almost completely reliable, the Fudge Factor makes the task of developing and applying theory much easier without any significant loss. If the reliability of a theory is too low and must be increased, some of the influences within the Fudge Factor will have to be identified and their effects determined by normal procedures. They can then be incorporated into the theory as additional rules and variables, or, more likely, added to the set of limiting conditions reducing the theory's applicability but increasing its accuracy. Thus if sunlight interfered with the operation of a theory, its influence, the amount of deviation from calculated outcomes it produced, could be determined experimentally. That information would serve as grounds for either changing the rules and content of the theory or limiting conditions of application, say by restricting use to periods of darkness.

The need for a Fudge Factor is particularly strong in fields of study where theory is likely to be rough and loose yet there is an urgent need for some basis for individual or collective action; the social sciences are good examples. The procedure allows the use of weak relations among variables as a basis for actions as long as the expected result is valued more than the risk of failure. Physicians will use a procedure that is successful only a small part of the time, knowingly, when there is no alternative— when it is the "best" option available. The Fudge Factor provides a way of determining the "best option" systematically.

Exercises

Review Questions

1. Compare systematically the structures and assumptions found in classifications and theories.

2. What are the two primary functions of causal relations in the development and use of knowledge?

3. What are the three basic questions that a valid theory must answer?

4. What is the precise meaning of "cause" in the sense required by a theory intended to serve as a basis for action?

5. Why is it necessary to limit the requirement that theory provide a basis for action to principle rather than practice?

6. Differentiate between the necessary and the sufficient conditions for an event to occur. What does the difference imply with respect to the use that can be made of instruments based on each form?

7. Discuss: Theory is always tested against more than one case.

8. What is meant by "isomorphism" between theory and observation, and why is it important?

9. Explain the role played by the Fudge Factor in theory? Why is it particularly valuable in social science?

Discussion

1. What kind of test could establish that something was a necessary cause of an event? Sufficient? Illustrate.

2. Why is the isomorphism of theory and observation always imperfect?

3. What kinds of problems appear when theorists attempt to produce theories for dealing with aggregates, such as automobile accidents?

12. Controlling Events II

Each time that an individual seeks to achieve a specific purpose in the world through action, a theory is required; actions intended to produce a particular effect must be based on an assumed causal relation between action taken and outcome expected. That may appear as a formidable limit on reasoned human action, but from another perspective, it is extremely encouraging. For each time that an individual actually produces the outcome expected from action, or succeeds in achieving an intended purpose, a valid theory has been acted on — barring pure accidents. The purpose achieved may be no more than inducing a member of the family to behave in a particular way, but the theory remains valid nonetheless. A great many such theories are available for use in everyday affairs, but for the most part they go unrecognized. Of course, the application of these instruments is likely to be limited to the immediate family or neighborhood, but that does not affect their validity as theories.

Theory, when it is taken to mean an assumed causal linkage, is not confined to science or the universities; it is an essential part of everyday life. Every effort to direct the flow of events on reasoned grounds must be based on a theory. Suggestions about how to "get something done" are derived from theories. The scope of the theoretical capacity available to the average person in modern industrial society is very impressive. Of course, powerful and sophisticated theories of the sort found in physical science are very difficult to produce in everyday life. They are also very difficult to produce in other areas of academic inquiry. And they are very hard to produce in physical science. Happily, broad and powerful theories are not needed for satisfaction of every human purpose. In many, and perhaps most instances, simple and crude structures are sufficient: A scalpel is not required for slicing bread. What does matter, however, is that the user be able to recognize "what is being done" when theories are applied, to know that a causal assumption is being acted on, and know how to test or improve the apparatus. Even if the user does not recognize the structure as a "theory," it remains possible to locate sources of error and stop depending on faulty assumptions.

Introductory

To facilitate recognition of theories in everyday affairs, the development of a simple theory, based on a story in literature, is examined in this unit. Such everyday examples should help to dissolve some of the mystique, and exaggerated expectations of precise and elaborate machinery, usually associated with "theorizing." Development and use of theories should be regarded as an essential component of everyday life, employed in even the simplest and most commonplace kinds of activities. In most instances, the first step in improving individual capacity to use theories is to generate awareness of their nature and function and improve the individual's ability to recognize them.

The example used here is literary and hypothetical, a product of imagination and not of experience. In genuine cases of theory development, the event that a theory is meant to control would appear in a concrete setting. That historical/cultural background, and immediate environment, is extremely important, for both the cause and the cure for the event must be found there, along with the limiting conditions that must be satisfied by the theory. One reason why imaginary events cannot produce genuine theories, and cannot serve as evidence in argument about theories, is that the constraints imposed by the real environment, which a real theory must overcome, do not appear in imagination and cannot be hypothesized without relying on yet another valid theory. Imaginary cases are useful only for illustrating specific and limited points.

In the illustration, as in a genuine case, theory development begins with a particular situation. Aggregated information is useful for calling attention to problems, and may be used to locate the cause of the problem, but solutions are worked out with respect to the particular event. The best model to follow is the way in which illness is treated in medicine. There, the point of departure for inquiry is always the sick person: no patient, no problem; no problem, no effort to produce treatment. Precisely the same limits apply to other aggregates. Information about the total number of automobile accidents in a given time period may suggest that something needs to be done to reduce the number, but the search for ways of controlling the frequency with which accidents occur begins by asking what causes them, and that requires attention to the individual accident. Aggregates do not always have single causes. Once the cause of a particular automobile accident is determined (tire failure, for example), a solution can be produced for accidents related to that cause. But accidents that result from other causes, which are always possible if cause is uncertain, may not be affected by that solution. If tire failure is one cause of accidents, and measures are taken to improve the quality of tires, accidents caused by driver error, brake failure, and the like will continue to occur, and will have to be treated separately. In general, a proposed cure or mode of treatment of a problem will work only in homogeneous applications, cases that respond in the same way as the case from which the treatment was developed. That is determined *after* a solution for the particular case has been found, generally, and there is little point in trying to classify cases in ways that are useful for treatment until causes are known and solutions for each cause are available.

The point is worth further elaboration as an illustration of the way in which theories develop. Suppose that careful study of a particular automobile accident suggests that the cause was drunken driving, that the accident would not have occurred if the driver had not been drinking. That drinking was a necessary condition for the accident may be difficult to establish, but we will assume the evidence is satisfactory. The theory suggests a simple remedy: Remove the drunken driver from the highways. Suppose the solution is generalized to automobile accidents as a whole, and all drunken drivers are taken off the roads. Will automobile accidents cease? Real-world experience suggests they will not, a signal that the class of events identified as *automobile accidents* is not homogeneous with respect to cause. Some accidents have different causes, and those causes will have to be identified, in some cases at least, before cures can be developed. The search for theories, for causes and cures for automobile accidents, can be expected to continue until the costs of further searching outweigh the benefits expected from success.

A Theory of Roasting

The structures and processes involved in everyday theorizing are very nicely illustrated in Charles Lamb's brief account of the discovery of cooking in China. In a story entitled "A Dissertation upon Roast Pig," a Chinese family living in an era when meat was still eaten raw went into town one day, leaving a litter of young pigs locked in their wooden house. When the family returned, the house had just finished burning to the ground and the embers were still hot and smoking. As the place cooled, the family began to sift through the ashes, searching for utensils and other family valuables. In the search, one member of the family happened to grasp one of the trapped pigs. Since it was very hot, the person's fingers were burned. The reaction to burning, then as now, was to place the fingers in the mouth to cool them. Some of the cooked flesh stuck to the fingers and was conveyed to the mouth. The end result was the first taste of cooked pork. The reaction was quick and positive: *Yummy Yum Yum!* It was delicious.

The sequence of events thereafter is readily imagined. The remains of the pig were brought from the ashes and sampled a second time; the resulting reinforcement of the original judgment stimulated further consumption. Other members of the family were invited to sample and reacted similarly. The rest of the piglets were located and consumed. When the orgy was finished, the family was hooked on roast pork. Now came the crucial question in theoretical development: How to get more?

All of the essential preconditions for stimulating theorizing have now been satisfied. A phenomenon (roast pork) has been observed; an evaluation (eating) has been carried out; the results were highly positive. There emerged an urgent desire to repeat the event, to do something that would produce more roast pork. How to convert the raw pig, which they recognized, into succulent roast pork? What had caused it? More important, how could it be caused again? There was only one case in which evidence could be gathered, and that had been only partly observed. Nowadays, it is taken for granted that the cooking (as it is now called) was due to the fire. In an era before cooking, that would not be obvious. Yet, if a connection was not drawn between burning and cooking, the phenomenon would not be repeated. Someone, somehow, made the necessary connection. Otherwise, the story would end with the first, and last, meal of roast pork. Doubtless, many such "stories" ended precisely that way.

The result of a successful connection of burning and roasting was a simple but adequate theory in the following form:

House containing pigs + Fire = Delicious food.

A set of nominal definitions (house containing pigs = *HP*, fire = *F*, and delicious food or roast pork = *RP*) allows us to convert that rather cumbersome equation into a simpler structure:

$$HP + F = RP.$$

Someone in the family proposed a theory; where it came from, or why it happened, no one can know, but the reasons for accepting it can be imagined. The proponent of the "fire" theory could argue that nothing else that occurred could possibly have caused the transformation; successive examination of possible causes, and the absence of any significant competition, perhaps carried the day. Or the proponent may have been the head of the household and in a position to force acceptance of the theory by the rest of the family. Whatever the course of events, the intervention strategy suggested by the theory, a simple repetition of the previous case, was clear enough.

A test was quickly arranged. The wooden house was rebuilt in precisely the same manner; internal arrangements were duplicated as closely as family memory allowed (there remained some uncertainty whether it was the whole house or its elements that played the key role in transforming the piglet). A somewhat larger group of pigs was placed inside, and the house was set afire. What happened? We must assume the experiment was relatively successful, else the enterprise would have been abandoned. A few pigs may have escaped; one or two were perhaps burned beyond consumption. But if a supply of roast pork was created, the theory had "worked," and a simple Fudge Factor would account for discrepancies.

Armed with a tested theory, the family's ability to produce roast pork would be limited only by desire and the availability of resources. But the quality of the theory was poor, the strategy suggested relatively inefficient and expensive, and some of the side effects were highly undesirable. Each dinner of roast pork required the construction of a new dwelling. Quality control was weak; in some instances, the meat was nearly raw, and in others it was burned to a crisp. The neighbors were getting restless because of the large number of fires taking place, and there was some talk of driving the family from the neighborhood to eliminate the curse. In brief, the level of control provided by the theory in its present form was inadequate. The family was being forced to choose between foregoing the production of roast pork, moving to another village, or improving the theory.

To this point, the story has all the fundamentals required for a television soap opera. Will the family produce a better theory? How will that theory actually develop? Did technology improve house building or cooking methods? Were better methods found for tethering the pigs? Were the neighbors invited to share in the roast to ward off ostracism? Such questions are fascinating, and relevant, but they cannot be answered. The source is only a story. The questions can only suggest some of the factors that might have entered into the development of modern cooking procedures and nothing more.

Lessons and Implications

What can be learned from the illustration? With a little structuring, a great deal. First, and perhaps most important, it illustrates the role that normative judgment plays in action. Without some human desire for repetition, for reproducing an observed event, there would be no impetus to theory development. The initial event may have been accidental; the recurrence was not, and it was fostered deliberately because of the family reaction to the first experience. Second, without the direct experience provided by the first fire, no theory could have been produced. A concept of roast pork is an essential prerequisite to a theory of roasting. Further, a neighbor supplied with some of the roast flesh, but told nothing of the course of events with which it was associated, could not possibly have developed a way of repeating the process.

Much abbreviated, the story illustrates what is probably the classic lesson of history: Human experience is so enormous, and so much of it has been recorded for such a long period of time, that there is no shortage of first encounters with the range of possibilities open to mankind—and new possibilities are emerging more or less continuously. What is required for improvement or progress is the capacity to deal with, or exploit, such first encounters in a productive manner. Unfortunately, that is a capacity that cannot be developed formally, except perhaps by stimulating an awareness of possibilities. What prompted the Chinese family to exploit the possibilities inherent in a situation that emerged accidentally? How can the same attitudes be fostered today? Such imponderables cannot be answered from history; the origins of most of our everyday knowlege are shrouded in time. But an examination and analysis of behavior in the present, systematic self-examination of current practice, is the best strategy available, all things considered, and that is the kind of enterprise for which the text was designed.

Analytically, the point that emerges most strongly from the story about the pigs is that as long as the theory remained formulated in terms of houses, fires, and pigs, it could not be improved very much. Better theory is contingent on conceptual improvement, or reconceptualization. If "burning a house" could be transformed into "placing the meat over a fire," considerable improvements in procedure would follow; if that concept was replaced by "heating the meat," the possibilities are really revolutionized: Fire implies burning in some fashion, whereas heating includes boiling and baking as well. Focusing on the pig, and transforming that concept into meat, can suggest the use of other animals, which would greatly increase efficiency. Without conceptual change, such extensions and improvements seem unlikely to occur.

The basic structures and processes involved in theorizing emerge very clearly from the story—given the advantages of analysis and hindsight. The practical effect of theorizing is to separate some set of variables from the rest of the environment and link them causally. In the case of the roast

pork, it was assumed implicitly that the cause of the transformation of the pig was the burning of the wooden house; the influence of other factors was ignored. The one limiting condition was the need to confine the pigs within the limits of the burning building. Structurally, the family produced a two-variable theory with a single rule of interaction that can be diagramed as follows: $(V_h\ V_m\ R_1) \supset \emptyset$
Where

$\emptyset$ = cooked meat.
V_h = the condition of the house.
V_m = the physical state of the meat (cooked or raw).
R_1 = as V_h changes from wood to ashes, V_m changes from raw to cooked.

The rule has precisely the same form as Ohm's law or the law of gravity, although the concepts and measurements involved are much cruder and less precise.

Within the theory, if the condition of the house is changed, whether by act of nature or by human intervention, the calculation shows that the condition of the meat will also change—the theory entails the desired outcome. That outcome is found *inside* the boundaries of the theory, although it is shown as an entailment. That is, the change in the value of V_m from raw to cooked *is* the desired event.

The amount of influence contained in the Fudge Factor required by the theory, as the family quickly learned, was large and significant. The results produced by acting on the theory could vary grossly. Rain might douse the fire; neighbors might put out the fire or release the pigs; the pigs might escape unaided. How much uncertainty was the family prepared to accept? One successful effort in five? In fifty? There is no way to answer, of course, but clearly there would be *some* point at which application would cease. If the sources of interference could be located, performance could be improved. If rain interfered, future efforts could be confined to dry days (a limiting condition of the theory). If the pigs escaped, they could be tethered or even slaughtered. If the neighbors interfered, they could be threatened or perhaps diverted by setting *their* houses afire. Such procedures would refine and improve the original theory, mainly by adding to the conditions limiting use. Once the user is satisfied with the costs and benefits associated with present use, development is likely to stop unless accidental improvement occurs or deliberate adaptation, based on experience in other, related areas, is undertaken.

New technologies, such as the invention of ovens or roasting pits, could certainly contribute to improvements in theory and practice, increasing reliability and reducing costs. Development of knowledge generally is likely to be even more important over the long run. There can be many theories linking a single event to a range of other factors; theoretical chains can be extended and branched in various ways. Since the costs and benefits associated with the use of each theory are likely to be different, additional knowledge serves to widen the range of choices available to the user, at least in principle. That is perhaps the most important benefit to be gained by living in a society where knowledge and technology are well developed, although the extent to which those potential benefits are realized, and how they are distributed within society, will depend on a variety of other considerations.

Exercises

Review Questions

1. Enumerate three claims or suggestions common in everyday affairs that involve a request for a "theory," as defined here.

2. Explain why valid theories cannot be generated from imaginary situations.

3. Discuss the importance of the Fudge Factor in the original theory developed in the story, and suggest ways of reducing its influence on applications of the theory.

4. Why was it important to reconceptualize the original theory? Illustrate.

5. Enumerate some of the ways by which technological improvements in other fields could contribute to refinement of the "theory of roasting."

6. Explain how the original theory could be generalized further and the effect such generalization would have.

Discussion

1. Write a brief imaginary account of the historical development of a theory and procedure for making bread. Include, among other things:
   a. the role of normative judgment
   b. the importance of accidents
   c. the effects of technological change
   d. the generalization involved
   e. the importance of conceptual change
   f. the role of the Fudge Factor
   g. the structural characteristics of the final theory
Assume that flour is already used in cooking and that milk is part of the regular diet.

13. Finding Causes

Reasoned control over events in the environment, and deliberate action in pursuit of human purposes, requires theories. Such theories in turn depend on the assumption of a causal relation between two or more observed events under specified limiting conditions. The relation may take one of two forms: (1) if one event is a necessary precondition for another, knowing that relation provides a means of preventing the other event from occurring; or (2) if one event is a sufficient precondition for a second event, that relation can be used either to prevent or to produce the second event. Given the importance of the function performed by causal relations in human affairs, the search for better means of locating them, and of justifying claims to have found them, is an important part of any knowledge system. That has long been understood, yet the question how best to seek causal relations, and how to argue convincingly that a causal relation has been located, remains without a definitive answer. Since no event is without cause, it can safely be assumed that the cause must lie in the events that preceded it. Various techniques have been devised to facilitate the search. One of the more famous of them is explored, together with its uses and limitations, in this unit.

One source of difficulty in finding causes is the human need to depend upon a conceptual framework, a set of conceptual "spectacles" for observing the world. Each conceptual framework includes some dimensions or aspects of the environment and excludes others; what is seen through one set of spectacles may not be apparent through another. And if the cause of event A is sought through a particular set of spectacles, the fact that event A may be visible in that conceptual framework does not mean that its cause will also be visible through the same lenses. Yet it is evident that both must appear in one structure if they are to be related systematically. A common example of the problem, and a possible solution, appears in academia, where a question that is insoluble within the conceptual framework employed by economists may find a ready solution within the conceptual framework of a sociologist or psychologist. One of the main virtues of interdisciplinary studies is their ability to show how a single problem appears in a variety of conceptual/theoretical frameworks and thus help sensitize students (and faculty) to the need to consider alternative ways of conceptualizing difficult problems. Such multiple frameworks are particularly valuable when the costs and benefits of an action are significant and no single framework is likely to reveal either all of the prime costs or all of the benefits associated with it.

Mill's Methods: How to Locate Causes

If an event occurs only once, its cause must be found within the historical situation in which it occurs. If an event occurs many times, its cause must be found for each occurrence, again in the unique historical situation where the event occurs. Causes refer always to unique events. The search for causes is much facilitated, however, if the event recurs often. It is easier to find the cause of a disease if there are many cases of it than when there is only one case, although success is not guaranteed in either situation. The reason is found in the variety of historical circumstances in which events appear. That variety allows for systematic comparison that can narrow the search for the cause for a particular event and perhaps isolate the cause completely.

Given a number of cases in which an event occurs, all sufficiently alike to warrant the belief they belong to the same class, and assuming that (1) no event occurs without a cause and (2) that cause must lie in the conditions that precede the event, systematic examination of antecedent conditions should bring the cause to the surface. Two things are then necessary for success: (1) a conceptual framework that will surface all potential causes; (2) a way of comparing events that will isolate or identify the genuine cause among the potential causes. The first problem remains unsolved in its essentials: We do not have, and do not have the capacity to develop, a universal conceptual apparatus of the kind required. The second problem, which presumes the first has been solved, is to systematize the search for causes among the antecedent conditions of an event. One of the more famous of the proposals for conducting such searches was devised by the English philosopher John Stuart Mill in the middle of the nineteenth century. Known as *Mill's methods,* the system comprises five techniques of locating causal relations. Judiciously used, with due regard to their limitations, they are extremely useful, and much of contemporary statistical analysis is based on the same kinds of comparisons.

The basic principle underlying Mill's methods, which makes a great deal of sense given the task to be performed, is to make a list of the factors that *could have* caused an event, then compare cases systematically, seeking to eliminate factors that could not have caused particular cases and isolate factors that could have caused all of the cases. There are some serious limits to the validity of the results. First, if the list is restricted to cases in which the event appears, it can overlook situations in which all the other factors are present and the event does not appear. Second, if the real cause of an event is not included in the list of probable causes, there is no way in which it could be found through comparisons of the kind Mill advocates.

Further, it should be noted that the strength of the evidence that supports the assumption of a causal relation does not depend on a count of the number of occasions on which two events are conjoined. Consider the case of the Indian tribe that believed the sun would not rise each morning unless one member of the tribe arose before dawn each day and entreated the sun to make an appearance. There would be a perfect correspondence between the rising of the sun and recital of morning prayers, and the longer the practice continued, the larger the number of favorable cases would be, yet who could agree that the increased number of cases provided stronger evidence for the causal linkage? And if the person assigned to perform the morning prayer failed to arise in time, thus providing a real test of the relation, and the sun rose despite the omission, to whom would such information be confided?

A different kind of danger encountered in the use of particular methods for locating causal relations, statistical or not, is that exceptions and failures are too easily overlooked. My mother always noted with pride that family disasters were invariably preceded by premonitions that she experienced. But the many cases in which disaster was predicted and did not occur were ignored. Mothers must, perhaps, be allowed some degree of license in these matters, but not systematic critics.

Further, the search for causes may be directed to either the necessary or the sufficient conditions for an event to occur. Both are useful, but the evidence in each case is different, and they are not interchangeable. Yet a search procedure targeted at the sufficient conditions for an event to occur may overlook evidence relating to a necessary precondition for that event. Research design must take both kinds of causal relation into account.

Finally, causal assumptions, strictly speaking, are created within the human nervous system and imposed on events and not found or discovered in nature. It follows that no formal or logical system can be produced that will create theories and guarantee their quality—or create the causal assumptions on which theories depend. There is no logic of discovery; the best that a logic can do is re-create its own content and assumptions. That means that no logical procedure can do more than *test* proposed causal relations among selected variables. Those tests cannot *prove* the causal relation. At most, they can rule out or eliminate one variable as the causal agent in a particular case or class of cases.

The Five Methods

In the system that Mill devised, there are five "methods" for comparing particular cases in search of causes. They overlap to some extent, and the number could perhaps be reduced, but the original form is retained in the discussion that follows.

The Method of Agreement

Assume that the cause of a specific event or phenomenon ($\emptyset$) is being sought and agree that $\emptyset$ has occurred on four different occasions. A record was made of each case, and four likely or possible causes of $\emptyset$ were searched for carefully. The results of the search are summarized in the following table:

Case	Factors Observed
1	A B C and $\emptyset$
2	A C D and $\emptyset$
3	A B D and $\emptyset$
4	A B C and $\emptyset$

On the basis of the evidence, B, C, and D are *ruled out* as possible causes of $\emptyset$; in at least one case in the set, $\emptyset$ occurred but B, C, or D did not. The only factor in the set that could be the cause of $\emptyset$ is therefore A, since it was the only factor present on every occasion where $\emptyset$ occurred. There is no way to say, from the data, whether there were cases in which A was present and $\emptyset$ *did not* occur. That information, if available, would greatly strengthen the case for assuming A as the cause of $\emptyset$, but such information might be very difficult and expensive to obtain.

With respect to the implications of the information supplied, two other possibilities could account for the findings. First, the real cause of $\emptyset$ may have been another factor *(Z)*, which did not appear in the conceptual framework used to study the cases and record the information. Second, the real cause of $\emptyset$ may not have been A per se but some particular element in A. The assumed relation between A and $\emptyset$ would therefore break down in other contexts. The classic example of this kind of error, found in nearly every text in logic, is the so-called Drunkard's Fallacy. Jones, the hero of the fallacy, was a drunkard, a determined consumer of strong drink.

After much pleading from family and friends, Jones agreed to cease becoming inebriated. However, he asked for time to determine the cause of his drunkenness so that his renunciation would be accurate and scientifically based. The family agreed. On Monday night, Jones consumed large quantities of scotch whiskey and soda and became gloriously drunk. Tuesday night, he essayed bourbon and soda water with the same result. Wednesday night was devoted to rum and soda, and again drunkenness followed. On Thursday he tried gin and soda, followed by vodka and soda on Friday night, concluding on Saturday with heavy infusions of brandy and soda. In all cases, drunkenness ensued. On Sunday, he sat down with the family to work out a solution to the problem. Using Mill's method of agreement, it was immediately apparent that the source of his drunkenness, the common factor in each case, was soda! He promptly swore never to drink soda again. The example is trite, an old professor's joke, but a nice illustration of the primary weakness in the "method of agreement."

The Method of Difference

The method of agreement is particularly useful for eliminating potential candidates for being the causal agent responsible for a particular phenomenon. Any variable not present when the phenomenon occurs cannot be its cause—as long as it does not appear in disguise, as in the case of alcohol. But application of the method may leave the inquirer with several potential candidates still in the running. The method of differences can be used to deal with that situation. Again, the reasoning is straightforward: If two cases of an event are found that are identical in all respects save one, and $\emptyset$ occurs in one case but not the other, the likely cause is to be found in the difference. For example:

Case	Factors Observed
1	$A B C D$ and $\emptyset$
2	$B C D$ but no $\emptyset$

By the method of difference, the likely cause of $\emptyset$ must be A. Again, however, the limitations and dangers discussed earlier must be guarded against. The method can only indicate the most likely candidate for causal status, *given that selection of variables.*

Joint Method of Agreement and Difference

As the name suggests, the two methods of agreement and difference can be combined. The method of agreement is used to reduce the set of potential causes to a handful, the method of differences to reduce the number still further—optimally, to just one.

Case	Method of Agreement		Method of Difference	
1	$A\ B\ C\ D\ E\ F$	$\emptyset$	$A\ B\ C\ D$	$\emptyset$
2	$A\ C\ D\ B$	$\emptyset$	$B\ C\ D$	no $\emptyset$
3	$A\ B\ D\ C$	$\emptyset$		
4	$A\ B\ C\ D$	$\emptyset$		

Again, the most likely cause of $\emptyset$ is A, given that selection of possible causes. It also remains possible that the cause of $\emptyset$ is some combination of variables, only partially included in the comparison. Whether this procedure deserves to be labeled a distinct method is doubtful, but Mill's judgment was positive, and it is usually respected.

The Method of Residues

Given a number of observed cases where an event occurs, and a range of potential causes, a somewhat different approach to locating the cause is to eliminate any factor known *not to be* the event's cause. The factor remaining when all others have been eliminated is again the best candidate available (from that list) for status as cause of the event. Thus if the Chinese family seeking the cause of the transformation of pork had made a list of possible causes, it might have included the shining sun, blowing wind, and many other factors besides the burning house. But if experience suggested that none of these factors caused the change (because they had been observed before, and the change did not occur), that would leave the burning house as the best potential cause of the event. As you can see, there is a considerable measure of overlapping among the methods, but there is some strategic value gained by separating them from one another.

The Method of Concomitant Variation

Although the most complex of Mill's methods, the method of concomitant variation is in some respects the most valuable. It sounds like a simple process for relating one change to another, but the underlying assumptions are actually more complex than that. An example from agriculture, where the method has widespread applications, can illustrate the relations captured by the method. If a farmer simply applies a fixed amount of fertilizer to a field of corn, and that increases the yield by a given amount, the relation is direct and immediate, and the information gained from the experiment is limited. The amount of fertilizer applied is linked to the amount of corn produced, but it would be very dangerous indeed to assume that doubling the amount of fertilizer would double the yield. The farmer cannot tell how much fertilizer is worth applying, even if the price of fertilizer is fixed and the value of the corn can be estimated accurately.

Suppose, however, that a field is seeded in the normal fashion, then divided into four equal parts. A different amount of fertilizer is then applied to each of the four parts, and the yield of corn from each part is duly recorded. The farmer now had the information needed to determine the effect of applying different amounts of fertilizer to a given planting and can calculate an optimal program of action. It may be the case, for example, that it pays to double the amount of fertilizer but not to increase it by a factor of four—the additional corn obtained will not cover the added cost.

In most statements of Mill's methods, applications are limited to static data; they can be modified quite easily, however, to deal with changes as well. Their uses and limitations remain the same in either case. At the risk of being irritating and overly repetitious, the *limitations* inherent in Mill's methods warrant further emphasis. Please remember that they can only suggest causal relations; they cannot prove or establish them. The results of using the methods are *evidence for* a causal relation and nothing more. The methods cannot guarantee the selection of potential causes included in the test; conceptual problems must be solved another way. The psychologist who continued to search for the cause of the pig's transformation into roast pork in the psychic condition of the pig because his conceptual apparatus did not contain any other variables that might account for the change would provide an extreme example of what can happen if the methods are not used critically—with awareness of limitations. And in the final analysis, suspected causal relations are tested in the environment by acting on them. Experience with assumed causal relations, in other words, supersedes or overrides all other results, whatever the methods used to produce them.

Exercises

Review Questions

1. What is the significance of being forced to use a limited conceptual framework in the search for causal relations?

2. Explain the basic assumptions underlying Mill's methods.

3. Assume a hospital is flooded with patients suffering from an unknown disease, believed to be caused by a germ. Show how Mill's methods can be used to locate the cause of the disease.

4. Using the same example, show how the Drunkard's Fallacy might occur.

5. Still using the same example, show how the "real" cause of the disease might be missed using Mill's methods.

6. Still using the same example, show how it might be possible to mistake the cause of the disease yet succeed in producing a cure.

7. Suggest any procedures that the hospital might follow in order to increase the accuracy and reliability of its diagnosis.

8. Enumerate the limitations on Mill's methods, emphasizing what they can and cannot be used to establish.

Discussion

1. Consider the parallels between Mill's methods and the use of the modern computer for data analysis.

2. Under conditions of near ignorance, how could the Drunkard's Fallacy be spotted? Under what conditions would it be desirable to institute a set of procedures for that purpose?

3. In general, would you prefer to see a very detailed examination of a small number of cases or a systematic comparison of a large number of cases using some version of Mill's methods if the resulting treatment was to be applied to yourself? Give reasons for your answer.

14. Criticizing Theories I

In principle, theories are relatively simple instruments, consisting of a causal relation embedded in a rule of interaction and a set of limiting conditions governing application of the rule. Any time that the set of variables included in the theory appears in the environment, and the limiting conditions are satisfied, the rule of interaction is expected to hold. In practice, theories are likely to be somewhat more complex, and application may involve a fairly lengthy chain of reasoning, using several theories. That provides plenty of opportunity for errors and makes criticism, location of error, or assessment of validity more difficult. Given the crucial role that theories play in efforts to maintain and improve the human situation, developing some capacity for systematic criticism of theories and their applications is an essential part of intellectual training. All that can be done in a short space is sketch the fundamentals, but awareness of these can be very helpful when proposals for action are being evaluated.

In general, criticism of theories and their applications focuses on three major questions. First, has the theory been developed and used for an appropriate purpose? The purposes for which theories are used must be of the sort that can be served by theories. Second, has the theory been applied correctly? Has the situation been properly diagnosed? Third, is the theory valid? That is, does the supporting evidence indicate that the theory holds with enough accuracy and reliability for the task at hand? The formal logical calculations required to apply a theory are not considered here; actions proposed on the basis of a known theory are assumed to be proper inferences. In real cases, the calculations bear careful examination. Mistakes are common and fallacies of reasoning and relevance occur frequently, both in personal and public affairs.

Is the Purpose Valid?

It may seem odd to begin a discussion of the quality of theories by asking whether the purpose for which they are developed or used is valid or appropriate, but people often try to achieve purposes that lie beyond the capacity of any theory that humans can create. Efforts to achieve such purposes as mounting to the top of a hill by performing actions not possible for humans—flying there by flapping the arms, for example—are not often seen and would rightly be scoffed at. But efforts to deal with a complex aggregate phenomenon such as poverty through a single policy or program are just as misdirected and equally unlikely to succeed, yet such proposals are commonplace.

A theory, in the sense that it is used here, can perform three basic functions: (1) it can show why a particular change occurred; (2) it can show the outcome to be expected if a particular change is made; and (3) it can show how to produce a particular change. Each of these tasks can be performed with a reliability that is something less than perfect even with powerful theories in physical science, and reliability can be very low indeed with the kinds of theories available in social science. Of course, theories can also be used to make predictions, but for that purpose, all that needs to be demonstrated is predictive capacity and not causal linkage. The first limit on the use of theory, then, is that the purpose sought must fall within the boundaries of those three functions.

If the purpose of the user can be satisfied by a theory of this kind, the next question to be asked is whether any of the theories currently available are adequate for the task. That will depend on the phenomenon to be controlled and the way the problem is stated—the limits placed on an adequate solution. To illustrate, suppose that a government agency wishes to care for a small group of badly undernourished children and asks for advice on how best to proceed. The advice that the agency receives, if its instructions are followed closely, will depend on the questions asked, and how they are formulated. To ask merely, "How can the nutritional state of these children be altered?" would be grossly inadequate. Taken literally, acceptable answers would include (1) starving the children further; (2) feeding them a tasty and balanced diet; and (3) providing each one with liberal amounts of alcohol. Each of these actions would produce a change in the children's nutritional state and thus answer the question as stated. Each can be derived from respectable theories; such actions *do* relate to nutritional levels. But assuming that the agency wished to act in the best interests of the children, only the second proposal is appropriate and helpful. Since everyone understands the intention, such facetious responses would not usually be heard. But the implication, that purposes need to be stated as precisely as possible, and limited as accurately as possible, is a serious matter. Too often, in both individual and collective affairs, purposes are stated in such slovenly terms that it is nearly impossible to determine whether or not they can be fulfilled.

The problem, of course, is that the more precisely purposes are stated, the more difficult they become to achieve. Theories that are acceptable at one level of precision may be grossly inadequate when purposes are more carefully stated. For example, there are dozens and dozens of ways to alter the physical condition of a human individual. As long as the direction and amount of change are ignored, such activities as eating, exercise, or the ingestion of lethal chemicals will each produce some change, but the direction and amount, and therefore the effect on the person, will vary greatly.

The range of usable theories available as a basis for action will narrow as limits are imposed on the solution, the outcome desired. If such particular aspects of physical condition as hearing or eyesight are to be altered, a considerable number of theories remain available—as long as the direction of change is not specified. Eyesight can be altered by sharp sticks, acid baths, medical operations, and so on; either cleaning the inner ears or puncturing the eardrum will affect the hearing in some degree. If the purpose is narrowed to specify that only *improvements* are acceptable, the supply of available theories is drastically reduced, and depends very much on the present state of those functions. How can perfect eyesight or excellent hearing be improved? Medical treatment or the purchase of a hearing aid can in some cases produce an improvement in hearing, but poor hearing, like baldness, is not easily remedied. A theory that can serve such a relatively narrow purpose will be much stronger, and the technology needed to implement it will need to be more sophisticated than was the case when the purpose was stated as a change in physical condition. And if side effects are limited in specific ways, the theoretical requirements for successful action become even more stringent. Almost anyone can cure any disease if the effect on the patient is disregarded. But if the patient's life must be saved, the task is more difficult, and if disfigurement is not allowed, the treatment is likely to tax the skills of a trained physician.

Beyond the problem of surface validity, an even more troublesome question can be asked of the purposes sought through the use of theories: Are those purposes worth achieving? I leave that question for later discussion, when the normative dimensions of action are being considered, but it remains perhaps the most important question that can be asked with respect to purpose. How that question is answered and justified largely determines the ethic that society produces.

The Diagnosis Problem

The various intellectual instruments developed for achieving human purposes in the environment must be applied before they provide any real benefits to humanity. In all cases, application requires a judgment by the user; the tools are generalized in form and therefore cannot be applied by rote or formal calculation. Someone must judge whether a concept fits an incoming flow of perceptions, whether a body of evidence supports a particular forecast, or whether a theory fits a particular situation. The problem of diagnosis is probably easier to see in the field of medicine than elsewhere, but it arises in every area where knowledge is used or applied, and with the same implication. In medicine, a well-developed treatment for a particular disease remains useless until particular cases of the disease have been diagnosed. For the same reasons, powerful theories are useless until it is determined, reliably, that they apply to particular situations.

The diagnosis problem refers to the isomorphism of theory and observation, to the degree of fit between the structures and processes contained in the theory and the course of events in a specified part of the observed world. In effect, diagnosis requires the user to determine whether the sets of assumptions contained in the theory are actually satisfied in the situation where the theory is to be applied. In practice, theories are applied to any situation where all the variables contained in the theory appear, and the limiting conditions attached to the theory are satisfied. If the diagnosis is accurate, the theory will "work"; the world will behave as the theory predicts or implies. The potential for error lies in the difference between the basis of diagnosis, which is observation of a set of variables and limiting conditions, and the central assumptions in the theory, which refer to the causal links among the variables. A further complication is introduced by the fact that different theories, different sets of assumptions, can be used to account for the same set of events. A theory may be mistaken, and a diagnosis erroneous, even if the predictions derived from the instrument turn out to be accurate.

An example can illustrate the kind of diagnostic problem that arises when more than one set of assumptions can account for a particular set of observations, and the assumptions are incompatible. At noon exactly, on the day when the sun lies directly over the equator, the following observations were made:

1. On the equator proper, a stick placed vertical to the ground on the earth's surface cast no shadow.

2. At a point 1000 miles to the south, another stick placed in the

ground in a position vertical to the earth's surface cast a shadow that was 14 1/2 degrees from the vertical.

How to account for the discrepancy? What set of assumptions is required to explain the difference between the two observations?

Given current knowledge, the question is readily decided. Knowing that *(a)* the earth is round and *(b)* the sun is very distant, that result must be expected. The sun's rays are very nearly parallel when they reach the earth's surface; given a curved surface on earth, the observations actually made follow logically. The results of accepting that set of assumptions is shown in figure 14.1. Since an angle of 14 1/2 degrees is about 1/25 of a circle, the observations, combined with the assumptions, suggest that the earth's circumference is about 25,000 miles—a figure now known to be correct.

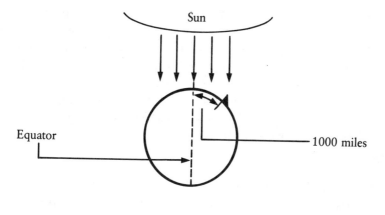

FIGURE 14.1

Assuming a round earth and a distant sun provides a good solution to the problem posed by the observations. But those who lived in an earlier era did not know that the earth is round or that the sun is a long distance from earth. They believed, in most cases at least, that the earth was flat and that the sun was very close to the earth. Suppose they devised an experiment that would test those assumptions, an experiment that produced the same set of observations recorded above. Would the evidence prove them wrong? Figure 14.2 on page 118 suggests it would not. Assuming that the earth is very close to the sun, the rays from the sun would not be parallel when they struck the earth. Therefore, the shadow produced on the surface

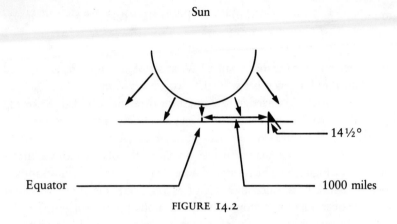

Sun

14½°

Equator ————————————— 1000 miles

FIGURE 14.2

by the second stick would also be expected. Moreover, the measurements would suggest that the sun was about 25,000 miles away from earth.

Both sets of assumptions correspond perfectly with the observations. How would a choice be made between them? Obviously, one step would be to design a further experiment that would test both assumptions. But if only one set of assumptions was common, what reason would there be to question them? Working out the kinds of observations or experiences that would lead people to question the assumption that the earth was flat and the sun was close will suggest some of the problems involved in improving existing theoretical structures, particularly if they are plausible in the light of present knowledge.

A Second Example

A somewhat different problem in diagnosis, taken from the field of medicine, illustrates the kind of dilemma that is more likely to occur in the social sciences. Suppose that a previously healthy person suddenly developed some alarming symptoms—high fever, severe pains in the abdomen, and frequent vomiting. What is the cause of such symptoms? Of course, the proper person to make such a diagnosis is a trained physician, but some very useful points can be made using the example. First, it is clear that a three-element pattern linking fever, abdominal pain, and vomiting would not be adequate. Those three symptoms must be linked to some fourth factor, otherwise one of the three must be the cause of the others and since they occurred simultaneously, that is very unlikely. Actually it is at least conceivable that the three symptoms could indicate two or more body malfunctions.

The tests that a physician would employ to produce a reliable diagnosis are too complex to deal with here, and in any case, the purpose of the example is to illustrate the effects of differences in the amount of knowledge available on the quality of diagnosis. Members of a community in which the level of medical knowledge was generally high would be likely to consult a physician immediately when such symptoms occurred. In other areas, family remedies might be applied. And in a few isolated communities, a witch doctor might be consulted. The implications of these differences for the patient's recovery, assuming a serious illness, are readily drawn.

For a trained physician, the symptoms described are not really adequate for diagnosis. Several different illnesses might produce the same effects. To illustrate the kind of problem involved, consider only two major possibilities. First, the source of the problem could be a severe case of indigestion, or intestinal blockage; second, the person might have appendicitis, a diseased appendix. Unfortunately, the two diseases require very different treatment. For indigestion, a laxative is needed; for appendicitis, the usual treatment is surgical removal. The diagnoses suggest different and incompatible modes of treatment.

One way out of the dilemma, often used in everyday affairs, is to select one of the two options and proceed experimentally—and slowly. But if the consequences of error are potentially serious, as in the example, that procedure is not advisable. Administering a laxative to a person with indigestion should solve that problem, but giving a laxative to a person with appendicitis could lead to a ruptured appendix, infection of the area, and even death. Removing the appendix, which will resolve appendicitis, is not usually fatal but it can be inconvenient, expensive, and uncomfortable, and physicians who remove appendixes that are not diseased tend to draw criticism from their colleagues and from the medical associations.

Improving Diagnosis

Two basic procedures are available for dealing with diagnostic problems with increasing effectivness. First, the richness and complexity of the set of indicators used to identify the members of the classes linked by theory can be expanded. In particular, those concerned with medical diagnosis look for symptoms that are unique to a particular illness or that can be used for differentiating similar illnesses. Of course, identifying the variables included in a theory does not guarantee that the causal assumptions included in the theory will hold, but confidence in the diagnosis can be improved.

The second procedure for improving diagnosis, like the procedure followed for improving forecasts, is to seek additional cues through further observation. The physician's confidence in a diagnosis is not a function of just the number of factors observed but the "diagnostic strength" of the factors. A single indicator may lead to a confident diagnosis, while multiple indicators may leave the diagnostician hesitant and uncertain. The only prescription that can be offered for improving the capacity to assess diagnostic strength is "experience." Experienced physicians do not always know the full grounds for their confidence in a diagnosis. Indeed, medical training, with its emphasis on supervised contact with real patients, takes the need for such experience into account. It serves to bring into play the extraordinary human ability to deal with very complex patterns without being self-consciously aware of them.

One final dimension of the diagnosis problem emerges if it is assumed that the example occurred at a time when appendicitis was unknown — when all such cases were diagnosed as acute indigestion. If laxatives were prescribed each time those symptoms appeared, as would be the case under those conditions, some patients would be cured, and those with appendicitis would presumably be made worse and would ultimately die. Would those deaths be taken as a warning signal by the physicians of the time? Not at all. It would be nothing more than a normal result of "indigestion" as then understood. Death would be an expected effect of the disease and not a warning of inadequate diagnosis. Consider how very difficult it would be for physicians in those times to question the diagnosis. Yet training for critical thinking and action must somehow prepare people in ways that would make it likely to occur, and not in medicine alone. At best, sensitivity to error, like willingness to acknowledge it, is not easily cultivated. About all that can be done is point out potential sources of error; if the errors were already known, they could be built directly into the training. That is not a very satisfactory solution to the problem, but there is nothing better available at present and so it will have to suffice.

Exercises

Review Questions

1. What are the three major questions on which criticism of theories and their applications should focus?

2. What are the three primary questions that can be answered using a theory?

3. Illustrate the way in which theoretical requirements are affected by the way in which the user's purpose is stated.

4. Explain what is meant by the "diagnosis problem" and why it is important.

5. How can isomorphism between theory and observation be established?

6. What techniques are available for resolving the problem created when more than one set of assumptions can account for a phenomenon?

7. Why are trial-and-error procedures sometimes inappropriate for diagnosis?

8. What techniques are generally available for improving diagnosis?

Discussion

1. Discuss the kind of training that might be provided diagnosticians in order to improve their performance.

2. Prepare a brief checklist of the points to be examined if a theory fails to produce expected results when applied.

15. Criticizing Theories II

When theories are criticized in broad terms, the central focus of concern is usually the set of purposes that a theory is expected to fulfill and the limits on application. From a different perspective, the validity of a theory is independent of any specific purposes that it can serve at the present time. That is, a theory may be trivial, or be wrongly applied, yet remain a valid theory, for validity depends on the justification offered for accepting and using it, on the evidence available to support it. From that perspective, the central element in a theory is the causal relation among the variables that it assumes; justifying that causal assumption is then the major problem in systematic criticism.

Introductory

The causal assumption on which a theory depends is incorporated into the rule that links the values of its variables. In a valid theory, the dynamics of the structure, the operation of the rule(s), will reflect the changes that are observed in the real world. Unless the dynamics are isomorphic, the theory cannot perform its expected functions. Put another way, experience controls not only the selection of variables but their interactions as well. The theorist must capture a causal relation; in order to do so, a set of variables is required to identify the things or events that are related. The causal assumption then allows the user to project the effects of deliberate action and not, as in a forecast, to anticipate the effects of an event after it has been observed.

The capacity of theories to project the effects of action plays a key role in theory validation; the evidence generated by deliberate actions provides the strongest reasons available for accepting the causal assumption. Predictive capacity based on observation alone does not validate theories. Internal consistency, and the degree of correspondence or fit with other established theories, plus the results obtained by application or testing in use, provide the primary evidence for the validity of theories, whatever the field.

In a number of important respects, theories are like maps—they serve as representations or overlays that can be imposed on a body of observations and used to deal with them. The kinds of criticisms that are properly directed at maps are also useful for dealing with theories. Maps, like theories, use conventional symbols to record and relate the results of observation. Maps are selective and abstracted; no map records everything that is observed, for that would be equivalent to a complete description. Like theories, maps are made by selecting a number of factors presumed to be important for the map user's purposes. That raises the same problems of design and costs encountered in theorizing. Maps can often be designed to serve a number of purposes economically, and designing a map for one purpose alone is often uneconomic. But a universal map that can serve all the purposes of all possible map users is out of the question. How broadly the map is designed depends on the kinds of purposes for which it will be used, and the amount of detail and precision those purposes require. Maps, like theories, must be tested for both accuracy and adequacy, for both aspects of performance are important. Without a knowledge of the purposes or uses to be made of a map, only accuracy or validity is testable. For testing validity, three points are important: (1) correspondence with other maps whose accuracy and adequacy have already been established; (2) the internal consistency of the map; and (3) the results obtained by using the map for the purposes for which it was intended. In mapping, as in theorizing, the ultimate test of the product is in application or use.

To extend the analogy between mapping and theorizing, theories, like maps, are not abandoned because of occasional failures. Instead, the areas of failure are noted and either the map is elaborated to deal with the problem or the use of the map is limited to avoid recurring failure. If a map intended for hikers does not include information about some danger points on a trail, for example, a note to that effect can be added to warn users of the omission. Otherwise, the map must be redrawn to include the omitted hazard. Finally, maps, like theories, vary greatly in range and application. Unlike maps, the more broad and general a theory becomes, the more accurate and precise it can become as well. But eventually theories, like maps, become too large and complex to be applied and must be broken down. Maps begin with particular areas, as theories begin with specific cases. As additional areas are mapped, it is sometimes useful to join them together into integrated structures; as other information about an area is obtained, it is sometimes efficient to add it to an existing map. But that procedure has limits. Eventually, it may be easier and cheaper to prepare a new map for a limited purpose, probably by extracting information from existing structures and combining them, than to use a large, multipurpose structure for a limited problem.

The Internal Structure of Theories

The concept of *theory* employed here is relatively weak, and such theories are more readily created than rigorously supported *empirical laws* of the kind preferred in philosophy of science. That weak definition is particularly important for the less developed disciplines, such as the social sciences, where very few structures of the precision and accuracy of the law of gravity or Ohm's law are available. Adding a Fudge Factor to a weak statement of relations allows the necessary logical calculations to be carried out without difficulty. Testing in use can produce an index of reliability that will inform the user how much confidence can be placed in the structure when it is applied.

The price of a "weak" conception of theory is uncertainty with respect to quality. The worst effects of that uncertainty are avoided if the purposes for which the theory can be used are specified carefully, and the reliability of the theory in the pursuit of such purposes is stated as accurately as possible. Theories must be judged in the same way that judges score particular efforts in diving contests. There, evaluation is based on two factors: the difficulty of the dive, which is assigned an index number, and the quality of the execution, also assigned a number. In that system, the imperfect execution of a very difficult dive may count for more than the good execution of a much easier dive. In medicine, analogous procedures may place a higher value on a treatment program that works only part of the time, but is directed to very significant cases, than on a treatment that works invariably but applies only to trivial illnesses. If the purposes are important, weak theories are better than no theories. Since the theories produced by social science are a critical factor in the conduct of human affairs, individual and collective, it seems preferable to have weak theories—theories that perform imperfectly—than to have none. And the more powerful theories fit the same pattern, hence they can be handled using the same critical apparatus.

Inspection of the internal characteristics of a theory can often produce an estimate of overall quality, particularly where the theory is seriously flawed. The concepts or variables included in a theory must be well defined, for a theory that links X and Y is not very useful if the meaning of X and Y remains unclear. A theory is equally worthless if the rule linking the variables is stated in confusing or ambiguous terms, or if reliability, the influence of the Fudge Factor, is not known. The structure must contain at least two variables, for theories function by linking the values of two or more variables by rule. A single-variable theory, a "theory of X" that did not link X to any other variable, would be meaningless.

The variables or concepts incorporated into a theory are usually symbolized; even if they are not, the concepts must be linked to real-world observations by a set of what are called *transformation rules,* rules that specify the meaning of the concepts or symbols in operational or observational terms otherwise the theory remains unstable.

Finally, the limiting conditions that control application of the theory must be specified. Otherwise, diagnosis may be impossible, or the theory will be applied improperly. When theories are well established and thoroughly incorporated into the training provided by those working in the area, there is a tendency to disregard or overlook some of the limits on application. Students of electronics are not reminded again and again that theories like Ohm's law do not function if the circuits being observed are improperly constructed or sited. The principal danger in such cases is that those coming to the field from other disciplines may not be aware of those limitations and will overlook them.

The Fit to Established Knowledge and History

In most cases, the degree of correspondence between a proposed theory and the body of related knowledge currently accepted by informed persons in the field provides the major test of the theory. In physics, for example, a proposed theory that was inconsistent with the law of gravity would be rejected, or treated with great skepticism, even if the author claimed that experimental evidence had been obtained to support it. In general, the role of the experiment in theorizing has been greatly exaggerated, especially by media such as television or motion pictures. In such highly technical and technological fields as rocketry, experimental success is truly cause for rejoicing because the experiment tests the reliability of the technology and not because it helps to establish the validity of the theories used to develop the rocket. In most cases, the theories involved were already well established before the first rocket was shot into space. In relatively new theoretical areas, where a solid body of well-established theory is not yet available, experimental results will play a larger role in justification. But in most of the older fields, experiments tend to validate expectations rather than produce new insights. Experiments are not undertaken simply to "see what will happen," in most instances at least; more commonly, before an experiment is performed, a theoretical resolution to the problem has already been produced; otherwise, the experiment itself could not be designed. What an experiment does is test the proposed solution to a problem, or more precisely, the set of assumptions on which that solution depends. Only rarely can an experiment be designed in such manner that it will actually *produce* a solution to a problem.

When theories must be tested, the social scientist is at a disadvantage compared to the physical scientist. There are few well-established bodies of theory available to serve as a base; experimenting in a laboratory tends not to be effective; on-site experiments are very difficult to control and in some cases impossible to evaluate. It is almost impossible to say, for example, what result followed from governmental "tests" of economic theory, say by reducing overall levels of taxation, or by allowing certain kinds of tax credits. Furthermore, natural-state experiments may not be allowed because the social consequences anticipated from the experiment are not acceptable, or the possibility of adverse side effects is considered too great. It is more difficult, therefore, to establish theories in social science than in physical science, other things equal.

In one area, however, social science has a clear advantage over physical science. The historical record tends to contain far more information about social events than about physical phenomena. History appears, therefore, as one of the major testing grounds for social science theorizing, the first checkpoint in an effort to establish or validate a theory. The materials that historians have recorded are not always what the social scientist would like to have, but on most problems some assistance is to be had from history, properly used.

The problems involved in the use of history to test social theory are well known. The historical record is always incomplete, often inaccurate, and frequently unreliable. The historical tradition, which controls what is included and excluded from historical accounts, has its own set of priorities, and they often differ from those of the contemporary social scientist. And the conceptual and theoretical framework that historians employ to structure their account of events can change over time, often quite dramatically. Comparisons of historical accounts for different time periods and different cultures are therefore risky at best, even for comparatively recent time periods.

Historical evidence, then, is less decisive, less convincing, than laboratory evidence, other things equal. Nevertheless, it is sometimes the only evidence available and must be used. Going to history with a purpose in mind, awareness of the evidentiary requirements for satisfying that purpose, and some awareness of the characteristics of the historical record—its limitations and weaknesses—is often unavoidable. At a minimum, history can be considered as an enormous suggestion box where concepts, relations, priorities, and other intellectual products can be found. History can provide examples and illustrations, suggest patterns that prove to have current utility, and most important, raise questions that need to be answered, whether or not it can provide answers for them. And knowing the answers that have been proposed to particular questions, and the effects that followed from reliance on those answers, can be invaluable.

In short, history remains as a central source of inspiration and direction, far better than literature because of the real empirical constraints built into the narrative. Shakespeare's kings can act in accordance with the poet's imagination, unfettered by real-world limitations; the historian's kings are real, and they behave as real kings behaved. Given the contemporary tendency to rely heavily, in social science particularly, on giant computers and masses of coded data, it is worth stressing the value of history to the social theorist, and the importance of the narrative form, or "storytelling," in conveying patterns that may be difficult to grasp in the abstract. History cannot serve all purposes, but it will serve some. At a minimum, it provides a place for imagination to feed, and imagination has nowhere else to seek such nourishment.

Experimentation

Because of the causal assumption contained in theories, the best single test of theoretical validity is to apply it and observe the result. In some cases, the situation in which the theory is applied can be isolated more or less completely from outside influences during the trial. If not, the influence of such factors can be aggregated in the Fudge Factor and estimated from the results of application. Successive tests can increase confidence in a theory, elaborate the conditions of application, and provide evidence about its scope and limitations in use. Understandably, experimentation, particularly in the laboratory, plays a major role in theory development in fields where it is readily possible, notably in physical science.

The relative worth of laboratory experiments and "natural state," or real-world, experiments is much debated. It depends on the extent to which the results transfer accurately to real world affairs, since that is the arena in which theories must ultimately be applied. That in turn is a function of the kind of theory being tested. Generalization about such matters is a very risky business. Some things can be said, however, about the strengths and weaknesses of the two experimental situations, and they may be of some value for the potential critic.

A "laboratory" need not be a separate room or building. Any situation that can be isolated from external influences can serve as a laboratory. Some laboratories are highly isolated; the extreme case is the laboratory located on a rocket in space, beyond most of the pervasive influence of gravity. Laboratories are ideal for determining the precise interactions among a set of variables. Their principal weakness is a function of the very isolation that makes precise measurements possible: Relations that hold within the laboratory may fail under real-world conditions precisely because of the effect of external influences. A system that functioned well only under no-gravity conditions would not be terribly useful on earth, or on any other material object in space of any significant size. It would resemble a program of treatment in medicine that required the patient to survive indefinitely without oxygen.

A natural-state experiment avoids the difficulties associated with laboratory testing but creates problems of its own. In particular, many of the factors that are operating in real cases remain unknown and cannot be controlled. Although their influence can be lumped together, if those factors are not identified, the limiting conditions under which the theory can be expected to function remain partly unknown, adding an extra element of uncertainty to applications.

To conclude, it should be noted that no amount of testing and experimenting, whether in a laboratory or in the real world, can eliminate all the risk and uncertainty associated with the use of theories. No theory can be "proved"; no theory can be "disproved" with finality either. The status of a theory cannot be fixed permanently and certainly. The weight of evidence may seem conclusive at one point in time, but subsequent observations and experiments can alter that assessment. The one question that can be answered, and not always very conclusively, is whether best knowledge in the present justifies accepting and using the theory to achieve a specific purpose under some stipulated set of conditions.

Exercises

Review Questions

1. Which aspects of theory are particularly important when the theory is being justified or validated?

2. In what sense are theories similar to maps, and subject to the same criteria of adequacy, and in what respects are they different?

3. What are the primary costs and benefits of accepting a "weak" definition of theory?

4. What form of test provides the most important evidence for the validity of a theory? Why?

5. Give reasons why social scientists in particular should be well grounded in the history of the kinds of events they are studying.

6. Compare the role of laboratory experiments and natural-state experiments in social science.

7. What role can systematic experimentation be expected to play in social science theorizing in the near future? Give reasons for your answer.

Discussion

1. What is the difference between "proving" a proposition and "disproving" that same proposition? Which task is easier? Give reasons for your answer.

2. What is the difference between adding another variable to a theory, and linking it with appropriate rules, and adding further limitations on the application of a theory? Which is preferable? Why?

16. Choice: Introductory

Analytically, the quality of human life is a function of two major factors: (1) the content of the natural environment; and (2) human capacity for molding or shaping that environment. The natural environment sets limits to what can be accomplished, positive and negative. Rich farmland and vast mineral deposits represent a very different potential for life than icy tundras or barren deserts. To some extent, the limits that nature imposes can be evaded, and the possession of resources does not guarantee their use. The evasion depends on knowledge and technical capacity (which is also knowledge), including ethics, for both whose wants and needs and which wants and needs are satisfied depends on the way human efforts are directed and the way benefits are distributed within society.

The channel through which human knowledge is applied to the environment is the choice or action. It serves as the focus of the entire critical or analytic system. The various instruments developed in the text are those required to place human choices or actions on defensible and corrigible foundations. The form taken by each instrument, and the criteria of adequacy applied to it, are also determined by the requirements of defensible action. Thus an instrument able to project the effects of human action on the future is essential for reasoned choice and is therefore included here. It is labeled a *theory* because it corresponds fairly closely to the use of "theory" in physical science. But it is included because of the function it performs. The remaining intellectual tools required for reasoned action are now to be examined more closely, then brought together to show how they are actually used.

Human life is usefully conceived as an endless sequence of actions or choices. Empirical or scientific knowledge, the ability to predict and control events, is an essential prerequisite to defensible actions, but knowing what to expect, or how to produce and inhibit change, is not enough. That kind of capacity must be directed, applied in ways that are controlled by a normative or ethical apparatus. In the ethic developed here, actions are directed to maintaining and improving the human situation for some population. Three aspects of the choice process are particularly important in criticism. First, areas where action is needed on normative grounds, where the existing conditions of life are not acceptable, must be located. Second, the options available to the actor(s) concerned with the situation must be projected. Third, one of those options must be selected or preferred. Each function requires justification. The next step in the development of the analytic framework is to identify the kinds of knowledge required for reasoned choice, the kinds of instruments involved at each step, and determine how such knowledge can be produced, tested, and justified.

The overall procedure employed to produce predictions and means for controlling events in the environment applies equally well to problems of choice or action. Human experience must be organized and generalized into patterns that can perform specified functions. Evidence obtained by applying those patterns can then provide reasons for modifying, improving, or rejecting them. In matters of choice, the critical base is provided by the human ability to react differentially to differences in the world, to prefer some situations to others. Those responses will have an affective or an intellectual base, or a rationale that combines the two influences, that can be used to justify the preference. The details of the process are explored in this unit and the next. The aim is to show the way in which human choices can be justified or criticized within the limits of human capacity. The focus is procedural and not substantive. That is, the goal is to clarify the way in which decisions can be made and not to make any particular decision.

Choice and Action

In everyday usage, the meaning of such terms as *choice, decision,* and *action* is not always clear; usage tends to be inconsistent. It is customary, for example, to speak of Smith's "choice" as either the set of options from which a choice must be made or the particular choice that has been made by Smith. Again, to "have no choice" means in some cases to be unable to act and in others to be able to act in only one way. The term *action* usually refers only to positive actions, although failure to act is sometimes included among "actions" in technical writings. The discussion therefore begins with a clarification of the meaning of basic terms as they appear in the critical framework.

The key to the meaning of action or choice as those terms are used here is an actor with the capacity to produce change. No action or choice can take place if there is no actor; if the actor has no capacity to effect change, there is again no action. An actor who has some capacity to produce change must *always* make a choice. Given capacity that can be exercised voluntarily, the actor is always faced with at least two options: Failure to act, to exercise capacity, will produce one option; positive actions will produce one or more others. Action is in either case inescapable. Capacity is a necessary and a sufficient condition for choice. The result of action, and its indicator, is a world that is different from what it would have been had the actor exercised capacity differently. In that context, action and choice are identical, two ways of stating the same thing.

That approach to choice and action allows us to concentrate on the set of outcomes or options that lie within the actor's capacity. The term *choice* can be used to refer to the full set of outcomes available to the actor or to the process of selecting one of those options; preference will refer to the option selected; reasoned action serves to produce the preferred outcome. Criticism of a positive action and criticism of the intellectual process by which a choice is made involve precisely the same set of considerations. Hence they are analytically or critically identical.

An actor with the capacity to change the environment will be able to produce two or more outcomes if capacity can be exercised voluntarily. The results of action, the content of the outcomes, can be projected, in descriptive terms, by an appropriate set of theories. The projection will appear as the set of values expected to be taken by a given set of variables. Choice or action requires a preference for one set of values for those variables over another set of values for the same variables. An actor able to move a large stone, for example, can choose from among a number of options, each a different physical position. The actor can examine all positions, express a preference for one, and provide a justification for that preference. The actor can also move the stone to the preferred position and then offer a justification for the action. The substance of the justification would be precisely the same in either case. That is the sense in which choice and action can be collapsed analytically. It follows additionally that the consequences of action or choice can always be expressed in the general form "This set of values for that selection of variables *rather than* these other sets of values for the same variables." Symbolically, if there are two options, A and B, then the consequences of the choice or action can be stated "A *rather than* B." Preferences are based on comparison and limited to the set of options to which they refer.

The options available to an actor are the consequences to be expected from the actions lying within the actor's capacity at a given time and place. Since the options always lie in the future, a theory is required to project their content. The projection will be stated in descriptive terms, but it will not be a description—only an anticipated description. Since the content of the options is a function of the actor's capacity, it can be determined objectively. That is, capacity, which determines outcomes, is independent of the actor's awareness, intentions, or other subjective states. If one of the effects of war is a serious reduction in the supply of talented young persons, then that *is* a consequence of war; whether it was intended, recognized, sought after, or even taken into account by those who make such decisions, is irrelevant. Unless the object of inquiry is to criticize the actor, there is no need to inquire into awareness or motives. The focus of criticism is always the substance of choice, the selection of one outcome in preference to specified others. The identity of the actor need be known only to determine the extent of capacity.

To avoid needless complications, criticism is limited strictly to actions and choices carried out by living humans. Dogs and cats may "choose" one food in preference to others, but they cannot generate the kinds of justification required for reasoned choices. True, dogs can be conditioned to select food that is more nutritious if less palatable than the alternatives, but in such cases the "choice" is actually made by the person who does the conditioning. For similar reasons, acts of nature such as floods or hurricanes, although they produce very significant changes in the human situation, are not amenable to criticism. There is no element of human choice or direction in such events. Of course, the individual who knows that a hurricane is approaching but fails to warn the neighbors has made a choice that *is* open to criticism, but blaming a hurricane is only an abuse of the language. Finally, when the actor cannot be identified, the available options will be indeterminate, and criticism is impossible. That can lead to serious conceptual difficulties with collective bodies such as legislatures. The alternatives may be very difficult to determine because of the decision-making procedure employed. If each member of a collective body can only choose whether to vote for a measure, vote against it, or abstain, no individual actually makes the collective choice. The collective decision is made by aggregating individual choices and applying a formal rule. Actions of such collective bodies come very close to being in the same class with hurricanes and floods, "acts of nature" of a peculiar kind. Some of the major problems raised by those situations are discussed more fully in another unit.

The options included in a choice must be real and attainable. It would be merely silly to speak of "choosing" to fly by flapping the arms, or "choosing" not to die when that is the ultimate fate of all living things. Neither the necessary nor the impossible is a part of choice. Ideals and utopias can therefore play only a very limited role in human actions; if they cannot be achieved, they are not part of choice. Worse, if they cannot be achieved, there is no way to determine whether or not a particular action moves actor or society closer to or further away from the ideal. If the route from city A to city B is unknown, there is no way to determine whether or not any particular step is a "step in the right direction." That requires knowledge of the complete route.

Finally, the objective here is to develop an approach to choice that refers to a significant form of human behavior and can be improved out of human experience. If choice occurs at every exercise of human capacity, real or potential, the significance of the focus could hardly be greater. If the quality of choosing and acting is to improve, instruments are required that can be justified out of experience and tested against experience. They must lie within human capacity. If reasoned choice or action depended on attributes available only in deities, humans could not make reasoned choices. Furthermore, the approach to choice should allow commonplace materials (such as you and I) to become competent critics. No certain grounds for choice or action can be created, but systematic analysis should be able to produce a level of agreement more than adequate for an ongoing society seeking to improve normative performance, or for an individual with the same objective in mind.

The Critical Focus

Choices or actions involve three primary elements: an actor, a choice or action, and a set of consequences flowing from the action. In principle, criticism could focus on any one of those elements or on combinations of all three. In practice, choice must be criticized by reference to consequences. Why that focus is necessary, and what it implies for systematic criticism, is explained in the remainder of the unit.

Given a commitment to using human actions to improve the conditions of life of human populations, the strongest reason for insisting that choices be justified or criticized by reference to consequences is that the alternatives will not work. Efforts to justify choices by referring to either the characteristics of the actor or to the qualities of the action produce anomalies and inconsistencies that destroy their value. What is called *ad hominem* reasoning, argument addressed to the attributes of the person, is today rejected almost everywhere. Although it may appear that such reasoning is honored, as when a physician prescribes a particular course of treatment for a patient, and the patient justifies following the advice by attributing it to the doctor, that is misleading. The real justification for the treatment is the one offered by the physician to his or her peers, and that justification will invariably refer to the consequences of the treatment, and the effects anticipated from the available alternatives. It is the latter procedure, the way in which doctors convince other doctors, that is relevant here.

Further, the intentions of the actor are equally irrelevant to systematic criticism of choice because of the absence of any necessary relationship between intention and outcome. Humans frequently intend one outcome and produce another, or produce what is intended but for the wrong reasons. Worse, humans often act without knowing why they act, knowing what effects their actions are likely to have, or even without knowing that they are producing an effect on themselves or others. The problem cannot be evaded by depending on the ethical characteristics of the individual actor. There is at present no agreed way to identify a "good" or "moral" person, but even if that could be done, it would not provide an adequate basis for action. If all the actions performed by a "good" person had to be accepted, that would be tantamount to considering every operation performed by a "good" doctor to be successful. Since the effects of action cannot be avoided, even if they are not used as the principal basis for justification and criticism of action, focus on the attributes of the person would lead unavoidably to anomalies and inconsistencies—approving or disapproving precisely the same action, with precisely the same effects, because of the individual involved. Any effort to judge the quality of actions independent of their consequences leads to precisely the same outcome.

That leaves only one possible alternative, justifying and criticizing actions by reference to their consequences. Happily, an adequate critical procedure can be developed from that base. It depends on a systematic comparison of the content of the outcomes from which choices are made and requires no more than a comparative rule of preference: Prefer *A* to *B, C,* and *D.* In everyday affairs, judging actions by their consequences is common practice, although use of that basis for justification in ethics has in some degree been inhibited by the old homily that disparages use because it implies that "the end justifies the means." It is a curious assertion, for if the outcome cannot justify the efforts to achieve it, what else possibly could? The confusion lies in an improper inference often drawn from the homily. Particular ends do not justify every and any means to achieve them; that would be possible only if a doctrine of absolute ends were accepted, and that is not necessary.

Comparison as the Basis for Preference

Every action or choice depends on the capacity to produce change. The difference produced, or the absence of difference when difference could have been produced, provides the leverage needed for developing justifications and criticism. By comparing the outcomes that could be produced by action, reasons may be found for preferring one to the other. Given the assumptions on which the present analysis depends, those reasons will refer to the conditions of life of those affected by the action. If no reason can be found for preferring one outcome to the others, the choice is a matter of indifference given the accepted ethic. If reasons can be found for differing with the choice made on the basis of the accepted ethic, those reasons provide a focal point for argument, clarification, and potential improvement. Of course, not every action or choice is reasoned. What identifies a reasoned choice or action is the element of deliberate weighing or comparing of outcomes, balancing the costs and benefits to humans of selecting each of the alternatives. When a choice is reasoned, some justification for the choice can always be produced; that justification fulfills the necessary preconditions for argument and improvement.

The concept of reasoned choice accepted here is weak and easily satisfied. Even the most perfunctory weighing of outcomes, and the most trivial of reasons for preference, satisfies the requirements. The quality of the reasoning can vary widely. Alternatives may be ignored or suppressed; calculations may be mistaken; the theoretical apparatus may be faulty; the level of uncertainty involved may be overlooked; and so on. But the process of reasoning, of offering a justification for preference, opens the way to criticism and argument, and that is all that can reasonably be required at present. The individual who offers no justification for choice is immune to systematic criticism but also without any capacity to convince others on intellectual grounds. Once reasons are proposed, their adequacy can be questioned, omissions can be identified, the implications of particular weightings explored, additions can be proposed, and so on. In the process, the justification can be strengthened, modified, or rejected in favor of a different decision. Whether in science or ethics, the train of processes required for improvement is set in motion when reasons are offered to support an assumption.

For the rest, the development of normative knowledge follows the pattern established with respect to empirical inquiries. The instruments of choice are created as a solution to a particular case; that solution can be generalized, applied to the class of cases exemplified in the particular. The instruments used need only compare the content of the options; it is not necessary to develop an external measure that can be applied to each outcome independently and uniquely—a much harder task. Over time, a system of priorities can be created that summarizes the solutions that have been made to particular problems in the past, and the modifications introduced as a result of further experience. That structure, properly termed the individual's or society's *ethic,* can be examined for internal consistency and for implications, and thus generalized and improved still further. In a sense, society's mores reflect such generalized solutions to choice problems encountered earlier in society's history. The difficulty with mores is the tendency to ossification that goes with their sheltered or privileged status; criticism of the basic mores is usually a difficult task in any society. As in theorizing, the procedures used to create solutions to normative problems cannot be formalized, but strategies of proven value can be developed for testing and improving the solution once it has been produced and defended. The critic's task, like the task of the reasoned chooser, is to examine choices systematically, looking for inconsistencies, omissions, and ambiguities, to suggest new aspects of the human situation that ought to be taken into account when choices are made, or to suggest modifications in existing priorities based on an assessment of their implications or consequences in future actions. In each case, the reasons offered to support action or criticism will link the action to the analytic requirements for making reasoned choices, to the substantive body of past human experience, or to both. Criticism is always both methodological and substantive, or it is incomplete.

Exercises

Review Questions

1. What are the two primary factors that influence the quality of individual life in a given society?

2. Explain why choice is defined by reference to an actor's capacity and not in terms of intentions or behavior.

3. Why are choices and actions analytically identical?

4. What is the basic form in which the consequences of choice or action can be expressed?

5. Why are the consequences of action, rather than the attributes of the actor or action, used as a basis for criticizing and justifying actions?

6. What are the advantages of basing choice on a comparison of outcomes rather than external criteria such as "goodness?"

7. What are the identifying characteristics of a "reasoned" action? Why is that considered a "weak" definition, and what implication does such "weakness" have?

Discussion

1. If the conditions of life are a function of the content of the natural environment and the knowledge available for dealing with it, discuss the requirements for a population able to maximize environmental potential.

2. Why is choice, considered as a process, such an important activity in determining the kinds of lives people actually live?

3. How does choice serve to integrate empirical and normative inquiries?

17. Choice: Instruments and Processes

Summarizing very quickly, choices or actions produce or prevent change, thus creating a situation that is different from what it would be if capacity were exercised differently. Choices are justified and criticized by reference to the content of the available options, the consequences of action. Consequences are stated in terms of the conditions of life of the population affected by action. As in empirical inquiry, the instrument used to make choices is produced by generalizing past experience. Since the fundamental assumption on which the analytic framework depends is that the goal of action is improvement in the human condition, such improvements provide the ultimate test of the various instruments involved in choice or action. And beyond that, the question whether or not an improvement has been made depends on the judgments and practices of informed and competent persons, as in physical science.

This text is concerned with the methodological dimensions of action, with the character of the assumptions required to make or justify choices and not with the psychology of action (the choices that *will* be made) or with the substance of action. The function of systematic analysis is to show the *kinds of* questions that should be raised in reasoned criticism rather than the questions themselves, and the *kinds of* answers that should be accepted, not the actual answers given. As it happens, when the effects of action are significant for the persons making the decision, the same general procedure is likely to be followed everywhere. The value of a systematic approach is that it can point to dimensions of choice that might otherwise be overlooked and suggests the kinds of reasoning that ought to be honored. To illustrate, a relatively commonplace example can be traced roughly though the decision process. It is assumed that Smith, an adult male with a small family, lives and works in the small city where he was raised. He is then offered a better job in the capital city. A choice must be made between the two positions.

Some of the preliminary considerations involved in the decision are fairly obvious but are worth mentioning in order to round out the discussion. Thus there can be no choice without a human actor or chooser; there must be a real person to make the choice. Further, the availability of different jobs does not in itself suffice to pose a choice, even if both could be filled by the same person. A worker cannot choose a job that has not been offered, though he or she could decide to apply for such a job, in effect, to try to create an opportunity to choose. The choice must be real, within the actor's present capacity. Moreover, the choice cannot be justified or criticized until the identity of the person involved has been established, since the costs and benefits incorporated into the options will vary with the individual. Finally, it is worth noting that the considerations that influence the worker's decision to accept a position or not may be quite different from the employer's reasons for offering the job to a particular person. Two very different decisions are involved, although they are of course closely related.

Determining the Options

The first step in reasoned choice is to withhold judgment until the implications of the various options have been examined. If Smith refuses another position out of hand, or "refuses to consider" the offer, the implications of such refusal are profound and extensive. In effect, refusing to consider any alternative means there is no conceivable option that is preferable to the present situation and the anticipated future. That is a truly staggering assumption, quite different from the position of an individual who hears out the details of an alternative position and then decides, after some deliberation, that change is undesirable. A reasoned choice is more than a direct affective reaction, although a reasoned choice may be directed by affective reaction if no reason is found to modify that reaction on intellectual grounds. Thus a child's decision to reject "healthy" food on affective grounds (it tastes bad) may be overridden, and with justification, although the decision is complex if the effect is to create a psychic state within the child that is even less desirable than a relatively "unhealthy" diet. In real-world affairs, affective reaction alone is rarely an adequate basis for choice. Indeed, affective reaction is not in itself a judgment or preference; the reaction is felt directly by the individual and reported as a *fact*. Unfortunately, the content of individual affect varies greatly with culture and is subject to conditioning or direction from external sources. In most cases, affective reaction must be combined with intellectual reasoning to produce the needed justification for preference; too many things that have an important effect on life are not accessible to affect. The individual can be conditioned to react affectively to "injustices" in the operation of government, for example, but the justification for such conditioning is intellectual, based on long-run considerations relating to the effect of institutional performance on the lives of affected populations.

To return to the example, once Smith has been offered a second job, action is not avoidable. That is the sense in which capacity forces action. Smith may, on various grounds, decide to accept or refuse the job on the spot and end the matter there. But if the decision is to be justified to a competent critic, certain requirements must be satisfied first. The implications of each of the available lines of action must be projected on the future and compared in terms of the conditions of life of the people affected. Those projections will be dynamic, film clips of the future rather than still photographs, and must extend as far as current capacity to foresee can be pressed. As a result, the projections will be problematic in some degree, and that uncertainty can influence decision. All of the normatively significant dimensions of the projected future are to be included. That places an added burden on the theories used to make projections, for they must be linked to an adequate set of normative variables. A worker who could do no more than project the economic implications of accepting another job or retaining the present job, leaving aside all the familial, cultural, social, educational, and personal implications of the choice, could hardly be said to have an adequate basis for decision, and would probably refuse to make the choice. Some aspects of the future will weigh more heavily than others, and weighting may vary from person to person (suggesting why it is highly desirable to have choices made as closely as possible to the place where individual preferences can count most heavily).

The point to be made here is that the outcomes must be weighted, without suggesting how or what the weighting should be. Two factors will influence the weight attached to particular elements in the outcome: (1) the probability that the projection is accurate, the level of uncertainty attached to the outcome; and (2) the significance of that factor in the hierarchy of preferences that are accepted by the individual. An uncertain but highly significant factor may count far more heavily than a less significant factor that is almost certain to occur. Thus a moderate risk of incurring illness from hazardous wastes may influence the decision to move much more than the near certainty of better transportation or even improved schools. Individuals differ greatly on such matters, and it is unlikely that unanimity can be achieved with respect to all choices; that is the reason why a collective decisioning apparatus, a social context, is an essential part of every human life.

In most cases, the choice of jobs will be treated as a simple two-option decision: The worker will either accept the new position or remain in the present job. In fact, there are usually a great many other options available, but they are overlooked or ignored. To take a specific case, if the worker is very nearly at retirement age, that option might be added to the set being reviewed. Other options, which may appear unreasonable, may nevertheless be available. The worker could vacate both jobs, abandon his wife and children, and run off to join the French Foreign Legion. In some cases, it might be possible to cease work entirely and apply for unemployment benefits, and so on. In most cases, such options are suppressed or ignored, but if they lie within capacity, they are real, and sometimes worth taking seriously.

The practice of suppressing all but a few of the real options available for choice is an important function of socialization. Consider a young woman who goes to the store to buy a purse. She examines the available purses (those she can afford) and chooses one—or in the case of my wife, rejects the lot and returns home. The alternate uses that might be made of those resources, which are virtually endless, are almost never examined. To justify the choice, she would refer to the kinds of purses available, their respective costs, and the degree of fit between purse features and her needs and habits. But the same resources could certainly be used to purchase food for hungry childen or assist the elderly to obtain medical attention. Told that she had chosen to add a new purse to her wardrobe rather than provide food for hungry children or medical assistance for the elderly, the young woman would be likely to become indignant. Yet precisely such choices are made every day when the exercise of capacity is examined realistically in terms of its scope. Each option must be weighed against *all* other options, both by chooser and critic. Socialization serves to suppress a very large part of the available alternatives and to legitimate the practice of limiting options in particular ways. That is one reason why a careful examination of current social practice, seeking to determine what is being included and omitted from individual and collective decisions, is badly needed in most societies. Few societies, however, have the institutional arrangements in place that could be used for that purpose.

Projecting the options from which choices must be made into the future is a little like dropping a stone into a moving stream. Depending on the size of the stone and the speed of the river, the pattern of waves created by the stone cannot be followed very far, or in great detail, before it disappears. Reasoned action requires that the options be projected as fully, and completely, as present capacity permits, but too much cannot be expected in the current state of knowledge. And present choices cannot be criticized in terms of future knowledge; the chooser can only do the best possible at the time of choice. If a choice is made under severe time constraints, as occurs in the real world all too often, that will also limit how well the options are arrayed. Experience can help by suggesting the kinds of actions likely to have significant consequences, and the kinds of places where significant consequences are likely to appear. Mistakes are unavoidable, but the real tragedy occurs when nothing is learned from either success or failure, and subsequent performance does not improve. An important goal of training in the use of the analytic framework is to facilitate learning from experience, first by providing a way of linking purposes to intellectual tools useful for fulfilling them, and second, by suggesting areas of great human significance for those concerned with choosing or criticizing choices.

The Normative Variables

The task of projecting the content of the options available for choice is both simplified and complicated by the need to employ normative variables to structure outcomes. In principle, a complete statement of consequences is impossible to achieve. Normative concern, however, focuses on certain kinds of consequences—those that involve significant dimensions of human life. That commitment to radical individualism simplifies the task of projecting outcomes, for anything that does not affect human life in an important way, either directly or indirectly, can safely be ignored. Nevertheless, the need to state consequences using normative variables means that the theories used to project them must make use of, or be linked to, a set of normative variables. Since theories, particularly in social science, are in most cases relatively scarce and are almost never stated using variables that refer directly to the normatively significant dimensions of individual life, that is likely to be a serious handicap for those responsible for social decisions.

In terms of the example used earlier, Smith's decision would depend on the effect of selecting one or the other of the options on the people who would be impacted by the change. If the only information available referred to wages and benefits, choice would be extremely hazardous. Of course, the economic effects of the choice would count heavily because they influence so many other dimensions of life directly and indirectly. But even the absolute level of wages and benefits would have to be balanced against relative costs, particularly of food, clothing, and shelter, as well as hidden costs such as need to send the children to private schools because of the inadequacy of the public schools. Other aspects of the situation likely to influence the decision would include job security, opportunities for advancement, kind of work performed, and even the physical characteristics of the workplace. Beyond these economic-related matters lie such concerns as the availability of medical, cultural, and recreational facilities; the quality of the schools; levels of public safety; ease of access to shopping and other requirements; and so on. Finally, a range of personal and familial concerns would probably be weighed before choosing. Leaving the family may be regarded as too high a cost to pay for a slightly larger income, particularly if family relations are close, or some members of the family are in poor health. Any factor that affects the kind of life that the family expects to lead, or is accustomed to leading, will be part of the set of variables used to deal with that situation.

The result of Smith's projections, calculations, and weightings can be brought together in a relatively systematic matrix, showing the input variables measured and their values, the normative variables affected by these input variables, and the weighting attached to each part of each outcome. Technically, such variables as "income" are not normative, in the strict sense; they are considered important because changes in their values will affect individual life. How they will affect individual life will be stated using genuinely normative variables. Their structure is quite complex, and discussion of their meaning and limitations can be delayed to another unit.

Input Variable	Normative Variable	Option 1 Value/Weight		Option 2 Value/Weight	
Income		$X	−	X + $50	+
Living costs		$X	+	X + 5%	−
Schools		Excellent	++	Poor	−−
Family relations		Close	+++	Distant and weak	−−

The weightings, which are the key to the decision, involve two levels of comparison. In the first instance, the two options can be compared with respect to income, etc., and a weighting attached to each continuum. Thus Smith may prefer more to less income, lower to higher living costs, good to poor schools, and so on. The more difficult decisions appear when increased income (less increased living costs) must be balanced against poorer schools and weaker family relations. Examination of that process too can be delayed until another unit as long as the principle involved is clear.

Assigning Priorities

Having projected the normative implications of each option as fully as possible, Smith now needs an instrument that will order the outcomes to show the preferred option. That instrument may already be available: Smith may already have produced a generalized structure that will apply to the situation. For example, if he has changed jobs and locations several times in the past, the family may already have decided that he would not change jobs again unless there were exceptional reasons—a major increase in income, a choice between moving and unemployment, and so on. The priority would assert that in choosing between jobs: "Prefer the present position to any alternative that does not include exceptional improvements." Since the choice to be made is certainly a case of "choosing between jobs," the pattern should apply. The new job is examined to see if it contains exceptional provisions, and that could be subject to some discussion. If it does not, the option that follows from retaining the present job is preferred.

If such a priority is not available, one must be created. The experience used to produce the instrument need not be direct. Other persons who have changed jobs can be consulted to obtain information about their reaction to the option chosen, and the information can be extrapolated to the present case—adjusted for any differences in personal or family likes and dislikes. Given the kind of general knowledge available in modern society, the relative desirability of a range of conditions of life can be considered more or less accurately without experiencing them directly. Finally, since experience will not usually refer to every aspect of the choice, some element of risk and uncertainty is likely to be involved in every determination of priorities. The family will not know "what it's like to live with" some of the conditions projected for the future, and will have to guess, or weigh the choice on other grounds and assume the unknown will prove tolerable. After all the weighing and comparing are completed, the particular decision must be made, meaning the preferred outcome must be identified and justified. That preference can then be generalized into a priority and applied to the particular case and other cases.

The reason for the additional step (justifying a preference, then generalizing the result) is analytic. Solving the particular case requires justification of a particular statement: "Outcome A is preferable to outcome B." Such particular statements do not provide a basis for action because the action must be inferred from the base and nothing can be inferred from a particular statement. The solution must therefore be generalized even before it is applied to the case from which it was induced. That case serves as a first test of the priority, and the experience obtained from the application can be used to strengthen or weaken the justification or modify the priority. The structure is then expected to hold each time the same set of outcomes reappears; the evidence that supports application is found ultimately in the willingness of informed users to rely on it.

Applying Priorities: Policies

Once a preferred outcome has been identified by applying or creating a priority, it remains to bring that preferred outcome into being, to reify the priority. A program of action, a set of rules of action, must also be created that will actually produce the preferred outcome. Those rules of action or action program will be referred to as *policies*. The need for a separate apparatus for applying the priority may not be obvious, but the separation is essential for justification or criticism. If Smith developed a priority and applied it, and the result was to show that the present job was preferable to the new position offered, some action would still be required to implement the intellectual decision. Refusing the offer requires an action program, which may consist in a simple phone call, a written refusal of the offer, or a message conveyed by an intermediary. There is a difference between making a decision intellectually and implementing it. The decision can be reached on the basis of a priority structure; implementation requires a policy based on valid theories. Usually, policies are developed out of the theories used to project the outcome from which choices are made. The theories must be practical, within the limits of present resources and technology, and not merely valid in principle.

To illustrate the importance of separating priority from policy, make the common assumption that fewer human deaths are preferable to more human deaths, other things equal. It follows that in the emergency room of a hospital, if a large number of persons is brought in at the same time and capacity is limited, the policy followed is to sedate the lightly injured and treat those with serious wounds. That policy tends to produce the preferred outcome very consistently. If the emergency room is located on a large warship engaged in combat, the same priority leads to quite a different policy: "Sedate the badly injured and treat those who can return to the battle." The reasoning is simple: If the goal is to save lives, saving the ship is the first order of business, and that is contingent on optimizing the availability of manpower at the battle stations.

Exercises

Review Questions

1. Differentiate between an ethics of action and a psychology of action. What question is answered in each case?

2. What are the minimum conditions to be satisfied before a reasoned choice can be made? Illustrate.

3. Outline the major steps in a reasoned choice.

4. Why is human affective reaction of limited usefulness in reasoned action?

5. What are the major differences between a still photo and the kind of projection of outcomes required for a choice?

6. How does socialization influence the content of a choice?

7. What are the functions of the normative variables in projecting outcomes?

8. Differentiate between a priority and a policy. Why is analytic separation needed?

9. What are some of the factors that limit human capacity to project the effects of action on the future?

Discussion

1. What are some of the normative variables that would be taken into account in selecting a college or university?

2. In what sense is an affective reaction *described* by the person who experiences it? In what sense is it more than a description?

3. Under what circumstances could an individual be expected to act in ways that would be detrimental to the self? What kinds of other effects might serve to offset those harmful results?

18. Choice: What Are the Options?

For each human individual or collectivity, life is an endless succession of decisions about the use of capacity and the resources attached to that capacity. In everyday affairs, most of the possibilities are ignored, or handled through habit or custom. Analytically, a choice is made to allow the drift course of events to continue unchanged by not exercising capacity. But in practical terms, the individual is unlikely to be aware of many of the decisions taken in this way. The choices selected for careful consideration are usually determined by the socialization process, including formal and informal education; such training alerts the individual to situations where the exercise of capacity has extensive implications for the future, particularly implications that are exceptionally harmful or beneficial.

Obviously, socialization may be faulty or inadequate, omitting things that are actually very important and overemphasizing other things. That is particularly likely to occur when society is changing rapidly. A horse-and-buggy childhood may produce an early-warning system, and a set of habits, not well adapted to the age of automobiles. In extreme cases, failure to develop an adequate set of indicators for the danger spots in society can actually be fatal.

Choices are made within the constraints provided by real-world particulars, and those constraints may in some cases be unique. What is actually the case in the environment must be known before the content of the alternatives from which choices are made can be projected. A general discussion of the process can show the structures involved and some of the complications that can arise, but cannot be used to create and justify particular rules of action or priorities. The priority actually attached to particular outcomes will depend on human experience generally, but it will be shaped and conditioned by personal reactions, individual knowledge, past upbringing, and a host of other considerations. In any particular instance, the relevant factors can usually be separated out and identified, but discussion of such problems in wholly general terms tends to produce confusion rather than clarification.

Projecting the Options

In making reasoned choices, the first question to be answered is always "What are the options available?" Reasoned choice proceeds from a systematic structuring of the alternatives to a comparison of their content and a solution of the particular case. The actor must be identified in order to determine capacity and thus project outcomes; a selection of normative variables is used to identify the significant consequences of each of the courses of action available. If the actor is a collective body, the legal capacity of the office or agency may provide a rough base for projecting outcomes, but there is often a significant difference between real capacity and legal capacity—and a significant gap between potential authority and the authority that is likely to be exercised. Individual characteristics do make a difference, even with respect to very powerful offices. The Congress of the United States may have the formal legal power to act in a particular way, but if those who currently hold seats in Congress refuse to exercise that power, the collectivity cannot act. It would be a mistake to regard the formal power as equivalent to real power. In such cases, it may take a fine sense of political judgment to determine whether or not formal power can actually be used.

Perhaps the best way to think of the options available to an actor is to imagine a set of film clips, each beginning at the point where action is taken, showing all the significant effects of action as they are projected by the available theories. Each alternative is a future scenario that can be brought about by actions within the actor's capacity. The content of the scenarios will be different in at least some respects, major or minor. There must be at least two such alternatives for every choice; usually there are many more than two, but most are ignored. The effect of action or choice is to produce one of the film clips *rather than* the others, and that provides the justification for basing preferences on comparisons rather than absolute measures. Technically, the consequences of action can always be stated in the general form: alternative A (which is projected using a set of normative variables) rather than alternative B (projected using the same set of normative variables, at least one of which takes a different value in B than in A).

Projections are always risky or uncertain. Since outcomes refer to the future and are projected theoretically, there is always some possibility that they will not be realized. That risk or probability must be estimated, however roughly, since it will influence the choice actually made. Given a choice between starting a war and triggering an outbreak of measles, only a monster would choose to start a war. But if the measles epidemic is a near certainty and the risk of war is infinitesimally small, then the risk of war may be the more reasonable choice to make. Compared to certain death, serious injury is preferable, other things equal. Nevertheless, a very strong justification for believing that death was certain would surely be necessary before serious injury would be accepted willingly. Psychologically, there is a pronounced tendency for humans to seek to deal with deadly choices by delay or procrastination. In all honesty it should be said that the strategy sometimes works, although only when expectations are actually very uncertain; in other instances, such as delaying treatment of a serious illness like cancer, the result can be lethal. Of course, delay that is intended, deliberate procrastination, counts as a mode of action and has its own consequences, which can be calculated in the same manner as any other action. The amount of risk, and the substance of what is risked, will often count heavily in choice. People differ greatly in their willingness to accept risk generally, as well as the amount of risk that will be accepted in order to obtain a particular outcome. Cowardice and foolhardiness are both common within the species.

Finally, it is worth noting that the options must be projected using the best theories available at the time when the choice is made. Those theories may prove to be very faulty, leading to outcomes that are almost wholly different from what was expected. Such errors provide evidence for criticizing and improving the theories used to make the projections, but they do not enter into the criticism of the choice. Choice is directed at a stipulated set of outcomes, which must be taken as stated—with a probability of success attached to each one. Criticism of the choice must refer to the set of outcomes at which the choice was directed, not the set of outcomes that actually appeared. Of course, it may be useful to criticize the individual who made the decision for failing to take into account the uncertainty attached to the outcomes, but that is a different problem.

Chain Reactions

Structurally, human actions trigger a sequence of chain reactions similar to those that follow the detonation of a nuclear device. One change leads to another, and so on through a series. Each set of outcomes is linked by an unbroken theoretical chain extending back to the original action. From one perspective, the resulting structure appears as shown in figure 18.1.

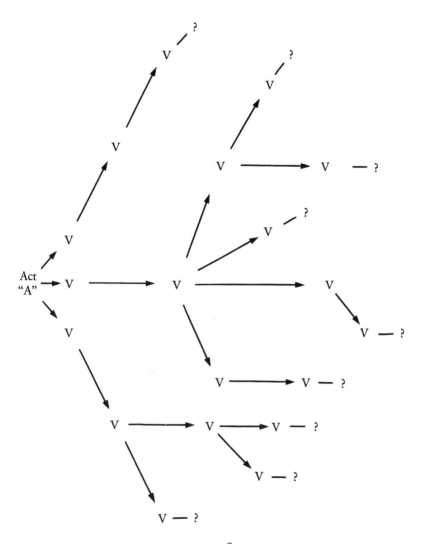

FIGURE 18.1

The set of chain reactions shown in the figure illustrates just *one* of the options available in a given choice. A separate set of reactions must be projected for each of the actions within the capacity of the actor. How full and complete must the chain be? Where does it come to an end? How can its adequacy be judged? These are difficult questions to answer in general terms. Ultimately, one limit on the content of the projections is the supply of knowledge available. But other factors, such as the amount of time available to make the projections, the cost of acquiring and process-ing information, the overall significance of the decision, and so on, will influence the amount of projection actually carried out. In principle, the full consequences of any action cannot be projected, just as a complete description cannot be made of any situation. This suggests that it is very important to develop procedures for monitoring the consequences of ac-tion, especially after major decisions have been taken, to determine the consequences actually produced, and particularly to locate significant de-partures from or additions to the expectations on which the decision was based. In practice, that is rarely done systematically and effectively, and where data *are* collected, they are not always processed and inserted into the decision-making machinery.

Realistically assessed, the amount of knowledge (theory) available for projecting the effects of major collective actions is extremely limited, even in such presumably powerful fields as economics. The film clips from which choices must be made may be fairly sharp and clear in the short run, but they blur substantially over relatively short time periods. The capacity to project future effects diminishes rapidly over time. There is little chance of improving the situation drastically in the short run, particularly with respect to collective affairs. And in any event, the danger in theoretical pro-jections lies as often in expecting or demanding too much as in having too little.

Out of necessity, humans live fairly close to the present. Past history tends to blur quickly with time, leaving aside exceptional events, and the "lessons learned" from these exceptions tend to become distorted very quick-ly. Events that provide subject matter for books become in a short time only chapters in books and then paragraphs — and then they disappear al-together in most instances. The future cannot be projected very far; the past fades quickly. That must be taken as one of the "givens" in human affairs, and a major handicap it can be. But it may also be a blessing, for too much memory could be a terrible burden, and too much capacity to foretell the future could be equally disastrous. In such matters, the only advice that can be offered is to do the best that is available to humans, not to be content with subhuman performance or demand superhuman deeds. Theories that provide a fairly reliable short-run guide for action can be used with profit; the ongoing human situation provides opportuni-ties to correct and improve very weak structures. That too is appropriate, for there is as little chance of learning all the strengths and weaknesses in a complex theoretical structure in a single application as in learning all the characteristics of a living human in a single encounter.

In the real world, collective decisions are simplified to some extent by the overriding importance of avoiding catastrophes or disasters. In the long run, learning what to avoid and how to avoid it may be far more important than learning how to achieve particular, positive results. In part that comes from the need to expect a certain amount of failure and therefore the need to learn how to benefit from such experience. If efforts to produce improvements in the human situation that fail are regarded as learning opportunities, some good can be squeezed from them. Failure to avoid serious disasters can put an end to experimenting. It can be argued, for example, that failure within the U.S. government to guard against disaster in the public housing program introduced in the 1937 Housing Act effectively ruled out the development of a viable public housing program for decades into the future. To some extent, the capacity to avoid disasters depends on the quality of the culture and the effectiveness of the socialization process, with complications already noted briefly. In stable eras, when life styles remain fairly constant between generations and levels of gross dissatisfaction are modest, the primary dangers to be avoided, and the choice situations with which they are associated, become fairly well defined—and populations are highly sensitive to them. When social conditions are changing rapidly, generations caught in the transition may face a much more difficult situation. To have danger cues for situations that no longer occur or are no longer dangerous is psychologically taxing at least. Not to have adequate indicators for what are real dangers can be lethal or highly disruptive. That creates a genuine social dilemma. Youth must learn the early-warning signals in order to survive; what is available to be learned may not be adequate. It follows that youth should be trained to develop their own warning signals, but that goal is easier stated than accomplished.

The Normative Variables

Actions generate a range of consequences, some trivial and others of great importance. Those consequences are stated in terms of a selection of normative variables and other, "nonnormative" variables. Each variable will refer to some attribute or characteristic of an individual or class of persons. Choices are argued and justified by linking the values taken by the set of normative variables in each situation to the conditions of life of the person(s) to whom the variables refer.

A small modification of the diagram of chain reactions produced in figure 18.1 on page 151 can suggest the way in which the normative variables (NV) are incorporated into the structured outcomes projected by theories.

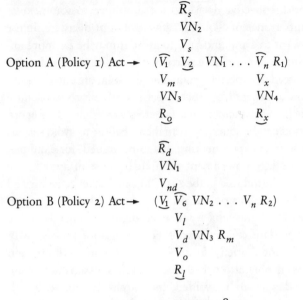

$$
\begin{array}{ll}
& \widehat{R}_s \\
& VN_2 \\
& V_s \\
\text{Option A (Policy 1) Act} \rightarrow & (\widehat{V_1} \ \underline{V_2} \ \ VN_1 \ \ldots \ \widehat{V_n} \ R_1) \\
& V_m \qquad\qquad V_x \\
& VN_3 \qquad\quad VN_4 \\
& \underline{R_o} \qquad\qquad \underline{R_x}
\end{array}
$$

$$
\begin{array}{ll}
& \widehat{R}_d \\
& VN_1 \\
& V_{nd} \\
\text{Option B (Policy 2) Act} \rightarrow & (\underline{V_1} \ \widehat{V_6} \ VN_2 \ \ldots \ V_n \ R_2) \\
& V_l \\
& V_d \ VN_3 \ R_m \\
& V_o \\
& \underline{R_l}
\end{array}
$$

FIGURE 18.2

To simplify the drawing, a choice between two options is assumed; see figure 18.2 above.

Assume that each of the actions available to the actor has the effect of changing the value of the first variable in the structure (V_1), but the amount of change will vary considerably. The repercussions that follow are captured in the chains. The normative variables appear at different points in the structure. The decision must take all the normative variables affected by the action into account; for ease in comparison, they are usually gathered together to form a decision matrix. The size and complexity of the matrix will depend on the number of actions available, the extent of the repercussions, the available theoretical apparatus, the normative variables employed, and so on.

One practical addition can be made to the structure. At the boundaries of present theoretical capacity there are usually a number of "gray areas" where relations are suspected but not yet firmly established. The relation between smoking and lung cancer, for example, was suspected long before it was firmly established, and firmly established long before it was fully accepted—and some continue to argue that the evidence is insufficient. Such suspected or "possible" relations can, under some circumstances at least, influence the decision to choose one option rather than another. For example, if experts generally agree that certain substances are a likely or possible source of brain damage in children, that opinion could, even in the absence of wholly convincing evidence, justify excluding those materials from baby food pending further inquiry. Much depends on the nature of the problem, the manner in which opinions are expressed, and the kind of reasoning or argument used to support the suspected relation; expert judgments are rarely formed on no basis whatsoever. A parent's assertion that local school lunches are likely to produce sterilization in children is unlikely to be taken seriously, other things equal; a similar judgment by highly regarded medical authorities would almost certainly lead to further inquiry and perhaps an immediate suspension of the lunch program. The structure of choices is readily extended to take such considerations into account.

The Decision Matrix

When the outcomes from which a decision or choice must be made have been projected to the limits of theoretical capacity, and any suspected important relations have been added in an appropriate place, it is usually helpful to select out the normative variables, each with a projected value, and bring them together into a matrix of rows and columns. Matrices serve to demonstrate the content of a set of options in a very economical way, and the structure greatly facilitates systematic comparisons. That is particularly true because it is usually good strategy in choices involving a large number of options to look for reasons to rule out certain options quickly. Matrices make it easier to locate normative variables that take grossly unacceptable values and therefore rule out the options in which they appear, other things equal. The physician, for example, will rule out immediately any options available in treatment that would lead to death or disfigurement for the patient if they can be avoided. Although it is useful to have fairly accurate measures of the normative variables, rough measures based on subjective estimates can be quite effective, especially as a point of departure.

A simple illustration is found in the following chart:

Normative Variables	Value Option 1	Value Option 2
NV_1	high	high
NV_2	76	81
NV_3	weak	unknown
NV_4	strong	moderate
Probability of occurrence	50%	60%

Even such weak measures as these can be adequate for decision, depending on the meaning of the variables. The matrix has the added virtue of emphasizing the need to accept a complete option, a full column of variables as they appear in the matrix. That rules out the common practice of focusing on the benefits expected to follow from particular actions and ignoring the costs attached to them.

The principal hazard associated with the use of such matrices to depict choices is that it will impart a static character to the outcomes from which choices must be made. A matrix appears as a cross-section of an ongoing process. Yet the consequences of action are extended in time; what is included in the matrix is limited by the availability of reliable theories. It would be wrong to select a point in the development of those consequences, freeze the action by determining the values of the normative variables at that point, and base the decision on that set of values. The chooser must take into account the full effects of action (and they extend over time), as far as they can be projected.

The solution to this problem is not a three-dimensional matrix, for the added complexity would greatly reduce the value of the structure. It is found in the normative variables, which refer to the projected over-time effects on individual lives of a particular action in a given situation. Those variables, to be examined in more detail in the following unit, serve to collapse the film clip of the future in which the effects of action have been captured into a still photo. They do so by referring to a life as a whole and not to the state of life at a particular moment in time. We can therefore expect the normative variables to differentiate between permanent and temporary changes introduced into the life, and to capture the "branching" effect on life produced by certain kinds of actions—as certain diseases affect more and more of the human body over time.

Exercises

Review Questions

1. What are the factors that tend to direct individual attention to particular actions or choices? Illustrate.

2. Enumerate some of the considerations involved in projecting the outcomes from which reasoned choices are made.

3. In what form are the consequences of action stated? Why?

4. How does the element of uncertainty or risk involved in projections of future outcomes affect choice? Illustrate.

5. Draw a simple chain reaction illustrating the effect at home of an announcement by you that you have decided to leave the university.

6. How does limited knowledge affect the film clips that contain projected outcomes of action?

7. What role can "suspected" relations play in real-world choices? Illustrate.

8. Why is the use of a matrix to show the content of the outcomes from which choices are made an advisable procedure? What risk is involved?

Discussion

1. What are the implications for socialization of the fact that an individual can "make" a choice and be wholly unaware that it has been made? Illustrate.

2. If a young person raised in sparsely populated country was suddenly transferred to the city, what parts of previous training would have to be abandoned and what kinds of new socialization would have to be acquired?

3. Discuss the broader implications of the rule "It is unacceptable to cure the illness by killing the patient."

19. The Normative Variables

In a theory of knowledge intended to provide a basis for action, the central concern is the individual choice, for that is where the empirical and normative knowledge created by generalizing experience is brought together and applied in an effort to improve the human situation. Such choices are criticized or justified by comparing the conditions of life of those affected by the action in each of the options available to the actor. Since every set of outcomes could in principle be conceptualized in any number of different ways, some selection of variables must be agreed upon, otherwise the options could not be compared systematically. Apples and pears can be compared in terms of any of their shared properties, and the fact that some properties are not shared can emerge from comparison and be expressed in comparative terms; but if one observer focuses on color and the other notes only the shape, the two observations are incomparable. Formally, comparisons depend on the fulfillment of certain conditions: There must be two or more things to be compared; and one or more continua must be identified and used to make the comparison. Otherwise, what occurs is discrete observations of two separate entities.

In reasoned choice, common continua are supplied by the normative variables. For reasons already discussed, those variables will refer to the significant dimensions of individual human life, taken as a whole. The normative variables identify the factors considered significant when the quality of an individual life is being assessed. There is no need for an absolute measure of quality, but the concepts that are to be used in such comparisons must be identified and the selection justified. In the process of justifying preferences, different weights will be attached to the normative variables as they appear in choice, but that is a function of the particular situation and does not affect the process by which variables are selected.

Structurally, the normative variables are very complex, as will appear shortly. Each variable will share two essential features, required by the initial assumptions on which the theory of knowledge depends. The first, already noted, is that each variable will refer to the significant dimensions of human life, considered as a whole. Second, the individual lives that serve as a reference point for the variables will be equal, in the limited sense that there can be no grounds for preferring one to the other unless additional information is available about the particular lives being compared. The effect of action, then, is to improve or worsen the condition of one or more human lives, and these effects are weighed in justification or criticism. There is no way to decide in the abstract what set of normative variables should be accepted and used by everyone, obviously, but the structures and processes involved in creating and applying the normative variables can be identified, and some of the problems associated with use can be discussed.

The Structure of the Normative Variables

The meaning, and unavoidable complexity, of the normative variables is best demonstrated by developing them progressively from the simplest possible base. A point of departure is provided by a descriptive account of the individual affected by action *prior* to the action taking place. Every person can be described fully, although not completely, in terms of the observed values of some selection of variables. In principle, the set of variables that could be applied to the person is infinite, therefore the description is always incomplete. Some set must therefore be selected to make the description; it can include any dimension of the individual from such purely physical attributes as height or weight through psychic states, learned skills or acquired capacities, legal rights, relations with others, and so on. Not every aspect of individual life is equally important, of course, and the importance of particular dimensions of life may vary over time. But some variables are so critical for the quality of life that others can be ignored. If the central nervous system ceases to function properly, for example, most other dimensions of life lose much of their importance. The life that serves as a reference point must be three-dimensional, including extension in time as well as breadth and intensity. And when choices are being made, the whole life is taken into account, for the meaning of particulars is indeterminate if the whole remains unknown. Which aspects will be included in any given choice depends on the situation, the actual effects of action, and the content of the ethic applied to the situation.

A descriptive account of any individual can be shown in a fairly simple diagram, as here:

$$[V_1 \ V_2 \ V_3 \ V_4 \ V_5 \ V_6 \ \ldots \ V_n]$$

All that is required is a selection of variables; the values of those variables are determined by observation at a particular point in time. For the moment, the "normative" variables in the selection can be ignored. The selection is shown enclosed in square brackets to indicate that it is not a calculable pattern or logic.

The effect of one person's actions on another person, or on the self, will occur in one of two ways: (1) the action may produce a change in the value of one of the variables used to describe the person; or (2) the action may prevent a change in the value of one of those variables that would otherwise have occurred. That is, Jones's action may change the value of Smith's "pain felt" variable from neutral to positive, or it may prevent such a change from occurring—say by interfering with the actions of another person seeking to inflict pain on Smith. Change is the basic indicator of action; unless some change occurs in the value of one or more of the variables that describe the person, or fails to take place when it is otherwise expected, there is no effect or impact. The first-order consequences of action can always be stated as a specific change in the descriptive account of the individual affected, and that is the first step in the development of normative variables able to measure the effects of action on the quality of life.

The immediate impact of action, the change introduced into a descriptive account of a person by another person's actions, is not in itself an adequate basis for choice. That is, the initial change produced by action is not always a good or adequate input of the impact of that change on the individual's life. A hypodermic needle may produce only a tiny hole in the human skin and yet cause near-instant death; in other cases, the body may be so badly mauled that survival seems unlikely and yet the long-run effect on the life may be trivial. Further, some of the variables used to describe an individual have no normative significance; they function as connecting links between external actions and the individual life. These connecting variables will be called *inputs* and symbolized as *(VI)*. In the first step in systematic analysis, the values of these variables must be linked to specific actions or changes by appropriate theories. In the developing diagram of the normative variables, these input variables can be separated from the rest, creating a subset of factors directly accessible to change by the actor, who may be another person or the person concerned. The result then appears as follows:

$$[[VI_1 \ VI_2 \ldots VI_n] \quad [V_1 \ V_2 \ V_3 \ V_4 \ V_5 \ldots V_n]]$$

$$\textit{Inputs} \qquad\qquad\qquad \textit{Description}$$

Both input variables and the complete set are enclosed in square brackets, since both are selections of variables, not connected by rule, and therefore not calculable.

The immediate or direct effect of action is the change in the value of some input variable that appears in the description of a person or the inhibition of such a change. How much impact that initial change will have on the life of the person depends on the kind of change that occurs and the mitigating effect of other characteristics or attributes of the individual. In some cases, the effect of the initial change is the same for virtually all persons, regardless of their other attributes. Thus, a bullet directed through the brain tends to produce the same impact for everyone. In other cases, the impact of a specific change will vary enormously from one person to another. The effects of a monetary loss, through theft or the imposition of a fine, will depend on the amount of the loss and the income or wealth of the individual concerned. In other words, some of an individual's attributes can mediate the effect of some kinds of changes, although not all changes can be modified in this way. These mediating or conditioning attributes are captured in variables that will be called *buffers* and symbolized as *(VB)*.

The effect of action on individual life, then, is a function of the input and buffer variables, acting in combination. If the buffer variables are also separated from the descriptive account of a person, the overall structure now has the following appearance:

$$[[VI_1 \ VI_2 \ \ldots \ VI_n] \quad [VB_1 \ VB_2 \ \ldots \ VB_n] \quad [V_1 \ V_2 \ V_3 \ \ldots \ V_n]]$$

| *Inputs* | *Buffers* | *Description* |

The structure has now developed a very useful additional characteristic: The set of buffer variables, taken collectively, can identify a class of persons who will be affected normatively in precisely the same way by a common change in the value of an input variable. A social policy intended to produce a particular impact or outcome will succeed only if it is applied to people who share a common set of buffer variables, each taking roughly the same values. Otherwise, the effects of action, normatively speaking, will differ from person to person. Thus the impact of a fixed payment each month or week, such as unemployment compensation, will be the same for all persons sharing the same set of buffer variables and values, and different for those who do not. Identification of critical sets of buffer variables, which will bound populations who are targets for significant collective actions, will therefore be an important task for those concerned with assessment or criticism of those actions.

Once the effects of action have been structured to this point, and both changes in the values of input variables and stated values for the relevant buffer variables are known, the way is cleared to assess the impact of the change on the individual's life. The variables used to make such assessments are properly identified as *normative* variables. Without trying to determine what they will be (and it is reasonably clear that they will include such things as state of health, levels of psychic satisfaction, access to resources, and freedom of inquiry and action), a great deal can be said about the apparatus required to determine their value.

Whatever specific normative variables may be employed, the value taken by those variables will be a complex function of the amount of change induced into the inputs by action and the values taken by the relevant buffer variables. To complete the apparatus, a set of rules must be created linking those two values to the value of the normative variable. In the case of a monetary fine, rules are needed that will combine the amount of the fine with, say, the level or income or of wealth, to produce a measure of the impact of that change on the total life, stated in terms of some normative variable(s), such as access to recreation or freedom from physical restraints on action. The rules need only be rough and loose, indicating cutoff points and other limits that mark desirable and unacceptable levels for the values of those variables. The variables themselves, as noted in the previous unit, must take into account both the amount of change and the duration of change, hence will refer to such things as "permanent physical restriction" or "temporary sensations of acute pain." As long as calculation will generate a preference for one set of values for the normative variables rather than another, the requirements for directing actions are fulfilled.

The structure needed to state the effects of action in normative terms can now be completed. It will include input variables, buffer variables, various descriptive variables that play no part in judgment and can be dropped, a set of one or more normative variables, and a set of rules for determining the values of those variables from the values taken by specific inputs and buffers. While it may seem large and forbiddingly complex, the fact is that the structure is a commonplace in everyday affairs, although use is not generally self-conscious and deliberate, and therefore not always very accurate. The reader need only project the effect on his or her own life of a large and unexpected expense or a major temporary disability to see how readily and efficiently the apparatus is handled in practice, and how adequately it deals with the kinds of considerations involved in assessment.

$$[([VI_1 \; VI_2 \ldots VI_n][VB_1 \; VB_2 \ldots VB_n][R_1 \; R_2 \ldots R_n]) \; [V_1 \; V_2 \; V_3 \ldots V_n]]$$

← —————— *A Normative Variable* —————— →

The normative variable is shown enclosed in parentheses ( ) to indicate that calculations can be used to establish the value of the normative variable by applying the rules to the values of the inputs and buffers.

The substance of the normative variables, the dimensions of life as a whole that should be used to measure and compare the effects of action, cannot be identified in general terms, although it is usually possible to deal quite effectively with particular cases. Most of them will be derived from current ethical systems, perhaps revised to meet the special requirements added when they are intended for use in reasoned choice or action. As in empirical theory, it is more important to develop the capacity to correct and improve over time than to attain reasonable certainty before application. If criticism begins with a real, particular case, some basis for a solution can always be found in the culture. That provides the essential point of departure for improvement.

Some Applications

Perhaps the most important thing to realize about the normative variables is that they cannot be generated in the abstract but emerge fairly readily in concrete situations—in combination with culture and tradition. The best evidence for the validity of approaching them piecemeal in this way is the universal availability of the apparatus in everyday affairs. There is a strong tendency to assume that normative variables applicable to every and all situations must be created at the outset. Focusing on individual cases serves to counteract that inclination at least partly. The goal in every application is a working solution to the particular case; the point of departure for the development of the apparatus is always the particular case, analytically at least. The normative variables required for dealing with a particular case will depend on the situation, but the effort cannot begin in a vacuum, else it will not begin at all. If a problem is recognized as a problem, that indicates that there is already some apparatus in place on which criticism can build.

To illustrate the ease with which the analytic apparatus can be applied, consider the situation discussed earlier of the worker trying to decide whether or not to accept a new position. Some of the changes in input variables (income, physical location, and so on) are obvious, and assuming an "average" family, with appropriate buffer variables, some of the normative problems involved are readily explored by those involved. The children, for example, would be separated from their present friends, recreational outlets, and from the grandparents. Discussion can handle such problems very easily. The physical separation is an input variable; what effect would a change in that variable have? Well, there would be a period of upset and unhappiness (normative variable), but that would not last long; the children are young (buffer variable) and make friends readily. On the positive side, the children would have the pleasurable experience of a new physical and social environment (normative variable). Further, it could be expected that the children would gain some amount of emotional maturity and stability from the move (another normative variable), perhaps offset temporarily by the effects of the new environment.

If the children were in close and frequent contact with the grandparents in the present location (buffer variable), separation might be taken more seriously by the parents. The effect of separation (input variable) would be felt in a different set of normative variables and by a different set of persons (not just the children themselves). The desirable effects of continued interaction on both children and grandparents, measured in terms of current pleasure as well as such things as formation of long-term behavior patterns or characteristics, might weigh heavily in the parents' ethical system, heavily enough to lead them to forego the benefits of the change to allow the children to maintain close contact with the grandparents. As long as discussion focuses on the quality of the life, taken as a whole, rather than on factors that contribute to the quality, it is not difficult to argue that particular outcomes are beneficial even if it proves very difficult to specify exactly what benefit is involved. The justification for arguing that a life that contains a particular element is preferable to a life that does not can rely on testimony from those who have tried both situations and reacted to them, the judgments of qualified experts who have tried to examine such effects systematically, and so on. The conceptual apparatus used for dealing with the normative dimensions of life does not have to be very precise to be useful and open to improvement, and that is the central concern, given the present state of the available knowledge.

The structure of the normative variables is complex, and the concept itself is difficult, and this has been a hard unit to absorb. Concentrate on the overall apparatus, on the way in which the apparatus is developed, rather than details. The problems raised are discussed and exemplified in other units. That clears the way for a discussion of the apparatus actually created for dealing with choices, the priorities and policies required for directing choices.

Exercises

Review Questions

1. Trace the evolution of a normative variable, beginning with a simple description of a person and isolating the input and buffer variables that influence changes in the value of the normative variable.

2. What are the limiting conditions governing systematic comparisons? How do they influence the projection of outcomes required for reasoned choice?

3. Under what circumstances would a normative variable be included in a projection even though it took a zero value? Illustrate.

4. In what sense do the buffer variables identify a class of persons affected in the same way by a given change in the environment? Illustrate.

5. Give an example of a change in an input variable for which there are no available buffers in individual life.

6. Give an example of a change in an input variable that will affect two different people in radically different ways.

7. How is the long-run effect of action reflected in the normative variables? Give an example of a normative variable that takes this into account and another example of a normative variable that does not.

Discussion

1. Compare the relative capacity of wealth and good health as buffers. Indicate some of the changes that each can and cannot influence or modify.

2. Any variable can be normative; it all depends on the situation. Discuss.

3. Discuss the relative usefulness of different sets of buffer variables for grouping the populations affected by collective action. Which variables would you want to include in a population inventory intended for developing social policies? Why?

20. Priorities I

Considered instrumentally, a priority is a structure or pattern that organizes the set of outcomes available for choice in a particular situation according to normative criteria. More precisely, a priority identifies the preferred outcome within an available set. In propositional form, it asserts: "Outcome A is preferable to outcomes B, C, D . . . N." The content of the priority is generalized and the structure applies to any situation in which the full set of outcomes appears and the limits attached to the use of the instrument are satisfied. When applied, the priority should *force* selection of one of the available options as the preferred outcome.

Meaning

The relationships embodied in a priority, the organizing principles on which it depends, are normative or ethical: A priority identifies the outcome that *should* be selected from a given set, the outcome whose selection can be defended or justified on normative grounds. The meaning is, of course, derived from the analysis. An instrument able to perform that function is essential for directing human actions on defensible, corrigible grounds. That meaning therefore serves to limit the kinds of reasons that can be used to defend priorities, and the kinds of applications that can be made of them. A brief summary of the more important characteristics of priorities, conceived in this way, will suggest the major limitations on development and use.

Priorities are created out of a systematic comparison of outcomes and applied to a range of outcomes; they are comparing devices. The preferred outcome identified by a priority is "preferred" only with reference to the other outcomes available to the actor. Priorities therefore do not provide an external or absolute measure of some property such as "goodness" or "rightness" that is to be maximized through action. The reason for limiting the instrument to comparisons is found in the requirements for reasoned choice and the limits on human capacity. Even if criteria of "goodness" or "rightness" could be agreed on, if choices are to be made it would still be necessary to find ways of locating the "better" outcome or the outcome that was "more right" than the others, and of choosing outcomes that were neither good nor right. Defensible choice requires a comparison of two or more outcomes in all cases. If more than one outcome were considered good, or if none of the outcomes was good, then "goodness" would not provide a basis for action. In human affairs, such situations are commonplace. Since choices are based on comparison, and refer specifically to the set from which choice is made, an outcome need not be "good" to be preferred, and may be preferred without being "good." Priorities identify comparative desirability or preference. That simplifies the task of justifying the priority but restricts the use that can be made of priorities for other purposes, particularly those purposes that are currently being pursued in moral philosophy or ethics.

From a slightly different perspective, the meaning of *preference* as it appears within the analytic framework differs significantly from the meaning of such other relative evaluative terms as *utility* in economics or *value* in decision making. "Preferred" refers to an assessment of the normative qualities of the lives of the population affected by action that is independent of the person making the choice. "Utility," in contrast, implies a referent, a person or collectivity that serves as a base point for measurement or assessment. Elimination of that reference point should reduce the likelihood that unacceptable biases will be introduced into the justification offered for action. Nevertheless, it requires development of procedures and criteria able to free the justification of priorities from any particular actor's perspective without sacrificing the validity of the justification—a requirement that will be satisfied here in due course.

Finally, the ethical dimensions of action captured in the priorities are quite different from the psychological dimensions of action sometimes used as "reasons" that explain and/or justify particular actions. A priority identifies the outcome that should be selected or preferred within a given set and not the outcome that is most likely to be chosen under specified circumstances. The "reasons why" an action is taken are not equivalent to the kind of ethical justification required for reasoned action. A somewhat nasty illustration can sharpen the distinction and suggest its importance. If a choice *must* be made between the lives of two children by reason of circumstances (a fireman in a burning building can save only one child, for example), and no information is available about either child, there is no basis for choosing one rather than the other. But if it is known that one child is normal and healthy, while the other is very badly disabled and unlikely to survive to maturity, the decision is readily made and justified, although it would be very difficult to implement. If, however, the mother of the disabled child were to make the choice, she could reasonably be expected to make, and give reasons for, a quite different preference. In both cases, "reasons" would be offered to support the decision. But the content of the two sets of reasons, and their ethical import, would be different. The critical apparatus used for assessing actions must be able to differentiate between these two kinds of reasons and adjudicate them.

Developing Priorities

Like any other intellectual instrument, priorities are developed inductively from the particular case, and tested or justified by reference to particular cases. The most important procedural requirement is that development begins with a real, particular case, for the same reasons that a classification of birds begins with observations of real, particular birds. Cases may be aggregated, but it is the particular case that matters. The reason for emphasizing the point so strongly is that a particular case must be solved *before* a priority can be created. Priorities generalize the solutions to particular cases; the solution must be available before it can be generalized. Of course, the reasons offered to support the solution provided for the particular case will refer to the whole body of relevant past experience, to a whole class of cases, and not to one case alone. The solution for the particular case is necessarily prior. If the essential features of an important class of cases is captured accurately in the generalized priority, it can be applied to each of them and may be a very useful tool. At the other extreme, the priority may be useful only for dealing with the one case — no further members of the class may appear.

To summarize, a priority provides a normative base for action, fulfills the normative requirement for action, in a particular situation or class of situations. The justification for the priority is found in its capacity to indicate the preferred outcome. The justification for the preference, which is the more narrowly ethical aspect of the process of developing priorities, is found in a comparison of the available outcomes by reference to past experience with the conditions of life that appear there. The preference must be justified before the priority can be created; the priority must be available before action can proceed, even in the case from which the priority was generated. What kind of justification is needed, and should be accepted, for a preference or priority is discussed in the following section.

Inductive Ethics: Advantages and Disadvantages

The inductive/comparative approach to developing priorities, beginning
with the particular case and generalizing, offers a number of distinct advantages over traditional or conventional approaches to ethics if the goal
is a guide to individual or collective action. Those advantages are secured
at a price, however; various limitations must be observed in the development and application of priorities, and they need to be made explicit. The
following discussion is again analytic, and the sequence of actions by which
priorities actually develop is unlikely to follow any particular pattern in
real cases, but all the requirements must be fulfilled, and limitations honored, else the end product will not function as expected.

Happily, human actions take place in an ongoing system, and all decisions are based to some extent on the apparatus already in place, on sets
of prior assumptions that are often incomplete, suppressed, or even unknown. The search for priorities cannot, and does not, begin with a blank
slate. If it did, little or nothing would be accomplished, for there would
be no normative variables available to identify significant events, no organized experience to use in justification for preferences. It would be literally
impossible to invent all those requirements first. The ongoing and at least
partly repetitive character of real-world events provides the necessary opportunities for articulating, elaborating, testing, and refining the various assumptions required for reasoned action. The full set of underlying assumptions, which would include the epistemology used as well, is almost certainly
unknown and may be unknowable. That is the reason for insisting that preferences be justified out of past experience using a pragmatic or purposeful
link; without these elements, the apparatus would not be testable or justifiable. Put another way, a systematic effort to analyze current practice, to
identify the basic assumptions on which present actions depend, is an essential feature of the maintenance and improvement of any ethic. Over time,
it can clarify points of disagreement, reveal conceptual inadequacies and
inconsistencies in reasoning, and provide a point of departure for further
improvement of the normative apparatus, individual or collective.

The primary advantages of the inductive approach to ethics have already been touched on. First, no more is required than *some* reason for
preferring one outcome to others; in the absence of competing reasons, any
reason can be decisive. There is no need to seek absolute measures of normative quality, which again simplifies justification. Within the epistemologi-
cal/methodological framework, reasons can be offered for accepting certain kinds of reasons for preference and rejecting others, and that provides
a foundation, however minimal, on which to construct a critical system.

Second, the inductive/comparative approach to ethics forces attention to the full costs and benefits of action, thus avoiding the common error of focusing on selected benefits and ignoring costs. What is chosen or preferred must be the complete set of consequences contained in the film clip that projects the expected results of action. That outcome cannot be chosen without prior comparison of the content of each of the available alternatives, avoiding the practice exemplified by the Roman emperor judging the two finalists in a singing contest: Having heard the first singer, he promptly awarded the prize to the second. Such judgments are beyond the capacity of ordinary humans. There is no avoiding a full examination of the relevant dimensions of all the options, insofar as they can be foreseen, with due regard for the uncertainties associated with the theoretical projections.

As a corollary, focusing on real, particular cases effectively rules out efforts to use the result of imaginary cases, literary illustrations, or hypothetical problems as evidence in argument about real-world actions. Imaginary cases are sometimes useful for clarifying meaning or illustrating a point, but they carry no weight whatever in argument. Of course, if there are reasons to suppose that at least some of the essential features of real cases have been incorporated into the hypothetical case, that is another matter— but in such instances, the relation is abstracted rather than merely hypothetical or imaginary.

Finally, the fact that a particular case must be resolved before a priority can be created forces development of procedures and criteria that are adequate for handling nonrecurring or unique choices. The decision to drop the first atomic weapon on a civilian population, for example, is both unique and nonrecurring. Given the enormous importance of some such events, a critical apparatus that could not deal with them would be seriously inadequate. What is needed is a sharp distinction between the recurrence of a specific case, the appearance of another member of a limited class of cases, and the availability of generalized prior experience, developed from a number of cases, that is relevant to the decision that must be made. If nothing in past human experience can be linked to the case at hand, the actor is helpless; there is then no alternative to pure trial and error, acting randomly to generate information that can be used in subsequent cases. Such conditions, if they occur at all, are extremely rare. In most instances, some of past experience can be linked to the case at hand providing a better-than-random basis for action. In such circumstances, proceeding experimentally and cautiously is probably a good strategy, but the uncertainty level will have been reduced to some degree, and improvements should come more rapidly, and at lower costs, than would be true with pure trial-and-error learning.

The principal hazard associated with inductive development in ethics, or in "bottom-up" development in any field of inquiry, is failure to notice and eliminate internal inconsistencies or contradictions. If each case is solved uniquely, and only real cases are dealt with as they arise, the overall priority apparatus or ethic is likely to develop unevenly. Some areas will be fairly well developed; others will remain virtually untouched. The opportunities to check internal consistency between one area and another will be limited, and since each element has its own independent existence and unique justification, there is little reason to seek support from allied areas. As the structure grows in size, the likelihood that inconsistency will not be noticed increases, for within each area a justification will be sought in the root cases in that area. Elements of the priority apparatus can be integrated or "reduced," as in scientific theorizing, and efforts to produce such reductions will reveal inconsistencies very quickly. But "reduction" is characteristic of well-developed disciplines and is unlikely to occur in ethics for some time. The possibility of generating a set of overarching principles that could be used to test every ethical proposition (from which every ethical generalization could be deduced) is not merely remote but impossible in principle, for even if that state were achieved, it would not be possible to give reasons for believing that it had been achieved.

A further complication is produced by the fact that not every element in a choice must be given a priority; all that need be identified is the preferred outcome. Where elements of the ethic intersect, a transitive ordering must be maintained, else the system may contain contradictions. That is, if A is preferred to B and B is preferred to C, then A must also be preferred to C, else there is a contradiction within the system. The need to identify only the preferred outcome in a set much facilitates the ordering: All that need be done is begin with any two outcomes, find reasons for preferring one and discard the other, then compare the "winner" with another one of the outcomes, discard the "loser" again, and continue until the full list of options has been exhausted. That procedure facilitates comparison, but makes it more difficult to maintain a transitive ordering. Further, combinations of variables are ordered as a whole and not by reference to their elements. If $(A + B)$ is treated as a unit, and preferred to C, there is no implication that A must be preferred to C or B must be preferred to C. That feature of priorities is useful because it provides a basis for compromise and negotiation, but it also tends to make internal consistency more difficult to achieve and maintain.

Eliminating Perspective Bias

In the justification of preferences, it is essential that the bias associated with particular individual perspectives, or special relationships between the individuals affected by action and the individuals who assess the action, be reduced or eliminated. In psychological terms, elimination of such bias is difficult at best and perhaps impossible. But analytically, a very simple procedure will lead to the desired result: In justification, the *identity* of the individuals whose lives are affected by action is separated rigorously from the attributes or characteristics of those individuals, including their relations with others. Nothing of substance is lost by the separation, for all the relations, and effects of relations, can be projected for a given situation and incorporated into the outcomes. While it might be desirable to suppress wholly the identities of all persons affected by action, that is impractical and not really necesary. But the justification used to support a preference for one outcome over the others must refer only to the conditions of life of those affected by action, to attributes and not to identity. Basing a justification or decision on the identity of those involved becomes *prima facie* grounds for rejection, a violation of the assumption that one life is the equal of any other, *qua* life. There may be differences in the weights attached to the various attributes of the individuals affected by action, or to the effect of action over time, but that is a matter for discussion and sufficient grounds for contesting the judgment.

Put another way, abstracting the identity from the attributes serves to separate the ethical from the psychological dimensions of action and allows justification to focus on what should be done, judged by the outcomes or consequences, regardless of the actor involved or the identity of those affected. That serves to rule out the use of such observer-relevant concepts as utility, and to eliminate pure selfishness or solipsism from justification. The separation of identity and attributes will not stop the use of identity in justification, overtly or covertly, but it does provide a base for locating and eliminating such indefensible foci without undue effort or analysis.

Avoiding Perfectionism

The strategy of inquiry in ethics, if an action orientation is accepted, tends to be forced by procedural and structural requirements. Clearly, inquiry begins with an examination of current practice, seeking improvements. That in turn implies concentration on the particular case. And most important, there is no reason to seek, and every reason to avoid, the kind of perfectionism that sometimes plagues philosophic ethics. A commitment to acceptable solutions to real problems means that the solution need not be any more precise than present capacity allows. Crude and effective measures, if they are the best available, can serve as a launching pad for improvements. So long as the "Caligula syndrome" is eschewed (the search for ethical structures that will function equally well in all situations, whether they are applied to moral monsters like the Roman Emperor Caligula or everyday people), improvement is possible. Despair and frustration can be avoided, together with their companion error, undue optimism. It is very difficult indeed to get very far above, or very far below, the currently accepted priorities in society. What is likely to happen in the long run is highly uncertain. The focus of concern is, necessarily, short-run improvements that can be justified as improvements. Surely a society that does not use torture to squeeze confessions from accused persons has improved its ethic over a society that continues the practice? If that much can be agreed on, future progress lies within human capacity.

Exercises

Review Questions

1. What is the precise meaning of "priority," and what function does it perform in action or choice?

2. How does a priority relate to a preference? Illustrate.

3. Why is a comparison required in the justification of preference? What implications does this have for the use of concepts such as "goodness" that are external or absolute measures?

4. What is the difference between the ethical and the psychological dimensions of action? Illustrate.

5. Trace the steps in priority development, using an example from experience.

6. Explain why a particular preference must be justified before a priority can be developed.

7. What is meant by "transitive ordering," and why is it important? Illustrate.

8. How can the influence of bias be reduced within the analytic framework? Illustrate.

Discussion

1. What are the major advantages and disadvantages of an inductive approach to ethics?

2. How does a strategy of avoiding perfectionism in ethics require acceptance of pragmatic criteria for justifying ethics?

3. Why is it impossible to follow the Roman emperor who heard the first contestant and gave the prize to the second? Under what conditions would it be possible to do this legitimately?

4. To what extent do the requirements for reasoned action focus attention on the particular case? In what circumstances would cases be aggregated?

21. Priorities II

Priorities are created by generalizing preferences that have already been established for particular cases. A priority is justified initially by showing that it can identify the preferred outcome in a given set of options. Ultimately, justification depends on the reasons offered for preferring that outcome. The principal normative or ethical task in reasoned choice is to provide a justification for preferring a specific outcome from among a particular set. Here we focus mainly on the set of conditions that an adequate justification must satisfy rather than try to justify any particular preference. The problem is far too complex to be dealt with adequately in a single unit, or even a whole volume, but some of the basic considerations involved, some of the limitations and possibilities, can be examined briefly.

Justifying Preferences

The first point that needs to be made about the justification of preferences is that any effort to produce generalized criteria of adequacy couched in substantive terms, to identify broad principles that can be applied to real cases, is almost certain to fail. The reason is simple: The act of preferring refers to such an enormous body of human experience, marked by so much variety, that specific generalizations are invariably subject to so many exemptions, complications, and limitations that the intellectual system overloads and ceases to function effectively. There is no alternative to focusing on the particular case if choice is to be dealt with in substantive terms. Given a real case, observation and relevant experience will usually serve to constrain discussion enough to make agreement, or fruitful argument, possible.

Methodologically, however, a great deal can be said about the procedures, possibilities, and limitations encountered in efforts to produce or evaluate justifications for preference without trying to support any particular preference or principle. At a minimum, the boundaries within which solutions to particular choice problems can be found are at least partly identifiable, and they provide a point of departure for further development.

Such general analysis will not solve the problems encountered in action, but it can suggest some of the conditions that real-world solutions must fulfill, and that is very useful, both for developing solutions to real cases and for justifying/criticizing/improving them.

Bear in mind as the discussion proceeds that in any inductive inquiry, there is no final or absolute standard for judging knowledge claims. In an inductive ethics of the kind suggested here, as in physical science, the ultimate court of appeal is the available body of informed opinion and current practice. That may mean all the physicists who specialize in a particular field, all the carpenters who construct particular kinds of furniture, or all those who can deal competently with a particular kind of preference. Informed opinion comprises those persons who are fully informed about the state of knowledge in a field and competent in the application of the conventions and criteria that control argument and judgment within that field. Much more is involved than firsthand experience with the phenomena in question. Informed persons must also be familiar with the available body of recorded human experience, with the criticisms or assessments of that experience voiced by others, and with currently accepted criteria for dealing with knowledge claims relating to the field. Having experience is not enough; that experience must be examined self-consciously, systematically, and competently. And when all is said and done, there remains an irreducible element of "judgment" involved in choice that cannot be specified fully and completely—and therefore cannot be automated or computerized. It can be tested only against another judgment.

When informed opinion is unanimous, or nearly so, its judgments will tend to be decisive in the field. That is, they will be considered adequate grounds for accepting or rejecting knowledge claims and the justifications offered for such claims, and an adequate base for directing the search for further knowledge. That gives informed opinion great power, but raises the danger of stifling innovation and creativity. If there is no consensus among the informed, knowledge claims will remain uncertain or be decided on irrelevant grounds. This construction of inductive inquiry and its implications may not fit too well with the notion of an exact and powerful physical science in which judgments are readily made and justified, but the inductive mode of inquiry is required in all areas, not just in physical science, and the results obtained by applying it vary considerably depending on the subject matter, and the state of knowledge.

Primary Assumptions

From a methodological perspective, the central problem in an ethics intended as a guide to action is to articulate the set of assumptions that make it possible to achieve the purposes of the inquiry—in this instance, to justify preferences for particular outcomes. Some of the primary assumptions needed in an ethics of action have already been noted and justified; four are especially important here. First, the focus of inquiry is always the particular case; efforts to create priorities begin there, and the priorities themselves are tested there. Second, the central normative concern is the individual human life; radical individualism in ethics is unavoidable. Third, with respect to life itself, one human life is the equal of every other life, although only in the limited sense that if none of the specific attributes of two or more lives are known, there is no defensible way to weight them differently in choice. Fourth, the justification for preferences must be found in human experience. Even taken together, these four assumptions do not constitute a sufficient base for developing priorities, but they are a necessary underpinning for any acceptable justification for preferences. They therefore provide grounds for rejecting some priorities and for ruling out certain kinds of justification, grounds that are particularly useful for assessing the quality or validity of collective actions.

The Human Focus

In any particular case, justification for preference will focus on the conditions of life of the population affected by the action; those conditions will differ in at least some respects in the outcomes available for choice. Reduced to essentials, reasons must be found for preferring one projected state of existence of one or more persons to other, different projected states for the same individual or group. Those projections must capture at least three primary dimensions of the human lives involved; or, to put the point differently, the normative variables must deal with three basic aspects of human life. First, there are the internal or subjective states of the person, directly accessible only to the individual concerned. Second, there are the objective or external attributes and features of the person, including relations with the external environment. Third, there is a social dimension to every life and action. All three aspects must be taken into account in justification.

In a very simple form of choice, only one human life is involved and two options are available, differing only in the value taken by one variable. But even in that grossly oversimplified situation, a complex range of considerations must be weighed or assessed. From the perspective of the individual, two film clips must be projected, beginning with the present. One projection contains the life expected to follow if the course of events is allowed to continue unchanged; the other shows the life to be expected if the capacity to act that makes choice possible is exercised. Each projection contains a life; the two lives are different; a preference for one or the other must be established (or the choice must be shown to be a matter of indifference given the accepted ethic).

Perhaps the best metaphor for the concept of life employed in comparison is a sustained and uninterrupted journey, which begins and ends for all persons in roughly the same state. What matters is the quality of the journey, taken as a whole. That quality cannot be judged by reference to the subjective, objective, or social dimensions of life alone; all three elements must be considered. Overall quality cannot be determined by focusing on the parts; the whole journey must be assessed. Further, comparison cannot be limited to what is observed; the critical apparatus must be able to reveal dimensions of life that are absent yet could be supplied. And finally, the implications of the choice for the other passengers taking the journey, and for the effect on individual life of the activities of the other passengers and the character of the vehicle involved, must be taken into account. Even a very simple choice raises the full set of considerations, requires attention to a range of influences and side effects that are themselves in a state of flux.

Some of the major implications for reasoned action of accepting that overall perspective on justification have already been discussed and can be summarized quickly. First, the normative variables used to structure the effects of action will refer to specific attributes of individual lives. Although the collective features of society, or the aggregate characteristics of groups, are very convenient to use, they have no intrinsic significance. They are useful in reasoned choice only if a relation can be shown between social features or aggregate characteristics and the conditions of life of specific persons. The model to follow here is the relation between a physician and his patients: There are various purposes for which it may be convenient to aggregate patient data and treat them collectively but not, except in very rare situations, for purposes of treatment.

Second, if individual lives are assigned a different weighting in choice, such differences require justification. The basic assumption, that one life is the equal of any other, is the bedrock on which a viable ethic depends. Of course, differentiation is justifiable in many different situations, but the basis for differentiation will be the relation between the *attributes* of the individuals concerned and the *purposes* for which differentiations are made. Selecting individuals to play on a football team serves to differentiate them, or weight them differently, but that differentiation is readily justified if it refers to the relation between player attributes and game requirements. If the differentiation is based on other factors, such as race or family relations, or any factor not linked to the purposes of the game, it cannot be defended.

Third, choices have a temporal dimension—what is chosen is a film clip and not a still photograph. The consequences of action may take years to work themselves out fully. The duration of specific effects, the sequence of effects and their timing, are often very important for assessing options. In contrast, comparison and weighting demand stability; the outcomes must be fixed in order to make comparisons. The problem can be partially resolved by using concepts that refer to the conditions of life over time rather than at particular moments in time, but success is difficult to achieve, and this aspect of justification requires careful monitoring.

Finally, each human life is in some respects unique, and that uniqueness is reflected in the outcomes expected to follow from action. If there are known differences among individuals, the implications of allowing the flow of events to continue, or of introducing a particular change, can be expected to differ to some extent from one person to another. That has great importance in collective actions. Unless outcomes can be structured to group together all those affected in the same way, normatively speaking, by a common action, justification of choice is out of the question. Even such seemingly "neutral" collective actions as the imposition of universal military conscription turn out to have very different implications for different subpopulations in society. And if exemptions from military service are allowed for such reasons as sex, physical disability, educational status, or occupation, differential impact is guaranteed if the grounds for exception are unevenly distributed within the overall population.

The Social Context of Choice

For all practical purposes, every human action takes place in a social context, in an environment that contains other persons as well as various organizations and institutions. That social context provides an important channel for affecting individual lives indirectly—not by direct action of other persons. Collective actions in particular produce changes in social conditions and institutional arrangements that are reflected ultimately in the conditions of life of members of society, and serve to differentiate them. To take a broad illustration, the potential for life of any given individual will vary with the economic, political, and social organization that characterizes the society. If one assumes a child with exceptional potential for mathematical development, for example, the extent to which that potential will be realized will vary enormously, depending on the society in which the child is born, the status of the child's family within that society, and so on.

The effect of the social environment, and of collective actions in particular, is to modify or "load" the content of the options available to individual actors. Of course, governments are abstract entities and cannot "act" in the same manner as an individual; governments act always through individuals. Those actions serve to alter the outcomes expected from individual actions within that government's jurisdiction. Thus a government accomplishes its purposes by rewarding specific actions in particular ways (paying its employees, for example) or by punishing or penalizing certain kinds of actions (fining those who speed on the highways); in both cases, the probability of reward and punishment can vary from near certainty to very low levels of likelihood. From the individual's perspective, assessment of options must therefore include considerations of the "loading" that government has imposed, with due regard for the probability of enforcement. The problem of individual choice is complicated somewhat by adding the social factor, but not altered in any fundamental way.

Examined from the collective perspective, a different situation appears. The central question, clearly, is "What options should be loaded, in what way, and for what reasons?" If collective actions are to be justified in the same manner as individual actions, and there seems no reasonable alternative available, then the basic evidence used to justify collective decisions will be the behavior of individuals within society in the absence of collectively imposed impediments or restraints. That is the sense in which government is the prime controller of the aggregate implications of individual actions freely taken. And that requirement provides the base from which a justification for democratic government, or more accurately self-government, can be created. Governments serve as instruments for developing and applying a collective ethic. From this perspective, the procedures and criteria used to judge collective actions are the same as those employed in individual choice. The consequences of collective actions are likely to affect larger populations than private decisions, and some problems will be encountered that may not appear in private choices, but the basic decision-making apparatus will be the same.

The existence of a multistate system, however, serves to complicate the situation. Governments must respond to the actions of other governments, and their actions will affect other governments. It follows that the members of a society may be very seriously and adversely affected by governmental actions targeted outside the society, and populations in other societies may suffer from collective actions that are ostensibly "domestic."

In principle, it seems unlikely that reasons could be found to justify the use of different standards for "internal" and "external" decisions. A human life is a human life, whatever the nationality of the person might be. In fact, however, all governments have tended to develop different sets of priorities, and very different normative variables, for dealing with foreign and domestic affairs. Indeed, if they did not they would soon lose their authority, for every organization depends on differentiation between members and nonmembers for its existence. The violation of the assumption of individual equality involved in the use of such dual standards, which can be justified by the value of the organization to those involved, has been extended radically and unfortunately by the widespread use of features of society as normative variables in justification of foreign relations—such terms as *national security* or *vital interests,* which have their domestic counterparts (*political stability,* for example), tend to shift attention away from the effects of action on particular individuals or populations.

In domestic affairs, the major problems in collective ethics tend to relate to the differential distribution of capacity for action, of the knowledge and resources needed to control the flow of events, that characterizes society. Such differences reinforce very strongly the tendency to differential weighting of human lives apparent in the history of human society. Clearly, if the collective ethic does no more than reflect the realities of power distribution within society, it can hardly rise above selfishness of a kind that is intellectually indefensible. History suggests that no society can rely on every individual to function in an ethically acceptable or defensible manner without coercion; collective action is normatively essential even if the collective effects of individual actions are ignored. Put another way, the kinds of lives that people actually live will be a function of the application of two sets of ethics, one individual and one collective. In case of conflict, the social ethic usually overrides that of the individual. Society appears historically as the primary instrument available for developing and enforcing a collective ethic that can be justified in reasoned terms. And since society can also become an instrument for augmenting and reinforcing the power available to private individuals, the self-governing society emerges as the best mechanism available for developing and applying an ethical structure that is optimally beneficial to all of society's members. Working out the meaning or implications of that possibility, and suggesting how it might best be achieved, has been the classic function of political philosophy and political science generally.

So much said, there are limits to what can be accomplished through collective actions, and to the human capacity for reasoned justification of actions, that bear noting. In general, reasoned decisions must be made at a level in society where the implications of the decision can be examined in sufficient detail, where the relevant experience is available in enough detail to allow for reasoned justification for action. That implies the fullest possible degree of devolution of decision making to the level of the individual actor. As far as possible, the individual ethic should control individual action; collective actions are almost invariably inferior in quality, other things equal. Further, however systematically choices may be structured, and however carefully arguments and justifications may be phrased, there will remain an irreducible element of judgment in the final decision to act. Put another way, choices incorporate a translogical or nonformalizable element that eludes complete specification. Ultimately, there is no alternative to providing the human individual with as much relevant information as possible and allowing that individual to control, and take responsibility for, his or her own actions. That condition may be regarded by some as a tragedy and by others as the triumph of the "human" over the mechanical; regardless of such assessments, it remains an immutable limit on social capacity.

Reasons and Justifications

From yet another perspective, the justifications offered for preferences can be seen as a combination of two elements or factors: (1) the affective reactions of living humans to the outcomes from which choices are made; and (2) the intellectual constructions of human life and its potentials or possibilities that determine what gives life meaning or significance and provides life's satisfactions. In any ethic, both elements are essential. Without affective support, the most sophisticated of intellectual constructions would lack force; without intellectual guidance, the most powerful of affective impulses could also be the most destructive.

Affectivity is simply the built-in capacity for differential reaction to differences in the environment that characterizes the human individual. Such reactions occur regularly; they are reported in factual terms. Affective reactions are therefore evidence that is useful for arguing about preferences. In some cases at least, they can be decisive. The principal weakness in argument based on affective reactions, of course, is that affectivity can be conditioned, and in all cases is socially/culturally linked. Since everyone lives in society and must function there, the linkage is extremely useful. But too many of the problems encountered in individual and collective action cannot be resolved by direct affective responses alone. At a minimum, some way is required to take into account the long-term as well as the short-term effects of action. Otherwise, harming the physician who causes pain in the course of healing the patient, and similar aberrations, could not be avoided. That means is provided by the intellect.

The justification offered for preferences, then, will depend primarily though not exclusively on intellectual reasoning, on an intellectualized conception of life as a whole. The effort to develop the necessary intellectual apparatus, or to adapt the existing structure to fit new limitations and possibilities as they emerge, is the most challenging task facing every generation in every society. As Michael Oakeshott once stated the problem, we sail a boundless sea without harbor for shelter or ultimate destination. In those circumstances, there can be no worse disaster than foundering the ship, and no greater accomplishment than finding ways of improving the lives of those on board. The tools available for the task are limited; all of them are derived from a history of past experience that is partial at best and never corresponds perfectly to the present. Yet that history is the only possible source of the information and knowledge needed for plotting the future, for developing the capacity to introduce modifications into that future, and for arguing that such modifications should be regarded as an "improvement" and not merely a change.

Exercises

Review Questions

1. Why does justification for preference necessarily focus on the particular case?

2. What is meant by "informed opinion"? What role does it play in the development of knowledge? What are some of the implications of that role for the settlement of disputes about knowledge claims?

3. What are the four primary assumptions on which the proposed approach to solving choice problems depends? Can you justify or defend each of them?

4. What are the three major dimensions of human life that need to be taken into account when justifications for actions are being produced?

5. What are the four major implications of focusing on individual life as the primary concern in choice?

6. Explain the function of government in individual choices and how that function is carried out.

7. What are the two primary factors that enter into justification of choices?

Discussion

1. Which of the three basic dimensions of life (subjective, objective, and social) should count most heavily when they conflict? Illustrate.

2. Under what circumstances should affective reactions be allowed to control actions without interference from the intellect?

3. What is the major limitation on what government can regulate from a central location, and what implications does it carry for the organization of governmental functions?

4. Would you oppose or support a proposal to install direct democracy in the United States? Why?

22. Policies I

The importance of something called a *policy* is recognized almost everywhere, whether it refers to public or private affairs. But in daily use, the meanings attached to the term are so varied that systematic criticism and improvement is out of the question until meaning is stabilized. In most cases, any formal statement of intentions, goals, purposes, ideals, or actions is accepted as a *policy statement* as long as it is made by an official spokesman, particularly if it includes the word "policy." The concept is extended to include everything from "it is our policy to pursue peace and stability in the Middle East" to "it is our policy to vote against recognition of any territorial transfer based on force." Even academic writings tend to leave the meaning of *policy,* and its companion concept, *theory,* undefined.

When the meaning attached to a basic concept needed for dealing with human affairs is defined in different, incompatible ways—in ways that do not allow for systematic criticism and improvement—that is a matter of concern for everyone. For if statements that use the term can have different meanings, then criticism, which is always directed at meanings, is effectively ruled out. So long as one person thinks of "policy" in terms of goals, while another thinks of it in terms of actions, they cannot communicate effectively. And if basic concepts remain undefined, the listener or reader is faced with propositions whose meaning cannot be determined and whose validity cannot be assessed. At a minimum, concepts require clear definitions and consistent application if the quality of intellectual performance is to be improved.

Policy: Meaning and Function

Concepts intended for use in the conduct of human affairs must have meanings that are consistent with experience, labels that are compatible with current usage, and a place in a critical framework where their uses and limitations can be examined. In the context of reasoned choice or action, a meaning for *policy* has already been established that satisfies those requirements. Once a preference has been justified for a particular choice and generalized into a priority, an action program is needed that will actually produce the preferred outcome. It will consist of two or more interlocking theories, linking specific actions to the preferred outcome. Such action programs are the best candidate available for the label *policy*. They are needed for reasoned action, they lie within human competence, and they can be justified and improved out of experience using the analytic framework. They are exemplified perfectly in the mode of treatment prescribed for a particular illness or in a cookbook recipe. Their meaning corresponds very closely to sophisticated usage in such places as government policy papers.

Although some of the better examples of policies that are reasoned and corrigible are found in such fields as medicine or agriculture, there is no need to look for complex problems or large and powerful organizations to study the policy-making process or to practice systematic criticism. All the essentials appear in everyday affairs. The football coach who teaches his players how to block an opponent effectively and reliably has provided them with a policy for producing the preferred outcome in a variety of situations that recur regularly in play. The retail store that refunds the purchase price of goods that have not been damaged if they are returned within a specified time period has developed a policy that all store members can apply. Even the individual who "makes it a rule" not to drive an automobile after drinking more than two glasses of beer or wine or one glass of stronger stuff has fulfilled all of the requirements for making "policy."

To satisfy the requirements for testability, an action program (policy) must be precise and detailed enough to force a specific set of actions in any situation where it applies. The reason for that requirement is very important. What is actually tested and improved in action is not the action taken. Actions are not improved; instead, actions are changed to produce a different outcome. Actions serve as a test of the assumptions that direct (force) the action. If the action is not forced, required logically once the assumptions contained in the policy are accepted, there is no test. If action fails to produce the preferred outcome, the assumptions that forced the action must be altered; the new set will force a different action in the situation the next time it occurs.

There is a limit, however, to the directive capacity incorporated into a policy. The most powerful policy that can be specified is so accurate and complete that it can be implemented through an automaton or stated in a computer program. Such policies may be possible in special circumstances, but they are not likely to be adequate for dealing with significant human affairs. The actions forced by most policies are stated vaguely enough to allow or require some interpretation by the person who applies them. The salesclerk responsible for accepting merchandize that has been returned to a store that allows full refunds if certain conditions are met must determine whether or not those conditions have been satisfied. The surgeon who performs an appendectomy will adapt a generalized set of instructions to the particular situation found during the operation. Interpretation, or modification, of policy is the rule rather than the exception in human affairs. Policy application is not button pushing. That characteristic of policy making has some significant implications for those who design policies, for those who apply them, and for those who train the persons who will apply them in future. The question how much leeway should remain in a policy, how much freedom of interpretation and action to allow those who apply it, is a nice matter for judgment in policy making. The answer will depend, among other things, on the kind of activity involved, the training and experience supplied to those who apply the policy, and the importance of the outcome.

One of the consequences of the incompleteness found in most policies meant for use in human affairs is an urgent need to incorporate an adequate monitoring system into every serious effort at policy making, and most particularly in collective affairs. That need tends to be obscured in the case of individual actions because the policy-making and monitoring functions are combined in a single person; no additional machinery is needed, although it may be useful to sensitize the individual to the need for monitoring the effects of action. The function of monitoring, and the need for incorporating it directly into policy making, is best seen in the context of the operating-room/recovery-room nexus in a hospital. Here, the monitoring apparatus is always installed in advance, and designed to provide early warnings of every significant change that can be anticipated. The reasons are obvious; waiting until the operation was performed to install a monitoring system could have catastrophic results for the patient. Of course, the monitoring apparatus may be modified in use, but that is another matter. Further, it is relatively easy to see why the kind of operation performed could under some conditions be influenced by current capacity to monitor the patient afterward. A policy or operation whose effects could not be monitored would be very risky and difficult to justify except in extreme cases.

The conditions under which collective actions are carried out tend to emphasize the value of creating an adequate monitoring system as policy is developed and applied. Public actions usually have an impact on large, mixed populations; the administrative apparatus tends to be cumbersome, and information flow may be slow and inaccurate. Yet the rate of change in industrial society can be very rapid, and the intellectual apparatus used in policy making is usually weak. In these circumstances, it would be foolish to expect a perfect program at the outset, and even if it proved relatively successful, modification could be expected at some future stage.

Since policy-based action tests both the policy and the priority involved, monitoring design must produce information adequate for testing both elements in the structure. Assuming the priority, a policy is tested by comparing results expected with results achieved; that requires information about the effects of action on the target population—a sufficient sample is needed to allow generalization to the whole of the affected population. Testing the priority is a more difficult task. Information is needed that will allow comparison of the conditions of life produced by the policy to the conditions of life within the alternative available outcomes, a comparison that is made in the context of informed opinion and current practice.

Finally, the effects of the administrative structure used to apply a policy, the "delivery system" currently in place, are part of the outcome produced by policy and need to be monitored together with the other effects of action. At a minimum, monitoring should identify changes in policy that are introduced within the administration, for the policy tested in action is the policy applied and not the policy adopted formally by an organization or government. More broadly, information is needed about the primary side effects generated by application, including such things as economic costs as well as less tangible effects caused by insensitivity or incivility.

Corollaries and Implications

Before defensible and corrigible policies can be expected, some fairly stiff requirements have to be satisfied. In some areas of policy making, individual and collective, personal and private, many of these requirements are already being met most of the time; in other areas, very substantial changes would be required. It is therefore important to note that those requirements are not arbitrary; they are no more than the consequences that follow from accepting the need to create action programs for applying priorities to human affairs that can be justified and improved. Further, the criteria can be and have been met; they are within human capacity. It may be necessary to reserve systematic criticism for special occasions, since it is likely to be time consuming and relatively expensive. But if policies are to be justified, the limitations must be respected. Otherwise, both policy maker and critic are like the drunkard searching for lost keys in a lighted area because it is difficult to see in the area where the keys were actually dropped.

Separating Policy and Priority

One of the more seriously misleading features of contemporary usage is stating policies in injunctive form. We are told: "Take two aspirins every hour," "Stop at all intersections," "Avoid alcohol while driving," and so on. Of course, policies must be stated in specific terms, otherwise they cannot be applied or tested, and the injunctive form serves to emphasize that requirement. But it also tends to suppress the element of comparison on which reasoned action depends and thus to collapse the policy and the priority structure into a single unit. That can lead to serious problems in justification and testing.

Stated fully, a policy asserts that "*if* priority P is accepted, then policy PO must be followed in situation S." The reason, of course, is that following policy PO will produce the preferred outcome as identified by priority P. Policies are rules of action, not statements of preference. If the policy and the priority are collapsed, the substance of the rule will be a preference and not an action. In effect, that substitutes an ethic of rules for an ethic of consequences and thus violates one of the primary assumptions on which the theory of knowledge is built. An example can clarify the point. The injunction "Do not remove any fish from this lake if that action will disturb the ecological balance of the lake" sounds like an action program in the negative. But it actually requires a prior preference ordering, a decision about the effects of action on the lake. If a policy is properly formulated, it serves to apply a priority, and that judgment (preference ordering) must already be made—no action rule could be formulated unless it had been shown that the preferred outcome would follow. To state a policy in that form, then, is already a clear indication of fundamental analytic confusion.

A further reason for maintaining the separation of policy and priority is found in the requirements for testing. Applying a policy, as noted earlier, tests a combination of empirical and normative elements and not just the policy alone. Examination of the results obtained may lead the actor to seek improvements in theory (the predicted outcome did not appear), in priority (the predicted outcome appeared but experience suggested it was less desirable than previously believed), or in policy (the rule did not produce the preferred outcome). Somehow, these effects must be separated. To illustrate, consider a choice among coins using a priority that asserts "Prefer more monetary value to less monetary value." A rule of action or policy such as "Choose the largest coin" will produce acceptable results given a choice between ten, twenty-five, and fifty-cent pieces. But if a choice is offered between a small and valuable coin and a large but almost worthless coin, the rule will not produce the preferred outcome. If the priority is examined and retained, the policy will have to be modified. Either the application will be limited to choices among ten, twenty-five, and fifty-cent pieces or a fairly complex set of rules (policy), of the type employed by coin dealers, will have to be created.

Suppose further that a choice is offered between coins of approximately the same monetary value: One coin is stipulated to be worth slightly more than the other, but the second coin has fairly substantial sentimental value for the chooser. Applying the established policy will satisfy the priority system based on monetary value and leave the chooser in possession of a coin with slightly more value than the other, but dissatisfied. In such cases, both priority and policy may have to be modified. If sentimental value is added to the normative variables, a fairly complex rule would be needed to show how that variable would be weighted against the other normative variable, monetary worth. Otherwise, use of the original policy could be restricted to cases where monetary difference was large and the value of other normative variables such as sentimental value was slight.

The use of the injunctive form to state policies is permissible, and even desirable, as long as such limitations are respected. But the common practice of treating ideals, aspirations, and unattainable principles as priorities from which policies can be derived, or as policies in themselves, is utterly unacceptable. Ideals, or unfulfillable aspirations in any form, are by definition goals that lie beyond human capacity—states or conditions that cannot be attained. Structures of that kind have no role whatever in reasoned choice. The reason is unimpeachable. Any goal that lies beyond human reach cannot be linked to a human act; there is no way to determine whether or not any particular action results in a shift toward the goal or away from it. Statements about the relation between action and goal, however, require an unbroken chain of connections between the two. Lacking such a chain, there is no guide to action. And if the road to the goal *can* be charted, then it no longer qualifies as an ideal or unattainable (in principle) outcome.

Causes and Cures

Every policy has a normative purpose, for it applies a priority. Put another way, policies are created in order to improve an observed situation or produce an improved situation as measured by the accepted ethic. In that context, policy making is very much future oriented; the policy maker is concerned almost entirely with cures rather than causes, with ways of improving existing conditions rather than reasons why existing conditions came into being. Knowledge of causes is valuable or essential only if (1) such knowledge is essential for producing a cure; or (2) it can be used to prevent a recurrence that would otherwise be expected. In fact, there is no need to know the origins of most human situations in order to improve them, any more than the physician needs to know the cause of a disease in order to treat it effectively. The classic example is diabetes, whose cause remains unknown but whose treatment is well established and reliable. Of course, knowing the cause of an event may greatly facilitate development of more effective or efficient treatments, in medicine as elsewhere. Knowing the chain of events that leads to malaria in a human individual can suggest a variety of intervention strategies for reducing the incidence of the disease—killing live mosquitoes, killing larvae, avoiding mosquitoes, and so on. The primary emphasis, however, should be placed on cures; the search for causes is validated by their contribution to the production of cures or prevention.

A useful corollary to the commitment to seeking cures rather than causes is the need to study successful actions rather than failures. To a surprising degree, systematic inquiry at present focuses on failures, particularly in social science. The addict is studied endlessly; the individual who acquires no addiction is usually ignored. The minority group that is discriminated against is examined carefully; the discriminating populations, whose behavior must be modified before a "cure" could be expected, are less frequently studied. Focusing on cures rather than causes would do much to remedy such misdirection. Further, a focus on cures should serve to emphasize the value of seeking ways to prevent outcomes rather than change them after they occur. To take a very common example, it is well known that a few simple rules of behavior that include eating proper food, getting enough rest, and exercising adequately would do more to improve health within the industrial nations than all the medical research that contemporary resources can buy. Yet the resources spent promoting such actions amount to only a tiny fraction of what is spent in the search for remedies. Parallel opportunities for preventive actions need to be actively sought, particularly in collective affairs. The progress made in health by immunization practices should also be possible elsewhere.

Composites and Aggregates

If policies are construed as guides to action, or action programs that will produce the preferred outcome in a given situation, that effectively precludes discussion of such composites or aggregates as "housing" policy or "foreign" policy. Such terms may be useful for indicating a rough collection of disparate policies that relate to a common administrative jurisdiction, but they are unlikely to be very useful for critical or analytic purposes. Formally, the use of gross aggregates, taken seriously, is only a special kind of division fallacy. A nation's "housing" policy can be improved only be dealing with its constituent elements; attacking "housing" policy in the aggregate is an exercise in futility.

A useful device for clarifying the status of policy statements that refer to large composites or aggregates is to use automobile accidents as a model. Until the aggregate of all automobile accidents is broken down to show causes, there is no way to know how to decrease the number of accidents short of removing all automobiles from the highways—the latter "policy" can be developed formally or logically. Reducing speed limits, often suggested as a way of reducing accidents, already supposes that a relation between rates of speed and number of accidents has been established. And in the event such a policy is adopted, accidents will continue as long as some result from different causes. In such situations, it is useful to speak of efforts to reduce automobile accidents because it simplifies a complex process. But there can be no "automobile accident" policy because the members of the aggregate will respond differently to different actions—they are heterogeneous with respect to cause. Instead, a range of policies is needed, each dealing with one or more of the specific, known causes of accidents. Those causes must be established before cures can be developed. The example is perhaps overly simple, but the kind of conceptual confusion it is intended to remedy is a very serious matter, particularly in collective affairs.

Exercises

Review Questions

1. Why is it important to have agreement on the meaning of the basic concepts used in a field? Illustrate from an area such as dentistry.

2. What is the precise meaning of *policy* as used in the text. Give an example from personal experience and another from collective affairs.

3. Why must a policy be able to *force* a specific action when applied? Illustrate.

4. What is meant by saying that policies are completed in application? What is the implication of that condition for policy design?

5. In what sense does action test both policy and priority? What are the implications for testing design and monitoring?

6. What are the minimum requirements for reasoned policy making?

7. What reasons can be given for maintaining a strict separation between policy and priority? Illustrate.

8. What are some of the uses and limitations of the injunctive form in policy making? Illustrate.

9. Under what circumstances is it necessary to know the cause of a condition in order to cure it? When is it unnecessary? Illustrate both situations.

10. What are the limitations imposed on the use of aggregates in policy making? Why are they necessary?

Discussion

1. Discuss the implications of having to design and implement policy at a level where the implications of action can be determined precisely.

2. What are the relative advantages and disadvantages of centralization in government? How can they best be exploited?

3. Why is it impossible to determine whether or not a "step in the right direction" has been taken until the entire trip has been mapped?

23. Policies II

Thus far, the primary focus of the text has been the various instruments and processes required for reasoned choice or action. In the present unit, the focus shifts to the use of those instruments in the pursuit of real-world purposes, to the policy-making process and the institutional setting in which it takes place. The treatment is highly condensed and is focused on the conduct of collective affairs in the industrial democracies, and more particularly, in the United States. But the structures and processes, and the guiding considerations, tend to be the same everywhere, in public or private affairs, in individual or collective actions.

Policy Making

Policy making emerges from the analysis of reasoned choice as a very complex and difficult kind of creative activity. That will not surprise anyone who has been involved with the management of collective actions. Considered very broadly, policy making is the application of human knowledge and resources to the conduct of human affairs. The central problem is to create action programs, rules of action, that will lead to the preferred outcome when a particular situation appears, when a given choice is to be made and acted on. A major constraint on the policy maker, of course, is the supply of resources and knowledge available; possibilities are also limited by such things as established attitudes and beliefs and existing institutions. From one perspective, policy making is a form of engineering, a reasoned effort to implement an ethical structure. Unfortunately, *social engineering* tends to be regarded with great suspicion in Western culture, yet that term fits the enterprise almost perfectly. The target population may be a whole society or only a single person, for reasoned action can serve limited and particular interests as well as society, but the focus of concern here is collective decision making or social policy making rather than individual action.

Because reasoned action brings together empirical and normative knowledge, and is criticized analytically or methodologically as well as substantively, almost any contribution to knowledge can find a use some-where in policy making, and the policy maker or critic will have to ex-amine every dimension of inquiry in the production, justification, and test-ing of policies. The intellectual requirements are formidable. Predictions and forecasts may be used to locate areas that require action—projected shortages of certain facilities, for example. Theories are needed to project the outcomes from which choices are made, and to suggest the policies needed to obtain the preferred outcome. Priorities must be available for ordering the possible outcomes; they in turn are dependent on the ade-quacy of the normative variables they employ. Policy making, in brief, de-pends upon adequate concepts, accurate measurements, adequate descrip-tions, sound forecasts and theories, and defensible priorities. They in turn imply an adequate language base, calculating capacity, and the institutional arrangements needed to provide the requisite knowledge. And above all, policy making depends on creativity, for policies are created, not "found" or "derived."

At another level, policy making is constrained by the availability of resources, the level of technology available, the information in hand about the target population, the legal and geographic boundaries established for the exercise of policy-making authority, the normative commitments of those whose agreement is needed before policies can be applied, and the kind of decisioning machinery the society employs. Moreover, beyond creat-ing and applying action programs, policy making is quite properly taken to include the development of an adequate monitoring system and the ma-chinery for modifying policy in use over time. Information must be ob-tained and processed, and the results must be entered into the policy-making machinery—gathering and processing data is not enough. Some of these factors will lie outside the competence of any individual policy maker.

The gap between this conception of reasoned policy making and actu-al practice in even the most advanced of contemporary societies is strik-ing. In general, established practice determines action, for system inertia is very hard to overcome. Significant modifications in existing decision-making arrangments will be needed to establish a sound base for policy making, and such changes are not readily made. The difference between present-day policy making and the kind of policy making that deserves to be labeled *reasoned* can be illustrated very dramatically by comparing present medical practice with medical practice as it would be if collective procedures in government were transferred to that field.

Within medicine, a prescribed treatment for a given illness is precise-ly equivalent to a policy. Medical policies are action programs directed at a well-articulated outcome. The overall purpose is so generally under-stood (to improve the patient's health at minimal cost) that it is not always stated explicitly. Medical treatments develop as generalized solutions to particular cases and are subjected to almost continuous testing and im-provement in use. Evaluation of policies takes into account all the effects produced in all particular applications, insofar as they are reported or iden-tified. In short, medical policy generalizes and summarizes a body of ex-perience with the use of a particular treatment program for a given illness.

If the everyday conception of policy found in current governmental usage were transferred to the field of medicine, it would produce some as-tonishing changes. There would be no effort to determine the needs of each patient or to treat patients uniquely. Instead, the symptoms of a large num-ber of patients would be aggregated, and treatment would be directed at the aggregate, specified in terms of averages. The cost of treatment would be subject to a predetermined ceiling, decided on nonmedical grounds. As far as possible, the effects of treatment would be ignored. If soaring costs or public outcry forced attention to the consequences of using the policy, only those effects favorable to the policy maker would be considered. And in due course, the treatment would be abandoned and replaced, even though it was known to work well in some cases and there was no satisfactory replacement. In many cases, treatment failure would be blamed on the pa-tient. Although it may be hard to believe, that parody is based on a genu-ine case—the development of a public housing program in the United States.

Institutional Arrangements
In the large industrial democracies, two major kinds of changes in current practice would be required if the concept of policy making advanced here were adopted. First, the effects of action would have to be weighed in terms of the effect produced on individual lives, assuming one life the equal of any other. Second, the institutional arrangements used to make policy, di-rectly or indirectly, would have to be modified significantly. Neither change is a real possibility over the short run.

The importance of basing the justification for action on its human con-sequences has already been examined in some detail. If the effects of social action are stated in other terms (social features or institutional changes, for example), the normative significance of the change cannot be deter-mined. Since the conditions of corrigibility then cannot be met, improve-ments in performance will be due mainly to accident. At present, collec-tive actions are only rarely justified or criticized by reference to specific changes in lives of identifiable populations. In fact, the information and knowledge that would be needed to produce such justifications is not generally available.

To be more specific, reasoned policy making requires enough baseline information about the population whose conditions of life are to be altered to determine the actions required to produce the desired change. But an adequate inventory of national populations is nowhere available. The data supplied by most national censuses are inadequate if not inaccurate. In the United States, such vital questions as the amount of unemployment in the society and the attributes or characteristics of the unemployed cannot be answered very accurately—only rough approximations can be generated. Further, it would be difficult and expensive to create an inventory of a large population that would be adequate for all social purposes. An eye specialist and a foot specialist may be concerned with the same patient, but each wants specialized information that would be of little value to the other. A single examination intended to serve both users would be expensive, particularly if it was applied to persons requiring neither kind of attention. Nevertheless, it *is* possible to develop in medicine a good general checklist, an inventory of the person, that is worth the cost and provides a solid base for more detailed examination. A similar structure is badly needed in society as a whole for dealing with an individual's "human" health.

The absence of a social inventory is a serious limit on the policy maker. At one level, reasoned policy making is only a special kind of inventory management. Inventories serve to locate portions of the overall population whose living conditions are so inferior to minimal needs, and to most of the rest of society, that urgent action is required. They provide a baseline for measuring inadequacies along particular dimensions. And they serve as a good indicator of the adequacy and humaneness of the society concerned. Such common practices as discounting the effects of action on minorities are readily visible in an adequate inventory, which may be one reason why such inventories are rare. The inventory also provides an indication of the quality of life that society is capable of producing—gives concrete meaning to such terms as *advantaged* and *disadvantaged* in the context of that particular society.

Because the discussion here is concerned with contemporary industrial society, it ignores the gross differences among societies, and some of the serious obstacles to improvement in the human condition found elsewhere. In some parts of the world, maintaining the present condition of the population may require unending struggle; in others, entrenched hostility to change makes improvement difficult. The capacity to make significant improvements in the lives of large populations is a recent human acquisition. Only a few societies actually have that capacity. Technological improvements and increases in wealth have in most cases improved the lot of the well-off far more than they have improved life for the disadvantaged. National incomes have risen rapidly without any improvement in the living conditions of the great mass of the population, or even with deterioration. The industrial nations are a special case on the world scene and not necessarily a bellwether for future changes elsewhere in the world.

Some Required Changes

The kinds of institutional modifications that would be required in most industrial societies to make possible reasoned policy making will vary with the society, but if the United States is taken as an example, three points are particularly important. First, some institution is needed where the whole range of collective decisions can be brought together and rationalized. In the United States, the absence of such an arrangement is considered a virtue, and change would be resisted strongly. Yet it is not uncommon for one element in government to reward what another seeks to discourage or even prohibits. One department may subsidize tobacco production, for example, while another agency spends large sums trying to reduce the incidence of smoking. Second, the legislature is at present used both to develop proposed policies and to decide authoritatively to adopt them. The effect of making both decisions by the same set of individuals out of the same set of pressures and interactions virtually rules out the development of policies that can be justified by reference to consequences. Third, the educational system is not producing the capacity for criticism that is essential for citizens in a self-governing community. The citizens of Athens, whom Pericles extolled as able to judge for themselves in collective matters, are today a rare species. For the most part, the citizen of today is an incompetent consumer of argument and unable to judge the adequacy of evidence used to support knowledge claims, particularly in collective affairs.

The absence of a single point in government where the choice among choices, the decision in which areas to make decisions, is a serious handicap on policy development. Over the years, the budget has come to be accepted as the central focus for national policy making. But, analytically, no budget can serve as a basis for decision, simply because the effects of a budgetary change on a particular population are usually impossible to determine. Even if it were feasible, budgetary practice mitigates against a realistic weighing and balancing of alternative competing courses of action. In most cases, the major segments of the budget—defense, agriculture, social services, education, and so on—are treated as independent elements.

The amount of resources allocated yearly is determined more by prior allocations than by assessment of need. Global limits are set for the overall budget and for each major division, but funds are rarely taken from one part of the budget and given to another because need is demonstrably greater there. That can and does lead to serious misallocations. It also reduces the likelihood that overall governmental performance, measured in normative terms, will improve over time out of experience.

The basic assumption underlying the argument for reasoned policy making is that it is intellectually feasible to provide a justification for acting in one way rather than another by comparison of the consequences produced. That assumption contrasts sharply with the view that policy must develop out of the conflict of competing interests within the political equivalent of the economist's marketplace, the government. Institutional arrangements greatly influence which of these perspectives on policy making will prevail in any given case. When one organization combines the power to determine the content of policy with the power to adopt policy authoritatively, that provides an ideal arena for the development of "interest-group" politics, an exchange of support among major interests so that each interest is satisfied. And since collective actions within legislative bodies are taken by formal aggregation of individual votes, that further supports the process. In such circumstances, responsibility for collective outcomes cannot reasonably be enforced against any particular individual, and the reasons why individuals vote one way or another may have nothing whatever to do with the reasons why a particular piece of legislation should be accepted or rejected. The actions of such collectivities are a special class of "natural" events like earthquakes or floods, analytically at least, and they elude normative criticism.

Various solutions to the dilemma of representation have been proposed, for the problem identified above is only a special case of the dilemma. None has proved very successful. If voters and their representatives both accepted the same concept of the representative's function, and his or her relation to constituents, that might resolve the problem in part, but no such agreement has been forthcoming. Various changes in institutional arrangements have been suggested — cabinet government, a two-party system, separation of the power to draft legislation from the power to enact, and so on. None has proved adequate. It would now be technologically feasible, in some countries at least, to introduce direct democracy, allowing each citizen to vote on every issue through a computerized network, but there is little enthusiasm for it at present — which is surprising, since representative democracy has always been a "second best" system of government required by the impossibility of bringing together all the citizens in a very large and widely dispersed society.

Other institutional arrangements currently in place tend to reinforce reliance on interest-group interaction instead of the search for reasoned policies. One very important factor is the concept of government embedded in the social ethos, the concept of the appropriate role of government that is widely accepted within the population. Very broadly, the American public is firmly committed to government that is "reactive" (not reactionary) in character rather than directive. In a directive system, best exemplified by China or the Soviet Union, the government is heavily engaged in productive activity, and future planning is an integral part of social development. In a reactive system, such as the United States, government does very little future planning and engages minimally in productive action—other than the provision of facilitating structures. Primary responsibility for the quality of life within society is assigned to the individual and not to government. Such political systems tend to react to external pressures, hence are much influenced by those able to generate such pressures effectively. That reinforces the tendency to develop policies out of interest-group pressures, not out of research into potentialities followed by reasoned efforts to optimize or maximize that potential. Indeed, given the substance of the ethos, efforts to generate policies targeted at future improvements might be regarded as incompatible with the basic principles on which the society functions.

A corollary indicator of the factors at work in society that will influence any movement toward more systematic and better defended policies is the use that is made of compromise. No society can function effectively without some capacity to compromise; it avoids the disruption that comes from open conflict. But no society can compromise every issue without a serious debilitation, or failure to develop, of its normative structure. For compromise functions by *evading* conflict over priorities rather than resolving it. If one group prefers *A* to *B,* while another prefers *B* to *A,* and neither can enforce its preference on the other, there is no alternative to compromise or conflict. The impasse can be avoided, however, by altering the content of the choice. That is, if some X can be added to the alternatives so that both groups prefer $(A + X)$ to $(B + X)$, then the dilemma is resolved; since the missing X is often found in the public treasury, that makes for a unique kind of political blackmail. Such compromises avoid a head-on collision, but at a price. Normative structures develop by changing the preference to fit the choice and not changing the choices to suit the existing preference. If the latter procedure is adopted, the normative structure remains frozen or deteriorates.

The massive failure that has characterized education in all the industrial societies is often noted but usually in terms that bypass social implications. By and large, the critical capacity and creative ability needed for self-government is not developing at anything like the rate needed to staff the government adequately, let alone provide a competent citizenry. Assessment of the reasons for the failure may vary, but the inadequacy of performance is not widely disputed. Some of the effects of educational inadequacy are masked by "prepackaging" necessary skills for a wide range of functions. That allows society to maximize the benefits obtained from the available supply of natural talent, but the kind of consumership required of the citizenry at large in self-governing societies is rarely produced. Nor is there any reason to suppose that those who control the schools have any clear notion of the skills required or how they might be fostered, and since knowing what is needed, and how to achieve it, is prerequisite to actual production, that tends to reinforce the judgment that the future outlook is bleak.

Again, there is an important corollary to be examined. In large societies, as in large organizations, there is a marked tendency for more and more decisions to be made in a central location, minimizing the degree of interpretation and judgment exercised at lower levels. Yet the realization that social problems cannot be handled effectively by a small handful of central decision makers is slowly and painfully emerging from contemporary experience, in government and business alike. As the scale of organization increases, the degree of control that can be exercised from the center decreases, and the cost of increasing that control escalates rapidly. The lesson is clear: Reasoned and corrigible policies must be developed and applied at the level where the full implications of the policy can be examined. Policy making is a local function. Central administrations are admirably suited for raising resources efficiently and for rationalizing competing demands on them, but they cannot dispose of their resources as effectively and humanely as local agencies, in principle at least.

The reasons why that dilemma emerges are clear enough. A corrigible policy must be made at a point in an organization where the consequences of action can be calculated accurately in human terms. The information required for such decisions cannot be aggregated without destroying much of its utility, even with modern computers. The process of condensing, aggregating, and generalizing creates a mass of information that cannot be unpacked without engendering enormous information costs. Increasingly, the central problem in government is to create the climate of trust and agreement required for using resources effectively to apply agreed priorities. If the common denominator in every choice is the effect of action on individuals, then increasing the scale of operations forces decentralization of policy making. Even if the common denominator employed is profit, that limitation seems likely to hold. Partly out of the pressures generated by increased demands on government coupled with decreasing capacity to fulfill demands accurately and effectively, most Western nations are converting gradually from reactive to directive systems. As that occurs, the need for intellectual competence will increase at all levels, and the cost of inadequate education will escalate. In that sense, the outlook for reasoned efforts to improve the human condition through reasoned action is intimately and inextricably tied to the future of the educational system.

Beyond the need to adopt and adhere to an adequate conception of policy and begin making the institutional modifications necessary to apply it, two basic steps are required to place policy making on a sound footing in the large industrial societies. First, the priorities and policies actually being used need to be identified and linked to their consequences for the various elements of the population. In effect, the experience that has been produced by past action needs to be collected and codified. Second, the social machinery needed to introduce an element of self-correction into government should be added to existing arrangements or improved where it is already in place. Social organizations, and private organizations, must be able to learn and put what has been learned to use. At present, even serious catastrophes produce little or no learning and future improvement. Partly that is a function of national dislike for governmental interference in individual affairs, maintained despite a vast increase in the level of dependence or helplessness of virtually everyone in society. The belief that efforts to plan lead to a social beehive is a fiction that has endured too long. The beehive is the unplanned product of "natural forces" and not an outgrowth of human reasoning. Indeed, it is human reasoning that informs us that the beehive is an inappropriate social structure and that it is not necessary.

The effort to prevent excessive governmental penetration into individual affairs has had a profound impact on the kind of society that has developed, particularly in the United States. There is a general unwillingness to supply the information needed for adequate policy making; there is considerable reluctance among the governors to try and collect it. The mystique that has surrounded the family, for example, has long shielded some of the appalling abuses perpetrated on the young and helpless by family members. If the role of government could remain small in the foreseeable future, that situation might be acceptable. But today government is the primary institution available for improving the human condition for most of the world's population, and there is no alternative. If it is not harnessed to the pursuit of ethically defensible purposes, then it is likely to be harnessed for the pursuit of purposes that are perhaps less defensible.

Exercises

Review Questions

1. What are the major intellectual requirements that must be satisfied before reasoned policies can be developed?

2. Why is creativity so important in policy making? Illustrate.

3. What are the principal constraints on policy making?

4. What are the major changes that would have to be made in most of the industrial democracies in order to place policy making on a reasoned base?

5. What factors in American society and tradition tend to support a continuation of "interest-group" pressures as the primary source of policies?

6. What are the principal uses of compromise, and what hazards are associated with it?

7. To what extent is a trend toward political centralization likely to reduce the quality of the policies being made by government? Illustrate.

Discussion

1. Why is the budget an inadequate instrument for controlling policy? Could it be made more effective? How?

2. What are the primary intellectual skills required for citizenship in self-governing communities? Why those?

3. Do you think the influence of government on individual life is likely to increase or decrease over your own lifetime? What implications is that likely to have for the educational system? Continuing education?

24. Propositions and Arguments

The primary goal of this text is the development of an analytic framework that can be used to guide or criticize human efforts to achieve specified purposes through action—in effect, to establish the intellectual foundations of reasoned action. The framework is built around the set of human purposes that must be fulfilled through intellectually directed action in the environment. Once those purposes have been established, the various instruments required to achieve them can be determined and ways of developing and testing them can be created. That overall process, which began with the initial organization of perceptions into descriptions and concluded with an examination of the policies used to direct actions, has now been covered, although much detail remains unexamined.

In this unit, the perspective shifts to the relation between the analytic framework and the kind of discussion of human problems that appears in everyday language. The limitations imposed by the overall set of purposes established at the beginning of the text are retained, but efforts to achieve those (and other) purposes are expressed in terms of propositions and arguments and not in the language of the analytic framework. The discussion is meant to serve two purposes: (1) to provide a link between the analytic framework and everyday usage; and (2) to allow a more thorough discussion of the role that formal logic or calculation plays in reasoned argument.

Propositions and Arguments

In the written and spoken language of everyday discourse, the descriptions, forecasts, theories, and justifications used in systematic analysis appear as the content of sets of *propositions*. A proposition states the content or meaning of a sentence; it relates to a sentence in much the same way that a message carried electronically resembles the electric impulses that carry it. A number of different sentences can carry exactly the same proposition or meaning. For example, "John is Mary's brother," "Mary is John's sister," and "John and Mary are children of the same parents" all say exactly the same thing—they contain the same proposition.

Even in relatively simple languages, the number of possible propositions is unbelievably large, and the content of each proposition can be extensive and convoluted. That potential cannot be exploited effectively unless the language is thoroughly learned and can be used to communicate and think both accurately and systematically. As knowledge expands, the need for an ever greater command of language increases also, and that has some important implications for populations that do not have access to a major language. Those implications extend to persons who live in a culture where the language is rich but who do not acquire very much skill in using it. Of course, the *kind* of language skill acquired matters a great deal: Excessive concentration on the way things are said rather than the content of what is said tends to produce literacy or grammatical skill without improving critical ability. Similarly, without basic language capacity, development of high levels of critical ability is very unlikely. Language skill and critical ability must develop together if they are to become an instrument for effective real-world performance.

The propositions used in reasoned argument or criticism all refer, ultimately, to human experience. It follows that no proposition can be regarded as certain or as self-evident (immune to argument or evidence). Reasons must therefore be required for accepting or rejecting propositions. Those reasons, which incorporate the criteria developed within the analytic framework, are also stated in propositional form. Taken together, they constitute an *argument*. Arguments, in that context, are sets of structured propositions that support or justify accepting other propositions. An argument will employ the various instruments developed in the analytic framework (forecasts, theories, priorities, and so on), stated in everyday language, to "make a case for" some proposition or set of propositions. The substance of the argument, the kind of evidence and reasoning required, will depend on the nature of the proposition to be supported—and the kind of evidence available within experience. Eventually, as in analytic criticism, an argument marshalls human experience, in generalized form, to support a set of propositions or assertions.

The Constituent Elements of an Argument

In broad terms, an argument consists of three main elements: (1) a body of generalized experience, organized into the instruments required for dealing with the problem at hand; (2) a set of judgments, required for creating and applying that body of experience; and (3) a set of formal calculations or deductive inferences that link the generalized patterns of experience to particular cases. In that context, argument must fulfill three basic purposes. First, it must show that on the basis of experience, some set of general propositions should be accepted; they may be empirical or normative in content. Second, it must show that once those generalized propositions are accepted, it follows logically and necessarily that certain specific propositions must also be accepted. And third, it must show that the judgments made in the development and application of those instruments are justifiable or defensible or warranted. The parallel to justification within the analytic framework is exact; only the language, the concepts employed, is different.

To illustrate, assume that the proposition to be argued asserts: "When certain types of clouds appear in the sky over Kansas City, rain can be expected to fall there shortly afterward." Analytically, that proposition is a forecast in the form "Observe A, expect B," without a statement of limiting conditions. The argument must establish the validity of the forecast. If the proposition is modified slightly, to assert: "Since clouds of a certain type have been observed over Kansas City, rain can be expected to fall there shortly," the proposition now refers to the *application* of a forecast. Much of the substance of the argument required for the two propositions will be the same in both cases, since each must establish the validity of the forecast, but the proposition that refers to the application of the forecast will require argument that includes additional evidence and reasoning.

To establish the forecast, an argument is needed that will show that what is asserted in the proposition accords well with past experience in Kansas City. That criterion is taken from the analytic framework, and without some such framework, there would be no way to decide *what* constitutes adequate evidence for the proposition. Essentially, the argument will consist of sets of statements that assert that in the past when such clouds have been observed over Kansas City, rain has followed in virtually every case. If the conditions under which exceptions occur can be identified, they can be used to limit application of the forecast. If not, then an estimate of probability can be produced if the body of recorded experience is extensive enough. If the proposition accords well with history, that provides an indirect test of the judgments made during the development of the forecast—in the process of classifying the clouds and generalizing the pattern of experience.

To support an application of the forecast to a particular case, the argument that validates the forecast will be produced first; once it has been established, the proposition containing the forecast then serves as a point of departure for calculating the implications of accepting it for the case in hand—in effect, the forecast is combined with a particular observation and used to generate a prediction. The logical skeleton of the forecast must be abstracted from the proposition, the content of the observation is formalized, and the two are combined formally. The result is a very simple syllogism:

> PROPOSITION 1. *If condition A is observed, condition B will follow* (forecast).
> PROPOSITION 2. *Condition A is observed.*
> CONCLUSION: *Condition B will follow* (the forecast).

Formally, the syllogism shows that once the generalized forecast, or the proposition that contains it, is accepted, and the condition stated in proposition (2) is observed, the predicted event (rain) must be expected.

That conclusion is contingent, however, on the validity of the judgments required to produce the two propositions, and a complete argument will have to deal with that point. The validity of the forecast itself has already been examined. To apply the forecast, an observer must make a judgment to the effect that the clouds observed over Kansas City are indeed members of the class of clouds referred to in the forecast. The argument would therefore consist of a statement of the attributes of clouds of the kind in question (the defining characteristics of the class) and a comparison of those attributes with observations made. If *all* the attributes could be identified, then the class is identified beyond dispute. If a decision is based on observation of only some of the class attributes, the judgment involved would be defended by propositions referring to the results obtained by basing judgment on that selection of attributes in the past.

The critical apparatus developed in the text is meant to be useful in everyday affairs and not merely in academic studies. Before the apparatus can be applied, the purposes and instruments on which it is based must be recognized in propositional form. In most cases, that is not very difficult. Complex propositions may have to be broken apart, but the elements are usually easy to recognize. Thus the proposition "If you provide the right kind of food, that bird will stay in your yard for the entire summer and in the autumn it will migrate, but the winter will be mild this year and it may stay through the whole year" combines a theory (if you provide food, the bird will stay), a classification used to produce a forecast (that kind of bird migrates), and a prediction about the weather to be expected in the winter that is only a prophecy as stated—the reasons for expecting the mild winter are not given—and a qualification on the original forecast (the bird may not migrate if the winter is mild). Happily, such propositions are not usually argued in detail, for it would take a number of propositions, and a whole lot of time, to provide a complete justification for accepting it.

An Extended Example

A somewhat more complex and fully extended illustration may help to clarify the relations between everyday language propositions and the coaching language derived from the analytic framework. Suppose that a young child was seen preparing to jump from the balcony of an apartment on the second floor of a large building. The immediate reaction of adult observers, of course, would be to prevent the jump if at all possible. Assuming the adults were successful and the child then demanded to know why his game had been interrupted, what kind of argument would be required to support the action (preventing the jump), how could the child be induced to accept the argument, and what kinds of counterarguments might be expected to emerge from the course of the discussion?

The initial adult response, which can serve as a point of departure for examining the argument, is simply, "If you had jumped from the balcony, you would certainly have been badly hurt and might have been killed." If the child were a careful listener, the proper response would be to demand to know why "jumping" would lead to such results. If the adults were capable of exercising self-restraint in the face of cheekiness, they would correct the proposition to say that the impact at the end of the fall would be severely damaging and perhaps fatal. The child, whose willingness to argue has already been demonstrated, can then demand to know why the explanation should be accepted. "Why," he asks, "should I believe that my body will be seriously injured and perhaps converted into a corpse by the impact caused by dropping from the balcony?" That question raises all the essential elements in a standard scientific argument; the response requires a valid theory, application of that theory, and correct calculations or inferences. Using current knowledge, a very powerful argument can be produced to support the proposition that the fall would cause serious injury or death. The velocity of the body at impact could be calculated with considerable precision using the law of gravity once the height of the balcony was determined. As long as the law of gravity remained unchallenged, the validity of the conclusion would be inescapable—the conclusion could be *proved* in strict terms. That is, it could be demonstrated that once the general statement that constitutes the law is assumed, together with the rules that constitute the mathematics in use, the conclusion cannot be challenged without self-contradiction. Assuming the calculations have been correctly made and are not challenged, the validity of the proposition relating to the rate of motion at impact has been established.

The child could, however, challenge the validity of the law of gravity, asking why the proposition that the body will accelerate at a rate of 32 ft/sec^2 should be believed. The argument can now move in one of two directions. First, it may be possible to show that the law can be deduced from some still more general law that has already been established. The child could challenge that general law as well, leaving the argument in precisely the same situation. The second option, which will be reached by any argument if pressed, is to begin arraying the experiential evidence that supports the law of gravity. Indeed, some of the effects or implications of the theory might be tested for the child's benefit, including, perhaps, throwing an object resembling the child in size and weight off the very balcony from which he was prepared to jump and measuring its speed at impact with a radar detector of some kind. Indeed, considering the nature of the argument thus far, some might be tempted to throw the *child* off the balcony, but it must be said that the information obtained could not be communicated to the child if the outcome was lethal and that would not lead the argument to a successful conclusion.

We can suppose that the child is overwhelmed by the evidence produced to support the law of gravity and concedes its validity. It then follows necessarily that the calculated speed of the body at point of impact must also be accepted. The child, obstinate to the end, refuses to accept the assertion that the body will be severely damaged, perhaps killed, if it strikes the ground at that speed. "I will bounce," the child asserts, "as I do on my trampoline." Evidence is now being demanded that will link the speed of impact to the damage caused to the body. Assuming again a substantial body of experience that shows that the effect of such impacts is almost invariably severe injury or death, those data can be arrayed for the child. Will the argument end there? Need the child be convinced at that point that the adults have acted properly? Not at all. Several lines of escape are available, in principle at least, before disagreement can be foreclosed.

First, the child seizes on the exemption clause in the evidence. "You assert," he says, "that the effects of such an impact are 'almost invariably' severe injury or death. Perhaps I belong to the exceptional class of cases." The point is valid. The injury or death *may* not follow. In fact, there have been extraordinary cases in which individuals have fallen from aircraft at quite high altitudes and survived with minor injury. The odds against such an outcome, which can be developed from experience, are astronomical. Reluctantly he concedes that the proposition that asserts that severe injury is likely to follow from the fall is correct. He can pause for one final gambit, however, by pointing out that the general rule applies to the class "human beings" and note that his membership in that class has not been established. The adults, who by this time may themselves doubt that class membership *can* be established, may nonetheless adduce the required data (relating to parentage, class attributes, and so on) and produce agreement on this point as well.

One last major ploy remains. "Why," demands the young monster, "should I care one way or another whether I am injured or uninjured, alive or dead?" The argument required at this point is no longer empirical but normative; the facts of the argument have been conceded fully, and the priority to be assigned to the outcomes available is now in question. Can the adults convince the child that it is preferable to be alive and uninjured to being either alive and severely injured or dead? In this situation, the reactions of those who have experienced life without injury and life with serious injury become relevant. The characteristics of life under the two conditions can be detailed, showing differences in levels of pain and discomfort, freedom of action, and various other significant aspects of life affected by injury or by death.

Of course, there is no guarantee that the child *will be* convinced, even though the evidence is so overwhelming that he *should be* convinced. But if the child continues to insist that he should have been allowed to jump, but can no longer provide reasons for taking that position beyond asserting "because I wanted to," the adults are then justified if they argue that the child's arguments are no longer reasoned and persuasive, and continued resistance on his part will result in severe punishment and loss of privileges.

I hope that the "overlay" of the critical apparatus on the propositional narrative is easy to see. Use of the critical framework in everyday affairs requires some capacity for making or detecting such overlays or parallels. Beyond underscoring the need for translation capacity on the critic's part, the illustration serves to bring out a number of important aspects of everyday argument. First, the critic must concentrate on the argument in hand, ignoring the source, or minor annoyances caused by extraneous particulars such as the intransigence of the child. The quality of the argument does not depend on the person who asserts it, or even on the tone and manner in which it is produced, although psychologically it has been demonstrated that such considerations significantly affect what *is* accepted. Finally, the quality of the argument is independent of the competence of the listener.

Quality is based on informed judgment about what *should* bring assent from a competent critic.

Second, note that there is no defense against implacable skepticism. If a proposition is questioned, and an adequate justification is provided, but the skeptic chooses to question the justification, and then the justification of the justification, there is no way out of the infinite regress. In one sense, every argument, in science or in ethics, could end with indeterminacy or an infinite regression. The critic can do no more than produce the best argument possible in the then-current state of knowledge. The unrelenting skeptic is self-defeating, for he or she can believe nothing and therefore cannot produce a foundation for action.

A third point, already encountered, is the importance of taking an argument literally, with as little interpretation as possible. It is both unnecessary and undesirable to engage in amateur psychiatric examinations of the author of an argument, wondering what was "really intended" or why the argument was made in a particular way. If an argument is incomplete, ambiguous, or merely inadequate, the critic need only say so and go on to something else. Of course, it is sometimes useful and even necessary to ask with respect to a proposition of great potential importance whether there *is* a good argument for or against it, disregarding the argument that has actually been offered. The quality of an argument is independent of the quality of the proposition being argued, at least to the extent that a good proposition may be badly argued—the converse does not hold. That does not, however, imply that poor arguments should be followed carefully in the hope of finding useful stimulation: A garbage can is not a good place to search for a steak dinner. And do not be frightened by diatribes against "destructive" criticism. There is no other kind. Indeed, one major function of systematic criticism is the demolition of ramshackle intellectual dwellings, and destruction is not contingent on the availability of a replacement. One does not have to have an alternative pill available before an individual can be dissuaded from swallowing a cyanide capsule.

Finally, the critic has the obligation to open his criticism to subsequent criticism, which means he or she must assert the grounds on which the criticism depends. The intellectual marketplace is one of the few places in human society where the law of the jungle, survival of the fit and death for the weak, is not only defensible but essential. Every proposition should, if challenged, be prepared to fight for its life against all comers. There is an obligation to criticize; an obligation to accept and try to meet challenges. No other basis is possible in the intellectual sphere if the knowledge that humankind must have to survive and prosper is to be produced.

Exercises

Review Questions

1. What is meant by a "proposition," and how does it relate to sentences?

2. Express each of the three primary purposes on which the critical framework depends in propositional form.

3. What is meant by an "argument"? How do arguments relate to propositions?

4. What are the three main elements in an argument?

5. What purposes must an argument fulfill?

6. State a proposition that applies a theory and another proposition that asserts a theory.

7. Express a priority in propositional form and a policy in propositional form, using your own experience as a base.

8. What is meant by saying, "There is no defense against implacable skepticism?" Illustrate from experience.

Discussion

1. Discuss the way in which argument using propositions relates to the analytic framework developed in the text. Under what conditions is the analytic framework useful or even essential in argument? Illustrate.

2. How can the individual be trained so that he or she *will be* convinced when they *should be* convinced? Can that be guaranteed? Why?

3. What is the primary reason for seeking to minimize interpretation in reasoned argument? Illustrate.

4. What is meant by "opening criticism to further criticism," and how can that be accomplished?

25. Creating a Checklist

This course has a very practical goal: to improve individual capacity to deal critically and effectively with real-world choice problems. Usefulness is not restricted to problems of national or international importance. The skills involved should also have value in school, at work, in personal affairs, and in the local community. To improve performance, the student must master the critical apparatus and learn how to apply it systematically. Both aspects of criticism are essential. The text has concentrated mainly on mastery of the critical framework, minimizing illustrations and applications. Experience with the course justifies that emphasis: Absorbing the critical apparatus takes time and premature efforts to apply it tend to interfere with learning by focusing attention on the details of particular cases rather than the generalized patterns and processes involved. And in any event, application of the critical apparatus tends to follow more or less automatically from acquisition. Students soon recognize "what is going on" in terms of the critical apparatus; they begin to "see," for example, that a classification is being used to make a prediction or that a word has been defined nominally and not in real terms—and to criticize accordingly.

In thinking, as in sports, once the basic skills have been acquired, improved performance is a function of practice. Effective practice needs to be regular, systematic, and comprehensive. The usual way of organizing sound practice, in sports or in such complex activities as piloting rockets, is to develop a checklist, a set of instructions or reminders. Checklists vary in size and complexity from the simple mental rules used to practice kicking a football to the extensive written instructions provided for pilots of commercial aircraft. Practice directed by the checklist serves to integrate technical skills into everyday performance, as good safety habits are built into everyday driving by sound training. Checklists identify the major elements in successful performance, whether in sports or in intellectual activity, underscoring the places where errors are most likely to occur. Such lists are useful both in practice and in performance—to both the performer and the critic or coach. They can direct efforts to solve real problems or provide guidance for practice intended to improve the quality of performance.

Probably the best way available for learning how to use the critical apparatus developed in the text is to create and apply an adequate checklist. In the preliminary stages of learning the apparatus, exercises such as those found at the end of each unit provide valuable practice. But the best form of practice is to deal with real problems or to criticize the efforts of others to deal with such problems as those efforts are reported in newspapers or other sources. The basic elements of a checklist that can be used in intellectual criticism are outlined below. It will have to be modified and expanded to fit individual requirements, for no single list is adequate for all persons in all situations, just as no single training schedule will fit the needs of all athletes. The list is a point of departure and not a finished product; it is left for the student to finish.

The content of an adequate checklist depends on the theoretical base that directs performance and criticism. The theory of knowledge used here links human experience to the fulfillment of a given set of purposes through a variety of structures and processes. Criticism proceeds by (1) identifying a purpose within the critical apparatus, (2) determining the structures and processes required to fulfill that purpose, and (3) examining those structures and processes by reference to past experience. To fulfill a purpose, a chain of relations must be created that can link experience to appropriate action inferentially. The chain is no stronger than its weakest link. Criticism of efforts to achieve purposes can therefore proceed analytically, breaking complex structures into elements and examining the quality of each element. The overall apparatus must contain all the elements required to carry out the intended purpose; each element must be justified by an appropriate body of evidence and reasoning. In everyday language, action or criticism begins by asking, "What are you trying to do?" or, "What is the purpose sought?" specified in terms of the critical framework. The tools needed to fulfill that purpose have already been established within the framework. Criticism or planning can focus first on the selection of tools, then on the adequacy of each tool, and finally on the validity of its application. That kind of examination can provide the evidence needed to assess the effort or suggest ways of improving performance.

To put the matter in another way, knowledge is here construed as organized human experience, created as a means of achieving human purposes. Reasoned efforts to attain a purpose within the purview of the theoretical structure, as well as criticism of those efforts, will focus on the relations that hold among purposes, instruments, processes, and human experience. In real cases, reasoned action and systematic criticism are concerned with both methodological and substantive questions, with analytic requirements as well as the substance of past experience. The difference between those two perspectives is simple but vital. Given a purpose, methodological criticism is concerned with the structural and procedural requirements for fulfilling that purpose; substantive criticism deals with the relation between the *content* of experience and the content of the structures used to achieve the purpose. It cannot be emphasized too strongly that both aspects of efforts to deal with intellectual problems must be examined in all cases. Methodological criticism can be decisive, but it can only rule out proposed arguments for solutions to a problem. Like Mill's methods, it provides reasons for rejecting but cannot validate. Substantive criticism is also incomplete, although in some cases decisive. If the content of experience does not correspond to the content of the instrument, the proposed solution is effectively ruled out. But the content of the instrument may correspond with experience yet fail to solve the problem if it is inadequately limited or improperly applied.

Adequate criticism requires both awareness of analytic or methodological requirements and familiarity with the appropriate subject matter. If a species of insects is to be eliminated from a geographic area, proposed solutions for the problem must be examined from both perspectives. Methodologically, it can be shown that the solution must contain a theory, an instrument able to link two or more variables causally, and if the solution does not contain such an instrument, it can be rejected. Substantively, experience must support the assumption that action based on a particular assumed causal relation can be expected to produce the desired result; again, failure to correspond to experience is grounds for rejection.

A Generalized Checklist

Given the way in which reasoned criticism or justification of efforts to solve real-world problems develops, a checklist for dealing with knowledge claims can be organized around three major elements: (1) the purposes sought through inquiry or action; (2) the instruments and processes needed to achieve each of those purposes; and (3) the relevant body of past experience. Obviously, there is no way to summarize human experience on all subjects and include it in the checklist. But the list can indicate the points in planning or criticism where such experience must be consulted and the kind of relation that must hold between experience and argument before the argument can be considered persuasive.

What Is the Purpose?

When there is a problem to be solved, or a proposed solution to a problem to be evaluated, the first step is to establish the purpose or purposes that the problem involves. These purposes must be stated in terms of the analytic framework, otherwise the critical apparatus will not apply. If the problem is to decide what clothing to wear, and that decision is contingent on the weather expected, then the purpose to be fulfilled first is to obtain a prediction of the weather expected on the following day. Either a theory or a forecast can be used for the purpose; in each case, the instrument used will have to satisfy specifiable criteria of acceptability.

It is usually easy to determine the purpose of one's own actions, but when problems are stated by others, it may be difficult or even impossible to determine precisely what purpose is being sought. For developing a checklist, it is useful to identify three basic kinds of purposes:

1. Direct efforts to predict, control, and choose—the application of one or more of the intellectual instruments.

2. Efforts to create the tools needed for achieving purposes—creation of intellectual instruments.

3. Indirect contributions to the achievement of purposes, which may refer to testing and refining existing instruments, creating new procedures (for testing or diagnosis, for example), or developing new techniques for measuring or assessing implications. The scope of the analytic framework is limited and excludes contributions to mathematics, formal logic, or existing language; such inquiries may contribute indirectly to the fulfillment of human purposes, but criticism is best left to the specialized subfield.

Within each category, both methodological and substantive criticism are required. Direct efforts to control events, for example, must employ the correct kind of instrument (a theory, in this case), and that question is decided on methodological grounds. The theory must also be valid—be justifiable out of experience—and that is determined on substantive grounds, by consulting past experience. If the purpose is to create a new tool, methodology can stipulate the structural requirements of the instrument, but substantive knowledge is required to test its validity. Indeed, no effort to achieve one of the purposes incorporated into the analytic structure can be assessed without reference to the appropriate body of accumulated experience. The implication, for both actor and critic, is clear: The first rule in criticism is "Know what you are talking about"; in effect, know the subject matter or be informed.

When problems or purposes are clearly stated and adequately conceptualized, translation into the critical framework is not difficult and systematic criticism can proceed confidently. Thus an effort to improve disease resistance in corn will clearly require the capacity to control the environment and will therefore demand a valid theory. But in real situations, purposes are not always so clear, and the concepts used to state purposes can vary widely. In some cases, the purpose sought is taken for granted or ignored; in others, traditional studies are replicated. And when goals such as "improved understanding" are set for inquiry, no translation is possible. Even efforts to produce a "model" or "theory" cannot be assessed until the meaning attached to each term is determined, for usage varies. Finally, purposes may be only partially stated and therefore closed to criticism until expanded. For example, an attempt to describe, that does not specify the purpose for which the description will be used, can be tested for accuracy, but its adequacy will remain uncertain. In order to apply the critical apparatus, the purpose of the critic or actor must be stated in terms that allow identification of performance criteria, the kinds of instruments needed to fulfill the purpose, and, ideally, the tolerable level of accuracy and reliability required.

The crucial step in systematic criticism is to identify the instruments, and the structures and processes, involved in achieving a stated purpose. In real cases, that task is much facilitated if four basic distinctions are rigorously maintained. First, efforts to predict, or to fashion instruments useful for predicting, should be separated from efforts to control events or create instruments for controlling them. The difference is vital, particularly where policy making is concerned. Control over events cannot be achieved without establishing a causal relation among the variables; for that purpose, evidence of correlation, or of predictive capacity, is not an adequate justification. Directly or indirectly (through another theory), the justification must refer to the effects of action.

Second, efforts to control the environment by preventing the occurrence of an event should be distinguished from efforts to control events by producing a particular event. To prevent an event from happening, an instrument is needed that identifies the necessary conditions for the event to occur; to produce the event, the sufficient conditions for occurrence must be known. It is much easier to produce and justify an instrument able to prevent events from occurring than to create an instrument that will produce events, or allow their production by deliberate action.

Third, efforts to determine the cause of an event need to be separated from efforts to modify or alter it subsequently. Even though the event remains the same, the instruments produced for the two purposes may be different. Knowing the cause of an event does not always provide a way of controlling or curing it that can be implemented; finding a cure does not always require knowing the cause. If the purpose is to cure, the search for causes of events for which no cure is required may also be construed as a waste of scarce resources.

Fourth, a distinction is needed between theories that are valid in principle and theories that can actually be applied in the present state of technology. Again, the difference is significant mainly in relation to policy-making requirements. In theorizing, there is no need to insist on applicability as a criterion of adequacy and some reason to take the contrary position. If an instrument can in principle provide control over events, and if it can be justified out of experience, whether directly or indirectly, there is no reason to reject it. The fact that the technological capacity needed to implement the theory is not available does not invalidate the theory. That situation does, however, rule out the use of the theory in policy making. If the purpose at hand is to direct actions, a theory that cannot be implemented is useless.

Structures

Assuming that language and a variety of logics is available, the number of instruments and processes required for dealing systematically with efforts to achieve the purposes covered by the analytic framework is very small — about a dozen elements altogether. Only seven basic tools or instruments are required: concepts or classifications, relational terms, descriptions, forecasts, theories, priorities, and policies or action rules. Each of the purposes covered by the theory of knowledge can be fulfilled by some combination of the seven elements. They provide a point of departure for either seeking to achieve those purposes or criticizing efforts to achieve them. Of course, purposes are likely to be combined in efforts to deal with real-world problems, but in systematic criticism they can be separated and dealt with individually. Each effort to achieve a purpose, or contribute to that end, must satisfy three criteria: (1) all the instruments required for achieving the purpose must be included in the solution; (2) each instrument must be valid, must fulfill both methodological and substantive requirements; and (3) the judgments made in developing and applying the instruments must be justified by current standards.

Once a purpose has been established, the first step in efforts to achieve it, or to criticize efforts to achieve it, is to determine the set of instruments on which success depends. For each of the three major purposes comprised in the analytic framework, those instrumental needs are summarized in table 25.1. The concepts employed may be either empirical or normative, depending on the purpose.

TABLE 25.1

Purpose	Instrumental Needs
Anticipate/predict or forecast	Concepts, relational terms, and either a classification or a theory
Control	Concepts, relational terms, and a theory
Choose	Concepts, relational terms, descriptions, theories, priorities, and policies

Once the purpose to be fulfilled has been established, the instruments involved are readily identified, which provides a base for either designing the research needed to propose a means of achieving it or criticizing proposed solutions — on methodological, not substantive grounds. If, for example, the purpose is to make a choice or to take action, that purpose can appear in one of two forms, general or specific. If the question put is "What can I do in this situation?" or "What can a specific actor *(X)* do in this situation?" the actor is identified and the alternatives available to that actor must be examined. If, however, the question is stated generally, in the form "What can be done in this situation?" potential actors must be identified first, and that will include everyone with some capacity to alter the situation. The alternatives available to each actor can then be projected and compared. In general, projections will be based on existing theory, unless there is time, and reason, to seek better instruments.

Once the projections are made, the relevant priority can be applied if it is available. Otherwise, a preference will have to be established and justified in each case. Finally, an action program must be created that will lead to the preferred outcome. In addition, such practical concerns as the availability of resources and the willingness to implement the proposed policy will have to be examined, but they fall outside the analytic framework. Each instrument incorporates a range of concepts, relational terms, and basic processes — observation, generalization, diagnosis, and judgment. In criticism, each element of a complete structure can be examined separately, in terms of its contribution to the overall effort. The experience actually applied in criticism cannot be specified until a particular case is identified, but a checklist can be constructed that will indicate points where errors occur most often.

Concepts/classifications. Concepts provide a good illustration of the way in which methodological and substantive criticisms interact in the evaluation of an intellectual instrument. Structurally, concepts consist of a set of variables together with rules that identify the selection and specify the range of values that each variable can take. The variables, and the range of values, identify the shared characteristics of members of the class. A special class of *simples,* exemplified by colors such as yellow, are defined by a single value of a single variable, but they are exceptional cases.

The best source of concepts, of course, is the language in current use in the field of inquiry. If none is available there, the concept may have to be invented, given a nominal definition, and introduced tentatively. Systematic criticism of concepts will consider four major points: (1) is the meaning of the concept clear and unambiguous? (2) does the meaning correspond to experience—does the concept have a valid real definition? (3) is the concept supplied with adequate indicators and measures, observables that are firmly linked to the meaning? (4) does the concept refer to significant dimensions of experience, measured against the purpose for which it is employed?

Relational terms. Practically speaking, relational terms are criticized in the same manner as concepts or classifications; they are concepts of a special kind. The primary concern is clarity of meaning and adequacy of indicators, the significance of the relation incorporated into the concept, its role in human affairs. Simple terms that refer to dimensions of time and space, such as size, distance, or direction, rarely cause difficulties. But such propositions as "Jones dominates Smith" or "Henry is more efficient than Charles" may be extremely difficult to deal with; meaning is not precise, and measures or indicators may be difficult to create and apply.

Descriptions. Descriptions appear as propositions in which the values of some set of concepts and relational terms are established through observation. Descriptive propositions are needed in every argument, explicitly or implicitly. Such statements as "The dog is black" describe explicitly; others, such as "That dog is larger than the other dog," describe implicitly, for they imply two descriptions whose content has been compared. Two points about description must be examined: (1) the accuracy of the descriptive account, which is a function of the quality of the concepts and the kinds of observations or measurements used to establish their values; and (2) the adequacy of the description, which is evaluated by reference to the purpose for which it is used.

Forecasts. A forecast must include at least two variables and one or more rules linking their values. Usually, a statement of the conditions limiting application, if any, is added to the structure. Beyond structural completeness (a single-variable structure is a prophecy machine), the primary test of forecasts is consistency with historical experience—and correspondence with other forecasts that have been established and accepted. Since the quality of a forecast must be judged before application, and the fit with prior experience cannot guarantee reliability, predictions of high significance should be reinforced by any means available. Since forecasts cannot be tested experimentally, all of the evidence available will be historical; there is therefore no good alternative to multiplying the number of forecasts used and perhaps seeking reasons why the forecast might not be expected to function in particular cases—extending limiting conditions.

Theories. Structurally, a theory consists of two or more variables whose values are linked by rules of interaction plus an assumption that the variables are linked causally—meaning that the rule of interaction is expected to hold regardless of the means by which change is introduced into the set. Such structures provide a basis for deliberate actions intended to produce specified changes in the environment. A set of limiting conditions is usually attached to a theory; if none is included, the theory is expected to hold any time that the variables included in it are observed in the environment.

Theories may incorporate either the necessary or the sufficient conditions for an event to occur; the evidence required to establish them will vary with the strength of the claim. Statements of the necessary conditions for events to occur can be used to prevent them; statements of the sufficient conditions of an event can be used to bring them about by deliberate action. The most difficult part of theory justification is to establish the assumed causal link between the variables. That task is facilitated by the availability of experimental evidence produced by acting on the theory. In addition, various conventions have been developed for identifying putative causal relations through statistical analysis (available in most introductory texts in statistics). Such conventions must be treated with care, of course, because they are subject to the same limitations as Mill's "methods," meaning that they provide evidence for causal links but cannot, by themselves, establish such relations. All theories are in some degree problematic or uncertain. That uncertainty is lumped into a Fudge Factor lying between theory and application, which serves as a measure of reliability. The concepts, relational terms, and descriptions on which theories depend are subject to criticism on grounds already discussed.

Priorities. A priority is a generalized structure, created from the preference orderings established in particular choices. It serves to order a set of achievable outcomes to show the preferred outcome. Each outcome or alternative is a dynamic projection of the expected consequences of action, structured using an agreed set of normative variables. Each normative variable is a complex structure used to indicate the conditions of a human life, fully projected, and not a simple cross-section of that life at a fixed point in time. The set of alternatives from which a choice must be made identifies the situation to which a given priority applies, subject to any limitations attached to its use. Priorities must be consistent with priorities already accepted by the actor or critic; they must also be supported by informed opinion or judgment, by justifications based on experience with the outcomes ordered within the priority. Finally, since a priority is applied as a unit, it is important to ask whether the set of variables on which the priority depends includes all of the normatively significant dimensions of the situations to which the priority applies—a matter of judgment based on experience and the results obtained by applying alternative competing sets of variables to the same situation.

Policies. A policy is an action program, a set of rules of action expected to produce the preferred outcome in situations where they are applied. Three aspects of policy are particularly important for the user or critic. First, the policy must be sufficiently comprehensive to *force* a particular action or choice. What is tested in use or application is always the set of assumptions on which action depends; unless those assumptions, incorporated into the rules that make up a policy, are sufficient to force or require action, there is no test. The action must be a formal logical consequence of accepting the policy. Second, the theories from which policies are constructed must be valid. Those theories will usually be tested when the options from which choices are made are being projected; the same theories are normally used for both purposes. Finally, since actions test theories and policies in combination, the testing design must make it possible to determine which of the two requires modification if the result is not satisfactory.

Processes

Knowledge is created, tested, and applied out of a dynamic, ongoing process that cannot be fully captured in static structures. Behind the structures, five major processes are at work. *Observation* or measurement is needed to generate the initial set of human perceptions from which all knowledge is created. *Generalization* creates the empirical and normative patterns used to bridge the gap between past experience and future events. *Calculation* allows a comprehensive and accurate exploration of the content or implications of such generalized patterns. *Diagnosis* is required to apply patterns to particular cases. Finally, reasoning or *judgment,* which is a very difficult process to isolate, serves to link evidence to conclusion, structure to situation. Each process raises a slightly different set of problems for the critic. Although process cannot guarantee product except in formal logic or mathematics, and there is no "method" for producing knowledge to be learned and applied, knowing the kind of contribution that each process makes to the development and use of knowledge, and the principal danger points associated with them, is an essential part of the intellectual equipment of both actor and critic.

Observation. Observation is the most widely discussed of the processes used to create knowledge. It provides the initial set of perceptions from which knowledge must be created and involves, among other things, discrimination of perceptions into entities, comparisons, and measurement against a variety of external standards or scales. With respect to any observation, there are two primary foci of criticism: the accuracy of the result produced and recorded, and the adequacy of the description produced. Accuracy depends on the quality of the concepts employed, the nature of the "things" being observed, the precision with which indicators for concepts can be measured, the kinds of scales available for carrying out the measurements, and the methods of observation employed. The most accurate observations possible occur in physical science where standardized concepts, very accurate measures, and widespread use of mechanical measuring devices make possible a level of precision beyond the reach of social science — at least at present. Accuracy can be fostered by such devices as concentrating on observation of public events open to multiple observers, emphasizing the need for different observers, and multiple measurements, but the crucial elements remain the concepts/indicators employed and the availability of adequate measures. The adequacy of descriptions generated from observations is a function of the purpose for which they are used, and that relation must be tested, but there is very little that can be said about the character of the relation in general that will assist the critic.

Calculation. Calculations, however complex, pose no special problems for actor or critic. They are performed *within* logic or mathematics and can be tested by any competent person in absolute terms. That is, a set of calculations is always either correct or incorrect, and that can be determined perfectly except in a few special cases. Happily, these cases are so rare that they can be ignored.

Generalization. The process labeled generalization produces the various patterns that make up the body of existing knowledge. The effect of the process is well known: It generates the patterns, or overlays, into which particular events can be fitted; those patterns serve to relate events in a variety of useful ways. The effect of generalization is to create a structure that is not limited with respect to time or place; that makes possible the transposition of past experience onto the future that dependence on the sensory apparatus enforces. How the patterns are created simply is not known, but it can safely be assumed that familiarity with the specific events organized within the pattern, if it does not guarantee that a pattern will be created, is nevertheless an essential prerequisite to creating it.

Two basic questions need to be raised with respect to generalization, both directed to its products and not to the process itself. First, what is the relation between experience with specific events and the assumptions or relations contained in the pattern? Second, how does the pattern relate to the conduct of human affairs, to the fulfillment of human purposes—is it significant? The validity of the process can only be tested against its products, hence there is always some element of uncertainty attached to generalization; acceptance is always conditional. The test consists in a comparison of the content of experience and the implications or content of the pattern. In some cases, experience can be created in order to test that relationship. How the test is conducted depends on the kind of pattern that has been produced. The significance of the pattern is a function of its use by informed practitioners and is distinct from its validity. In most academic disciplines, tests of validity are all that is required of generalizations, but where the focus of concern is the development of knowledge adequate to serve as a guide to action, that test is not enough.

Diagnosis. Generalizations create patterns; diagnosis is the name for the process used to apply patterns to particular situations. Two questions, one far more difficult than the other, call for diagnosis. In the simpler case, the question raised is "Does the particular event belong to pattern P?" It requires a systematic comparison of the defining attributes of the generalized pattern with the specific attributes of the event. If the two coincide, the event has been diagnosed. A much more difficult problem is posed by the question "Is there a pattern within existing knowledge that applies to this situation?" Here, what is required is a search of any and all relevant patterns in the knowledge supply to determine whether a pattern can be found whose generalized attributes correspond to the particular case. Diagnosis of medical conditions is perhaps the most common example of efforts to deal with the second question; success, obviously, requires a very extensive knowledge of the available patterns and some skill in fitting one to the other. When the patterns are complex, and there is a very large number of them, and the results of diagnosis are highly significant, as in medicine, specialization can be expected, for it narrows the search field for a suitable pattern. It carries the danger, however, that a pattern is available in another specialized area but will not be applied because it falls outside the area of specialized knowledge available to the person making the diagnosis.

When full information is available about the event to be diagnosed, the process can be expected to produce accurate and reliable results, subject only to the quality of the available supply of patterns. But in most cases, diagnosis will be based on partial information. When classifications are used to make predictions, such "partial" diagnoses are essential. Where this occurs frequently, as in medicine, conventions governing diagnostic requirements will tend to develop. In less formal circumstances, individuals will acquire "experience" that can be brought to bear on a particular diagnosis. In effect, such experience serves the same function as diagnostic conventions in more formalized fields, and in some cases the results of experience can be articulated, tested, and transferred to others. But in many situations, such as locating fish in a given lake on a given day, it may not be possible for the expert "diagnostician" to give reasons for choosing one spot rather than another, although the actual performance may be quite satisfactory.

Judgment/reasoning/argument. Finally, there is a dimension to the development and use of knowledge that is somewhat amorphous, difficult to isolate, yet analytically necessary to account for human performance. It has been here labeled *judgment,* but it is sometimes indicated by references to *reasoning,* or even to *argument.* Judgment appears when evidence is marshalled to support a conclusion, when a diagnosis is asserted, when a theory or forecast is accepted or rejected, when a priority or other pattern is applied. Unfortunately, the only test of judgment is another judgment, and if informed judgments conflict, there is no way to resolve the difference pending further evidence or additional reasoning. That is the primary sense in which the current body of informed opinion in a field of inquiry is the ultimate test of knowledge claims, and the reason why such tests are never absolutely conclusive.

Purposes, Instruments, and Processes

A. Purposes that involve use or application of instruments
1. *Anticipating/predicting*
Instruments: concepts, relational terms, and classifications, forecasts, theories
Processes: observation, diagnosis, calculation, judgment

2. *Controlling*
Instruments: concepts, relational terms, descriptions, theories
Processes: observation, diagnosis, calculation, judgment

3. *Choosing*
Instruments: concepts (empirical and normative), relational terms, descriptions, theories, priorities, policies
Processes: observation, diagnosis, calculation, judgment

B. Purposes that involve creation of tools (excluding logic)
1. Description, which may be seen as creation or use of tools, requires observation, diagnosis, and judgment

2. All other instruments are based on observation, generalization, and judgment

C. Indirect contributions to knowledge
Includes all efforts to test and/or improve instruments or processes.

Instruments

Concepts, relational terms, descriptions, forecasts, theories, priorities, and policies

Processes

Observation, generalization, diagnosis, calculation, and judgment

26. Writing and Reading

Nearly everyone will agree that learning how to use a language effectively, how to read and write, talk and listen, is an important part of education. And much of every student's time in school is spent acquiring language skills. The results of such training are not, however, equally useful for everyone. In general, academic language training treats language use as a single, homogeneous activity, and training is expected to apply to all uses or applications. But language is used in many different ways, and the skills involved are not the same in all instances. For example, language is used to provide background noise, chatter that is heard but not listened to for content. The language skill involved is merely the ability to make the right noise at an appropriate time. Again, language can be used to trigger preconditioned responses, as with military commands or parental orders to children. Here, skill in language use means knowing the preconditioned responses and the appropriate words for producing them. The actual meaning of the words need not matter, for people can be conditioned to respond to commands in almost any form. Moving in a different direction, language is used by poets and fiction writers to evoke memories, stimulate particular emotions, excite, or titillate. In such usages, language mastery requires knowledge of the reactions associated with particular words, phrases, and scenes in the society or culture to which the writing is addressed. All such uses of language, and there are many more, are perfectly legitimate. Each has its own skill requirements, and they will differ, often substantially.

In argument or criticism, the primary function of language is to serve as a vehicle for stating, defending, or criticizing knowledge claims, or the use of knowledge to achieve stated purposes. The focus of concern here is the substance of the message, the meaning of what was said, and its acceptability.

Language is usually taught in the schools as a separate subject by persons whose primary field of interest is language, literature, or drama and poetry; and most language texts adopt that emphasis. In general, the "literary" approach to language determines standards of performance applied to reading and writing at all educational levels. Unfortunately, the techniques and strategies of reading and writing that are adequate for literary purposes are often inadequate and even counterproductive when used for argument or criticism focused on real-world substance or content. There are at least two major differences between language use in argument and criticism and language use in literature. First, the content of the two kinds of writing and their purposes differ greatly, and the student must learn "what to look for" in each case. Second, there are major differences in the implications of adopting specific writing techniques or strategies for application to the two areas. In criticism and argument, writing is controlled by the criteria that determine the adequacy or acceptability of an argument in a substantive field. Neither the "things to look for" nor the criteria of adequacy that control reasoned argument are included in language training offered at the secondary school or university, with very rare exceptions.

From a somewhat different perspective, the most important difference between language use in literature and in systematic argument emerges as a major difference in the approach to reading. In argument and criticism directed at real-world affairs, the reader must deal with the text rigorously and literally, minimizing interpretation. Of course, every sentence in every language involves some minimal level of interpretation, but the goal in reading is to determine exactly what was said and not what was meant or intended. For those who write in this mode, the corollary is the need to write as accurately as possible, minimizing the need for such interpretation. Criticism of "what the author intended" is not equivalent to criticism of "what the author said." For this reason, the use of metaphors or evocative writing in argument and criticism is almost invariably unacceptable, for it tends to foster rather than minimize interpretation. In literary writing, in contrast, such usage plays an essential role and could not be eliminated from the writer's repertoire.

With respect to writing techniques, the primary difference between literary and critical writing lies in the way material is ordered and arranged. In writing intended to amuse, techniques that increase dramatic tension are desirable, and surprise endings may be considered "good theater" and entirely appropriate to the writer's purpose. In a serious argument, a conclusion that came as a surprise to the reader would be an unmistakable indication of poor writing—and poor argument. For reasoned argument proceeds, necessarily, by leading the reader or hearer step by step from an initial set of assumptions through a body of related evidence to a forced conclusion. Each step must usually be agreed on as it is taken, particularly in a long and complex chain of reasoning. Clearly, such differences in technique will enforce significant differences in language training and the kinds of exercises used to foster skill.

Some of the rudiments of the kind of reading and writing demanded by systematic argument and criticism about real-world affairs are sketched below. The positive suggestions, potential hazards, and suggested remedies are based on a considerable body of experience teaching such writing, but they are only a beginning. Awareness of these aspects of writing should lead to improvement, but do not expect the reading and writing habits of a lifetime to disappear overnight. Further, external assistance is essential, for few writers, however experienced and skilled, can do an adequate critique of their own products. Those looking for assistance may not find the help they need.

Writing

The primary emphasis in language training directed at criticism and argument should be placed on writing. In general, arguments must be written rather than verbal, for complex verbal arguments cannot be followed in detail and retained with sufficient clarity to allow adequate criticism. That is why lectures are such a poor teaching mode, a device that allows information to flow from one person's notes to another person's notes without passing through attentive consciousness. Verbal discussion is ideal when a variety of possibilities needs to be explored rapidly, or in efforts to illustrate a point and thus clarify its meaning. But the precise content of a lengthy verbal communication simply cannot be held together long enough to expose it to systematic examination. And if the verbal barrage continues, as in lectures, while the listener is trying to sort out precisely what was said earlier, there will be serious gaps in communication. Until an argument is reduced to writing, its status will usually remain uncertain. Indeed, some physical scientists prefer to reduce arguments still further to mathematical symbols and notation, but that is at present impossible in most areas outside of physics or chemistry. Training can improve the individual's ability to handle verbal discussion, but the written argument will remain the central focus in the development and improvement of knowledge well into the future.

The first rule in substantive writing is to have something to say, and to know what it is. The writing must answer a question, assert a knowledge claim, set forth an argument to support or attack a knowledge claim, or pursue some other purpose that has been legitimated in an appropriate intellectual context. The purpose of the writing is not to produce an effect on a reader but to set forth an argument and have it accepted by a competent reader. The purposes that can be served by the writing are bounded by the epistemological and methodological apparatus that will be employed to criticize or justify it. In the context of this text, such writing will attempt to describe, classify, predict, state a causal relation, make a choice, advocate a policy, and so on—or to defend or criticize efforts to fulfill one of these purposes. Put another way, the primary purpose of critical writing is to answer such questions as "What has been observed?" "What outcome is predicted in this situation?" "What caused that event to occur?" or "How can that event be made to occur?" The question asked will largely determine the kind of argument that will be needed to support an answer, or criticize an answer, and will therefore determine the content of the written argument as well.

Once the writer is clear about "What is to be said?" or "What is the purpose of the writing?" it remains to tell the reader *everything* that is needed to make the argument convincing, assuming normal competence in both language and substance. Those writing in a given field can take for granted the "generally accepted knowledge" of the field, but even then, uncertainty should be minimized. The reason is obvious. The reader or critic can deal with the content of the argument only by reference to the purpose set out by the author. If the writer's purpose is not clear or cannot be determined, the argument can be criticized only by reference to the reader's construction of the author's purpose. The author's purpose must be stated at the outset, otherwise the reader will not know "what he or she is reading," and that causes annoyance and an unreceptive attitude at the least. Since the purpose of writing is to get agreement or acceptance, it is self-defeating to antagonize the reader needlessly. Of course, agreement must be had on acceptable grounds. Advising the writer not to antagonize the reader needlessly does not mean appealing to support based on pity or other irrelevant considerations.

Once the purpose of writing has been established and made known to the reader, the author must specify the kind of evidence and argument required, in the author's judgment, to fulfill that purpose. The reader will also develop a set of assumptions about the requirements for fulfilling that purpose, the kind of evidence required, and so on. If they do not coincide, it will at least be possible for the reader to identify the points of difference that separate the two perspectives and perhaps assess them equitably. The writer, in effect, must identify the content of an argument that should, in the writer's judgment, fulfill the purpose of the writing given a competent reader. There is no guarantee that the reader will be competent, of course, but there is no guarantee that the writer is competent either. These are the points that systematic criticism, open to informed opinion, must decide.

In the process of working out the kind of argument needed to fulfill the purpose of the writing, the author will produce an outline of the proposed writing more or less automatically. Both criteria *and* outline should be conveyed to the reader. The reader will, of course, decide which criteria to apply to what is read, but by providing criteria the author may head off criticism based on inadequate or inappropriate grounds, and in any event, the reader is then in a position to see whether the author has fulfilled the purpose of the argument, using the author's own criteria. Ultimately, the question what criteria apply to such arguments is a matter for judgment by "informed opinion" within the appropriate field.

Organization

Reasoned argument involves much more than setting out a question, providing a body of data, and stating a conclusion. Arguments have organization. There is a beginning, an ordered set of steps, and a flow of reasons and evidence leading to a conclusion, all determined by the purpose of the argument and the character of the evidence. Further, there is a psychology of reading that must be taken into account. Working out the organization or development of an argument in detail is therefore an important part of argument. If A is contingent upon B, then B must be stated first. If the reader must realize X in order to accept Y, then X should closely precede Y. In effect, the writer should map the argument in advance, from the perspective of the reader, with due regard to the requirements of competent argument. Awareness of that organization pattern infuses and influences what is said at every stage of writing.

The reason for attending so closely to organization is that reading is a very peculiar activity. What is read enters the neural apparatus like a single thread. Complex patterns are formed by linking elements of the thread after the elements have been introduced. One cannot depend on the listener or reader to make the necessary connections. A good analogy to the process is found in the way a moving dot is used to produce a two-dimensional picture on the surface of a television tube. If the argument is complex, and what written argument is not? the writer must map the route for the reader in advance, then refer back to the map regularly as the journey through the argument progresses. Structure and organization are maintained by such map references. Summaries may be needed periodically, particularly in longer pieces of writing, together with "future pointers" that remind the reader where the discussion is leading.

Ultimately, the organization of an argument, written or verbal, is determined by the analytic requirements for successful argument accepted by the writer. That set of requirements determines the subheadings included in the writing, as well as the topic sentences in each paragraph. In a criticism of someone else's work, as in an original argument, the topic sentence will *always refer to the writer's point.* Thus, in a critique of a work by Jones, paragraphs must begin with such sentences as "The use of concepts in Jones's work is very poor" or "Jones ignores some of the earlier work done on the topic." The evidence to support the proposition will then be produced in the remainder of the paragraph. If a paragraph in a critique begins "In the second chapter, Jones begins by treating crime . . ," a serious mistake has been made—almost as bad as appending the sophomore's classic "Jones also deals with . . ." at the end of the paragraph. Such sentences may be useful for *condensing* what was said; they have no place in opening sentences of critical paragraphs. The work being criticized is referred to or cited *only* to illustrate the critic's point.

An author who begins with a clearly stated question or purpose can check on the progress of the argument, and the maintenance of relevance, by returning to that question or purpose at the end of each paragraph and asking how or what that paragraph has contributed to the argument— and comparing achievements to its anticipated function as set forth in the outline. In effect, the overall purpose of the writing determines the sets of subordinate purposes to be fulfilled before the overall purpose can be achieved, as in the development of an analytic or critical apparatus. That structure, which should be reflected in the prewriting outline, should identify the purpose that each paragraph will fulfill and indicate how that can be done. Changes will occur during the course of the writing, but that must be expected. A simple check on the final product is to make a sentence-summary of each paragraph and compare it with the organizational outline of the requirements for fulfilling the purpose.

All of which adds up, as the reader is no doubt aware, to a program of very hard and sustained effort. What is written must be planned beforehand, outlined carefully, written, read, analyzed, rewritten, and so on until it will fulfill the intended purpose in the hands of a competent reader. However well planned a piece of writing may be, the actual writing process will almost invariably lead to changes and modifications, usually in what has already been written as well. *No one* can write competent finished copy on first draft. A beginning paragraph may take several efforts, even from a professional writer. For university students, that poses a serious problem. If several term papers must be written each semester, as is normal, it is literally impossible to treat each one in so rigorous a manner. Professors should understand the problem, and many do, but it is usually left for the student to sort out—by selecting courses, in most instances.

The purpose here is to show what is involved in written argument. It may not be possible to apply such standards to written work in the university, but every effort should be made to do so if you are concerned to learn how to perform well when good performance is essential. For learning how to write well, or argue well in writing, takes time, patience, persistence—and competent criticism. That is most likely to be found, and be willingly provided, at the university. Competent readers are scarce, perhaps even among university faculties. Asking anyone to read your work carefully and provide systematic criticism is asking a great deal, for careful reading and criticism is as difficult and time-consuming as good writing. Further, the amount of assistance a skilled reader and critic can provide is directly proportional to how well the writer has done his or her work. Roughing out a crude draft to be organized and integrated by someone else may be a good indicator of "cheek" but is unlikely to attract the kind of prolonged assistance that improvement requires. If the original writing is too poor, a competent critic can do little more than return it for rewriting; writing must reach a minimum standard of coherence before criticism can actually begin. In effect, submitting grossly inadequate written work to be read and corrected by others amounts to asking the reader to do the most difficult part of the writing.

Finally, do not be entrapped by the kind of "supercriticism" that seizes on one procedure, such as definition, and demands a clear definition for every term used in argument and then for every term used in the clarification of the original terms. Although good writing is largely self-contained, no author can define every word or delineate every rule of grammar used in writing. Nor is there any need to do so. If common usage is too vague for the purpose at hand, it can be sharpened by precising definitions. For the rest, common sense and a firm commitment to purpose, coupled with self-conscious efforts to write carefully, will go a long way toward producing adequate writing. Poor writing usually results more from carelessness than from incompetence or stupidity. Most students have acquired any number of bad habits of which they are unaware. To be made aware of habitual errors, and of the results of carelessness, is usually all that is necessary to remedy most of them.

Some Dos and Don'ts

There is no way to head off every mistake that can be made in writing, and no need to try. The best strategy for improvement is to make the mistakes, learn what they are, and correct them. Indeed, students told to avoid error X will in most cases deny ever committing such an error; students allowed to make the error will not usually make foolish claims of that nature. There are, however, some general principles that are worth following, some mistakes that recur so often they are worth pointing out, and some rules of performance that past generations of students have found useful. They are offered here in that spirit.

1. Be simple and direct. Sentences that plod may be dull but they are much better than sophomoric phraseology, needless verbiage, or complex obscurity. Style can develop in due course, and if it never develops, that is small loss if clarity results. Even grammar, in the sense that it is concerned with split infinitives, can safely be ignored if you concentrate on what had to be said and what was actually said, read very literally. Poor spelling is another matter because it will lead the reader to suspect the writer is a semi-literate dolt and prejudge content accordingly. The function of punctuation is to keep meaning straight; use if for that purpose. There are some useful conventions to remember, such as the rule that states that commas, periods, and question marks almost invariably go *inside* quotation marks in American writing. For the rest, consult a writer's manual: *The Chicago Manual of Style* is one of the more widely used of the standard works.

2. Use familiar words rather than unusual words, active and direct verbs rather than passive verbs, and concrete terms rather than abstract terms. For example, instead of "Blizzard conditions can be expected," merely say "A blizzard is coming." Rather than "The claims are of a far-reaching nature," use "The claims are far-reaching." Avoid "empty" sentences, even if they are technically correct. I mean here the written equivalent to clearing the throat with a "Harrumph." "The whale is an extraordinarily important animal," for example, says little until the reason for its importance is known, hence that should be included with the introductory statement. Realize that you are looking through a window through which the reader cannot see. Merely to comment on what is visible to you is extremely frustrating—for example, to be told "There is something important going on out there," which amounts to "The whale is an extraordinarily important animal."

3. Keep related terms together; it minimizes ambiguity. Such sentences as "There was discussion yesterday of sexual behavior in the Dean's office"

can cause confusion and comment unless order and punctuation are clarified. Compare also "The difficulty can only be alleviated by surgery" with
"The difficulty can be alleviated only by surgery" and imagine that two
physicians make such statements in discussing *your* case.

4. Avoid clichés, unless you intend to become a sportscaster. Don't
have your meat "done to a turn" or leave your friends to the "tender mer-
cies of the mob." There is rarely need for an "acid test," even though it may
be considered "part and parcel" of your program. Remember, if you are
"watching for the next swing of the pendulum," you may not see the automobile that kills you.

5. AN IMPORTANT PART OF WRITING IS KNOWING WHEN TO STOP.

Parting Advice

Nearly everyone can learn how to write adequately. Everyone should. It
takes practice and effort — and a teacher. A mere handful of points can improve performance greatly.

1. Be self-conscious about writing. Know what you are writing, what
is involved, what the reader must be told, and why. If you are writing for
someone else, try to be clear about what is required or expected — and try
not to get too impatient if the person who sets the exercises is also unclear
about what to expect. It happens.

2. You must accept the work involved. Jones's calisthenics cannot develop Smith's muscles, even if they are done in Smith's name in gym class.
Expect to rewrite again and again. Don't hand in first drafts. Ever.

3. The heart of writing is structure; the basis of structure is purpose.
Use the analytic framework if it is appropriate to the writing you are doing. It gives you a critical base to work from.

4. Simplicity is the writer's greatest virtue. If the argument is good,
complex presentation may kill it.

5. Grammar and punctuation must flow from the purpose of the
writing. They are like scales in piano playing: if they sound like scales,
they were not played properly.

6. Read! Read a lot. And read with an eye to what the author is doing
as a writer. If possible, read good writing. Where to find it? The *New Yorker*
magazine is usually well written. So is Bertrand Russell's nontechnical writing. *Science* usually contains some pretty good stuff, but you must be selective. The better columnists in the *New York Times* or the *Washington Post*
do pretty well. They also sometimes do pretty badly, but you can usually

spot the disasters. Just ask if you can tell what is being said and whether it makes sense. And read them as *writing,* not substance.

7. Write. And write often. But only if you write carefully. Sloppy writing is not practice in good writing but practicing bad writing. Write *for* someone whose judgment you respect—your toughest and most competent critic.

No one of these points, nor all of them together, will solve all your writing problems. It takes much practice, good emulation models, and sound criticism. Mastery of content is the essential first step. Awareness of some dimensions of the writer's craft can help change knowledge into communicable knowledge and mere belief into capacity for legitimate persuasion. The transition is worthwhile if you have something to say.

27. Critiques

One of the more common tests of student performance in the university is the written or oral "critique," usually of a book or major article in one of the academic journals. Since it is often less than clear what is being demanded of the student, a brief statement of the kind of "critique" expected in this course seems required—and may prove useful even in other academic programs.

To begin, two negatives: First, a critique is not a string of negative criticisms, a response to "What's wrong with this paper/book?"; second, a critique is not a summary or condensation of a written document. A critique, as it is construed here, is an overall assessment or evaluation of a piece of purposeful writing. In most cases such assessments will include five major points:

    1. A statement of the author's purpose(s)

    2. An evaluation (by the critic) of the significance of the purpose(s)

    3. A judgment of the extent to which the author achieved his or her purpose(s)

    4. An argument to support that judgment

    5. Additional commentary, which may refer to mode of presentation, use of language, organization, sources, etc.

Each of these points may require a number of paragraphs or pages. Much will depend on the amount of space available for the critic's use. In general, it is better to restrict the length of a critique fairly drastically, since that forces an assessment of the relative significance of the different points raised.

The form and content of critiques, whether written or oral, are largely determined by the functions that a critique must perform. At one level, the critic goes through precisely the same set of considerations as the author; many of the same problems arise in both writing and criticism. At another level, however, the two tasks are quite different—criticism must state self-consciously and directly the kind of assessment that the author should have made but does not always make. That difference is particularly marked in the form of exposition followed in the two tasks—writing and criticizing—if only because of the differences in the target population or audience addressed in each case. Writing involves one author and a reader: The author examines a topic that is at least partly inaccessible to the reader and seeks to fulfill some intellectual purpose within that context. Criticism inserts another level of readership between the original author and the critic's audience and that additional layer must be taken into account in the writing. Schematically, those relationships can be laid out in the following form:

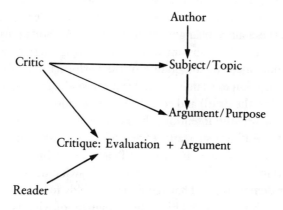

The structure and content of a written critique is determined almost entirely by the complex and overlapping relations between author, subject matter, purpose, and argument on the one hand, and between critic, subject matter, author's purpose and argument, and critic's purpose and argument on the other. The critic's exposition is determined by the needs of the critic's reader, and, of course, what the critic finds in the author's argument. In all cases, criticism must be stated in a way that will expose the critic's judgments and argument to further criticism by the critic's reader. To simplify, the discussion will be limited to three elements, the original Author, the Critic, and the Critic's Reader, who will be referred to as the "Reader."

For both Author and Critic, the central focus is the Author's purpose with respect to the subject matter. The Author's first task in writing is to state his or her purpose as clearly as possible—that is not always done, of course. The reader must then be told what, in the Author's judgment, is needed to fulfill that purpose. The Author then proceeds to fulfill those requirements as fully and systematically as possible—or try.

From the Critic's perspective, the Author's purpose will always be stated in two contexts: substantive and methodological. Authors only rarely state the methodological aspects of their purpose in writing, except implicitly or in statistical terms (which are not always adequate). The Critic, however, must deal explicitly with both aspects of the Author's argument. The methodological purpose must be stated within an analytic framework or epistemology in which purposes are linked to the intellectual requirements for fulfilling them. The methodological purpose can vary widely. In the system we are learning here, for example, the Author may seek to describe, predict, make a choice, project the effects of action, or produce and support an action program or policy. The purpose may be to create an instrument, test the instrument, apply the instrument, or provide an argument for accepting the instrument. And the purpose may combine any number of these aims in single argument. If the Author's purpose cannot be determined in either substantive or methodological terms, that is already a serious indictment of the quality of the performance. The Critic can, in such cases, go on to examine *possible* purposes (particularly if the Critic is being paid by the word) and complete the evaluation by reference to them (e.g., "If that was the intention, the performance was a dud").

Once the Author's substantive/methodological purposes have been determined, the Critic must inform the Reader what (in the Critic's judgment) is required for fulfilling those purposes—what the supporting argument must demonstrate. That requirement holds for the Critic whether or not the Author has stated his or her judgment of what is needed. That statement becomes the base for criticism, both in methodological and substantive terms, and it opens the way to subsequent criticism by the Critic's Reader.

Analytically, the next stage of criticism is to pass judgment on the Author's performance, to inform the Reader whether, and to what extent, the Author has succeeded or failed in achieving his or her purpose. A critique is an assessment or evaluation of the Author's performance. The Critic's readers will in turn assess the Critic's performance, the extent to which the Critic's purpose—which is to support the evaluative judgment—is fulfilled. Obviously, the order set forth applies to writing, and not to the Critic's reading of the Author's work.

The remainder of the critique will be devoted to arguing the case for the Critic's judgment or evaluation. The Critic must give reasons for the evaluation of the Author's work. The reasons will be substantive (how well does the Author's argument correspond with experience—observations, theory, etc.) and methodological. In effect, the Critic must link what the Author *did* to what the Author *should have done,* according to the Critic, to fulfill his purpose(s). Evidence for methodological inadequacy will come from the Author's writing, viewed through the methodological framework accepted by the Critic. Evidence for substantive inadequacy, or inadequacy, will come from the Critic's knowledge of the subject matter.

Some implications:

1. Because the critique makes the *Critic's* case, the topic sentences in a critique will be assertions *by the Critic*. Statements by the Author are only evidence for the Critic's judgments. If a paragraph begins "The Author says . . ." or "The Author then goes on to say . . ." the Critic is summarizing and not criticizing.

2. Methodological criticism is possible even if the Critic knows nothing of the subject matter, but it can only provide reasons for disallowing what the Author has written—it cannot establish an argument.

3. Author and Critic may disagree about what is necessary for achieving the Author's purpose(s). That should be acknowledged by the Critic, though the Author's judgments may be overridden if reasons are provided for doing so. Usually, a Critic will assess the performance using *both* sets of criteria, for it is often useful to point out that an Author succeeded according to his own standards, but the standards themselves are not acceptable.

4. When the Critic is stating the assessment of the Author's performance, the reasons for the judgment will be summarized at the same time —up front in the critique. Thus the Critic will say that the Author "fails by reason of conceptual inadequacy, ambiguity, lack of evidence, and so on." That initial statement usually provides an overall framework for writing the critique. The Critic, in other words, states the judgment and its grounds in broad terms, then goes on to provide evidence (from the Author's writing or from general knowledge) to support the judgment, drawing examples from the work criticized. Normally, points are taken up in the same order as they appear in the summary, progressing from the highly significant to lesser points that may be made. No criticism of the Author is valid until the evidence for it is produced. If space is limited, that may reduce the number of points that can be made. Enough must be done to validate the assessment.

5. The Critic has as much responsibility for clarity, organization, and lucidity as the Author, and perhaps more. The Author's inadequacies do not, in other words, justify the Critic's inadequacies. That is why poor writing and argument are much harder to criticize than good writing and argument. And in all cases, KEEP IT SIMPLE!!!

6. The order of presentation in the Critic's argument must follow the steps set out on page 238. Until the Critic's evaluation is known, the Reader

cannot assess the argument. That depends on a prior statement of the Author's purpose. And if the whole thing is trivial, there is no reason to do so, hence the significance must also be evaluated.

7. Criticism should include references to the manner in which the Author organizes and presents the material, the quality of the writing, and so on. To make a good case badly is almost as bad as making a trivial case well.

An Illustration: X on Values and Social Inquiry

Considered as a contribution to the continuing discussion of the role of human values in social inquiry, X's paper is grossly inadequate and even perverse. The judgment is harsh, but the inquirer's choice of topic determines the criteria applied to the performance. Very complex and fundamental questions of the kind that X raises here require extreme care and great analytic skill and precision from those who seek to answer them and equally rigorous standards of criticism from those who evaluate the answers. Because such questions impinge directly or indirectly on a very wide range of beliefs or assumptions about the meaning of knowledge and the means by which claims to knowledge are developed and tested, they provide numerous opportunities for surfacing inconsistencies and inadequacies in conceptualization, analysis, and reasoning. And when a set of questions has been widely and thoroughly discussed, as in the present case, the limiting conditions for adequate response tend to be fairly well defined, hence lacunae in argument are more readily visible than might otherwise be the case. In short, X undertook an exceptionally difficult and perilous intellectual voyage. That the enterprise failed, and to some extent why it failed, can be demonstrated by reference to three aspects of the performance: (1) the quality of the reasoning; (2) the adequacy of the conceptualization; and (3) the overall conception of the nature and purpose of social inquiry that guided the effort.

The number of minor and major reasoning flaws in the essay is far too large; even in a much less ambitious undertaking, that would be sufficient grounds for demurring from the conclusion. Whether they are a function of carelessness, arrogance, or ignorance I cannot say, but they sum to argument by assertion rather than reasoning from and to evidence. The frequency of simple non sequiturs is astonishing for so short a piece. For example, even if the end purpose of human life is agreed to be survival of the species, it does not follow that men should return to hunting and gathering because they survived in the past using those techniques. Logically, that ignores the difference between returning to and evolving through a technological stage. More generally, it ignores the need to examine *all* the available options in order to make a reasoned choice. Again, the fact that the living standard in the United States is higher than elsewhere is not evidence of superior performance by the American political-economic system. That judgment requires evidence of superior performance compared to other systems operating under comparable territorial and resource conditions. The rich family may enjoy a diet that is to be preferred to the diet of a very poor family, yet eat very badly when measured against its own potential. To take a third illustration, it is not an argument against cultural relativism to show that different people in a culture learn different things; the cultural relativist claims that there are some things that *no one* in a culture will "see" because of the nature of the culture. The fact of differential learning is simply irrelevant to that claim.

Another relatively simple and basic canon of reasoning much violated in the paper is the need to specify fairly precisely the limits of application of any rule or principle employed in argument. If the reasons used to support a judgment are not limited to fit human experience, the argument is faulted merely by extending it to any situation not excluded by the terms of application where it will produce absurd results. For example, if the significance of inquiry depends on the generality of the phenomenon studied and the ease with which the question can be answered, then learning why dogs scratch should be far more important than the study of riots, revolutions, or recessions. Again, if people should not be made to feel ashamed of excessive income because guilt feelings, persisted in, are unhealthy, then the criminal courts and their attending institutions should almost certainly be eliminated. The reason for requiring the limits is fairly simple: Accepting any assertion means accepting its implications, and when unlimited principles clash with experience, the principle, not the experience, must give way.

Charity, generosity, and humaneness (which have no place at all in rigorous criticism) might lead us to attribute such relatively minor errors to carelessness and forgive them out of consideration for the pressures of time and space on the author. The conceptual inadequacies in the paper are much too serious for that. If "what we are talking about" is unclear, then what has been said is beyond test. Acceptance, in these circumstances, is a matter of faith or ignorance. The base from which concepts are examined is quite widely agreed. The meaning of any concept is determined by a combination of usage, limitations introduced by the user, and the extensions of the context in which the concept is employed. Since all concepts must be grounded in observation (concepts are ordinarily defined as instruments for organizing perceptions), the ultimate test of the adequacy of any way of conceptualizing a situation is the experience of those familiar with the application. That is why the use of such technical terms as "dependent variable" should be avoided; they tend to shield the argument from the experience of the listener or reader by introducing a memory-translation problem and overemphasize the formal dimensions of the argument at the expense of experience. The signs of inadequate concepts are unmistakable: Statements employing the concept will tend to be vague or ambiguous and the empirical claims contained in the statements will be tendentious or involve unusual and "strange-sounding" claims.

Space limitations restrict discussion of the conceptual uncertainties in the paper to the two most crucial to X's thesis. First, a distinction is attempted between values concerned with something called the "purely intellectual" characteristics of the social sciences and values that lie beyond disciplinary boundaries. Since the meaning of "purely intellectual" is not obvious, it must be sought in the exemplification. But the only example provided for an "internal" value issue is the question: "What are the really significant kinds of research, both empirical and theoretical?" Now, that really opens the conceptual Pandora's box and raises a very fundamental issue about the context in which "significance" is assessed. There is one limited sense in which the importance of any action or process can be judged "within" the system in which it occurs. Thus, the significance of the system of checks and balances contained in the U.S. Constitution can be assayed in terms of the operation of government. But all such actions or processes will also have significance in a wider context, that extends to the population affected by it. The checks and balances in the Constitution also affect those who live under the Constitution by influencing the kinds of laws that are passed and the kinds that are ignored and so on. In academia, the significance of a particular piece of research can be assessed both within the discipline and in the wider arena of human society. To allow the first and ignore the second is unconscionable and without justification. Moreover, it opens the door to incorrigible scholasticism controlled and directed by self-fulfilling ordinances elaborated by self-appointed authorities.